Fountain House

9/30/96

God bless you
all I love you.
Christ be with you
love daughter &
you Sister
Edi

Fountain House

Portraits of Lives Reclaimed from Mental Illness

Mary Flannery

and

Mark Glickman

with a foreword by

E. Fuller Torrey, M.D.

 HAZELDEN®

Hazelden
Center City, Minnesota 55012-0176
1-800-328-9000 (Toll Free U.S., Canada, and the Virgin Islands)
1-612-257-4010 (Outside the U.S. and Canada)
1-612-257-1331 (24-hour FAX)
http://www.Hazelden.org (World Wide Web site on Internet)

ISBN:
1-56838-128-X

00 99 98 97 96   6 5 4 3 2 1

Book design by Will H. Powers
Cover design by David Spohn
Cover photograph by John Roth, New Frontier Club
Typesetting by Stanton Publication Services, Inc.

EDITOR'S NOTE

Hazelden offers a variety of information on chemical dependency and related areas. Our publications do not necessarily represent Hazelden's programs, nor do they officially speak for any Twelve Step organization.

All stories in this book are based on actual experiences. The names of
Fountain House members and some details of their stories have been
changed for privacy reasons.

To Fran
Mary-Claire, John, Rosemary, Dan
and
To Cynthia

Contents

Dedication   V

Foreword by E. Fuller Torrey, M.D.   IX

Acknowledgments   XI

Introduction   I

1   *Each Rung I Climb Up, I Fall Down Three*   3

2   *Please Don't Knock. Walk Right In*   17

3   *Too Young to Know Anything Could Go Wrong*   32

4   *It Can Change Your Life*   50

5   *I Was Standing On My Self-Esteem*   65

6   *How Can I Escape?*   81

7   *I Think I Am an Alcoholic*   93

8   *What Do I Do Next?*   112

9   *But Still, By God, They're Working*   128

10   *You Don't Know Who I'm Going to Be Someday*   145

11   *Membership Is Voluntary and Without Time Limits*   164

12   *There Are Many "Fire Souls" in This Room*   177

Appendix A: Directory of Clubhouse Programs   197

Appendix B: Standards for Clubhouse Programs   218

Foreword

The clubhouse model, of which Fountain House is the prototype, has emerged as one of the most effective means of psychiatric rehabilitation and a book describing it is long overdue. The house which became Fountain House was purchased in 1948, almost a half century ago, yet no article describing the program was published until 1982 and clubhouse standards were not set until 1991. Fountain House, in short, has been one of the best-kept secrets in the field of psychiatric rehabilitation except among a small coterie of individuals who have been fortunate enough to visit it. Many of these people then started their own clubhouses.

During the almost fifty years that Fountain House has existed, the need for its services has increased enormously. In 1955, when Fountain House was just getting off the ground, there were over 558,000 seriously mentally ill individuals in state psychiatric hospitals. Fountain House was in fact started by a small group of these individuals who had been discharged from New York's Rockland State Hospital. Today there are only approximately 71,000 individuals left in those hospitals. Subtracting 71,000 from 558,000 means that approximately 487,000 seriously mentally ill individuals who would have been hospitalized forty years ago are living in the community today. But that does not tell the whole story because the 558,000 hospitalized individuals was based on the 1955 United States population of 164 million people. Today the population is 260 million, so if we had the same proportion of people in the state psychiatric hospitals today, the number would be over 821,000. The real magnitude of deinstitutionalization then, is 821,000 minus 71,000 or approximately 750,000 people. That is the same number of people as who live in San Francisco or Baltimore. The need for Fountain House replicas is therefore enormous. Clubhouses provide seriously mentally ill individuals with a supportive network, friends, a sense of belonging, friends, educational opportunities, friends, housing, friends, and jobs. Jobs, through the Transitional Employment Program, are one of the major reasons why Fountain House and its offspring have been so successful. When I have visited clubhouses around the country, from large ones like Fellowship House in Miami and Thresholds in Chicago to smaller ones such as Alliance House in Salt Lake City and Rainbow House in Rome, New York, the members are usually proudest of the jobs they are holding. For those who want to work, there is no substitute.

The major reason why clubhouses are not more widespread is because of our thought-disordered mental health funding system. We provide fiscal incentives to encourage states to discharge individuals from state psychiatric hospitals so that states can shift the cost of care from state government to the federal government (e.g., SSI, SSDI, Medicaid, Medicare, food stamps). But we provide no fiscal incentives for providing the aftercare that is needed, including the rehabilitation that clubhouses so skillfully provide. The federal Medicaid program is driving the system, but Medicaid does not cover most vocational or educational rehabilitation. Anybody with an IQ greater than that of a turnip should have been able to predict that the present funding system would inevitably lead to discharged mentally ill individuals ending up on the streets rather than in clubhouses.

In summary, community services for seriously mentally ill individuals who have been discharged from psychiatric hospitals are on the best days merely in crisis and on the worst days much worse. Fountain House and its clubhouse offspring are a large part of the potential solution. Mary Flannery and Mark Glickman have provided an excellent overview of the clubhouse model and as such, the book deserves a wide readership.

E. FULLER TORREY, M.D.
Clinical and research psychiatrist
Washington, D.C.
author of *Surviving Schizophrenia* and
Out of the Shadows: Confronting America's Mental Illness Crisis

Acknowledgments

We are indebted to the clubhouse community and especially the members and staff of Fountain House, who revealed themselves courageously and without reservation.

We also thank all those we interviewed in the mental health community who patiently answered our questions and supplied important background information.

We are also grateful to the following individuals:

Kenneth Dudek, executive director of Fountain House, for giving us complete access to the clubhouse and to the members and staff. Kenn allowed us to write the Fountain House story as we saw it. We deeply appreciate his trusting and supportive attitude.

Steve Anderson, a staff worker at Fountain House for sharing his invaluable research into the history of Fountain House in his unpublished manuscript, "Mental Illness and Normal Life: Fountain House and the Development of Clubhouse Culture."

Rose DeWolf of the *Philadelphia Daily News* for her generous advice and enthusiasm.

Mary Carley, Judy Glickman, and Bill Wedo for all their effort and time in helping with the manuscript.

Our editor, Tim McIndoo, for his belief in this book from the beginning and his encouragement that helped see it to fruition.

And our parents, Jack and Rosemary Flannery and Jack and the late Mary Glickman, for their love.

This project began with a 1993 Kaiser Media Fellowship for health care reporting awarded by the Henry J. Kaiser Family Foundation to Mary Flannery. We thank Drew Altman, Penny Duckham, and Eileen Shanahan for their support.

Introduction

Each year in the United States, 5.5 million people experience a severe mental illness, defined as schizophrenia, bipolar disorder (manic depression), and major depression. Typically the illness strikes those between the ages of fifteen and twenty-five, before a life really begins. Often the person struck down never resumes a normal life of school, career, or marriage. And this affects many other lives. Families spend a lifetime trying to find effective help for their ill family members. Unfortunately, they find few programs that work and must watch helplessly as their loved ones cycle in and out of mental hospitals or languish without a job, decent housing, or hope for the future.

Our book is about a program that helps people who have suffered from severe and persistent mental illness, a program that in fact has helped tens of thousands of people. The program is called the Fountain House model. It started in New York City in 1948 and its success has led to the creation of more than 250 programs around the world based on this model. (See the appendix for a complete list of these programs and the set of standards that inspired them.)

Fountain House is a comprehensive program that offers vocational, residential, and social services under one roof. Using a straightforward and commonsense approach, Fountain House focuses on the strengths and talents of people recovering from mental illness. It is this focus on the healthy and contributing aspects of its members (formerly called patients) that makes the Fountain House model of recovery unique. This approach often succeeds with those who had been considered the most ill and hopeless. Members of the Fountain House program frequently return to apartments and jobs in the community.

Taxpayers spend about $17 billion each year for all forms of public mental health services. At a time of great concern about shrinking federal and state budgets, Fountain House is a cost-effective means of helping people recover in the community while avoiding expensive hospital stays. A year in a New York State mental hospital costs about $120,000 per patient. A year at Fountain House, including housing, costs about $42,000 per member.

While the problem of the homeless remains an intractable dilemma nationwide, Fountain House has successfully dealt with its share of the problem by developing a network of decent, low-cost, independent housing in the community from which thousands of members have benefited. As members of Fountain House shift from recipients of entitlements to working taxpayers, the public benefits significantly as well.

But the program's triumph lies in helping thousands of former psychiatric patients make the transformation from persons without hope or confidence into productive, contributing members of their communities.

This book is the story of some members and staff of Fountain House as, together, they move forward on the long and difficult road of recovery. It is our hope that this will lead to a better understanding of the Fountain House model and thus to greater opportunity and hope for people everywhere who have suffered from mental illness.

Each Rung I Climb Up, I Fall Down Three

Linda Pierce took off her gloves and checked her watch. In a few moments, it would be 1 P.M. An aide would unlock both sets of metal doors and visitors would be admitted inside to see patients hospitalized on the second floor of the Myers Building at the Manhattan Psychiatric Center. Anyone who'd been there more than once called it MPC.

A public facility for short- and long-term care of people with mental illness, MPC consisted of several sand-colored buildings on Ward's Island under the Triboro Bridge. MPC was built in 1957 to hold 1,000 patients, but with the increasing emphasis on community treatment, usually only 500 were there at any time.

On this Thursday afternoon, February 3, 1994, only one other person waited for visiting hours to begin. She was gray-haired and carried a plastic bag. Linda could see the outline of a Hershey bar and a *Sports Illustrated* in the bag. The woman was holding a take-out cup of coffee, probably bought in the grimy, windowless luncheonette on the first floor. Linda kept on her winter coat because the hallway outside the ward was drafty.

Linda carried that day's *New York Daily News* tucked inside her large leather pocketbook. She didn't know the man she was visiting, except that his name was Victor Cook. She hoped he might enjoy reading the newspaper. Visiting Victor was part of her job.

As a member of the Connections team at Fountain House, a social service facility on Manhattan's West Side where people with severe

3

mental illness came each day, Linda was assigned to look up those who'd either dropped out of the program or were hospitalized. Linda's assignment this day was to let Victor know that people at Fountain House hadn't forgotten him and that they were looking forward to his return.

Linda took satisfaction in making these Connections visits because she remembered how abandoned she'd felt when she was hospitalized. No one came to visit her. The only magazines she saw were dog-eared copies that she cadged from other patients. Sometimes she'd force herself to walk through the knots of patients talking outside the luncheonette, dig a dollar bill out of her jeans' pocket, and buy a cup of coffee. But most often, she had stayed on the ward.

Linda had thought she was nobody. She was dedicated to self-destruction. Every day, she woke up and thought about committing suicide. On numerous occasions, she tried.

Now that she was finally emerging from the haze of her own mental illness, she was glad to lend a hand to help others recover. And she realized that by helping others, she helped herself as well. She had to admit, it was fulfilling to walk into the ward and see someone's face light up simply because she was there.

Her responsibilities to the Connections program and to the people at Fountain House kept her focused on living, not dying. She no longer thought about dying. Now she had too much she wanted to do.

"Victor Green," Linda said to the aide when the doors swung open. The aide nodded and walked down the corridor while Linda took a seat in the day room.

After a few minutes, a man in his late twenties walked in, head down. He was wearing jeans, sneakers, and a maroon sweatshirt with "I Love New York" printed across it.

"Victor? I'm Linda Pierce. I'm with the Connections Program. From Fountain House."

Victor smiled and sat down.

"What's the weather like outside?" he asked. The frosted panes of glass embedded with wire didn't offer much of a view.

"It's cold, but it's not snowing."

Victor lit a cigarette. Before his most recent bout of mental illness and hospitalization, he'd been working at a temporary, part-time job that Fountain House had arranged. But when he began talking aloud to himself at work, answering the voices in his head, his boss called Fountain House in alarm and Victor had to leave the job. His therapist convinced him that going into the hospital, where the effects of his medications would be monitored daily, would help him get stabilized again.

"They said I could go back to Fountain House next week on day passes," Victor said. "But I can't."

"Why not?" Linda asked gently.

Maybe he thought he was barred from returning, but that wasn't true. Once someone joined the Fountain House program, he was always welcome to return.

"I feel like, well, like a failure," Victor whispered.

Linda reached out and took his hands in hers.

"This isn't failure. This is learning. We all learn when we fail."

*

Linda was fifteen years old when she told the doctor that she could see her stepmother shouting at her, could see her lips move and knew words must be coming out, but heard nothing.

"But you can hear me now?" Dr. Nelson asked Linda.

"Yes, sir."

Dr. Nelson, who took care of Linda's immediate family as well as her cousins, aunts, and uncles living in Savannah, put down his pen and closed the thin manila folder with the records of Linda's checkups and toddler ear infections. He didn't waste time looking for a biological explanation. He sent Linda and her father, George, straight to Memorial Hospital. Linda was assigned to see a young psychiatrist in the Clark Pavilion who had stacks of charts on his desk.

When the young doctor read the scribbled note from Dr. Nelson, he immediately looked interested.

"Tell me about yourself," he said gently.

In a flat voice, Linda explained what had happened. She didn't divulge anything beyond the bare facts. Her stepmother, Anne, had been screeching at her, louder and louder. And in some part of her brain, Linda knew this shouting was going on. But she didn't hear it. Anne's voice was somehow erased in her mind.

She knew what she had admitted sounded awful. Her brothers already were calling her crazy. Why give them any more reasons? So Linda didn't tell the psychiatrist the other strange occurrences that had been happening in her life: That she saw and heard things that weren't real. That it seemed sometimes as though a movie was playing in her head, drowning out the sound of her stepmother, her teacher, even her friends.

She never mentioned the time when she was lying in her bed on a clear, humid summer night and voices came from her brown leather shoes lined up under her chair. Deep, masculine voices. They told her to pray to the moon. The window was open and she looked out at the big white moon. No one else was in the room. No one to hear the voices. Her parents were on the front porch. Her younger brothers were sleeping.

The voices got louder, more insistent. "Do it, do it, do it," they growled. And Linda did as she was told. She stood up in the middle of her bedroom, lifted her arms, and prayed to the moon with the same words she used at Sunday church services.

"Dear Lord, dear Jesus, help me. Please help me," she said over and over. But the voices were not satisfied. They wouldn't stop until she fell asleep exhausted just as the sun was coming up.

During lucid moments, she wondered what was wrong with her.

The young psychiatrist told her father that she must be admitted to the hospital right away. George agreed. He didn't know what else to do. While he and the doctor went to the admissions department, a nurse escorted Linda to a hospital room. Linda took off her shorts and blouse, folded them up and slipped them into a plastic bag for her father to take home. She put on a white hospital gown that was so large, it slipped off her shoulders. So she had to sit in bed with her shoulders scrunched up to keep her modesty.

She stayed for a few weeks, the first time she'd ever been away from home. Several times she talked to the young doctor and to an older one. They asked her questions. She couldn't focus on what they were saying.

"Nervous breakdown," the young doctor told her father, handing him a prescription for medicine. "Possible schizophrenia," the doctor wrote in her chart.

Her father never had the prescription filled. All along, he was sure he knew what was wrong with Linda.

"It's voodoo," he said. He was deeply rooted in voodoo. Anne didn't really believe in all that stuff, but she went along with him when he insisted someone was working a spell. Linda went along with that explanation too. In their Savannah neighborhood, it was better that everyone thought she was under a spell, that she was hoo-dooed, than that she was crazy.

George took her to several voodoo doctors. One told her to wear a small leather bag around her neck for nine days. Linda never knew what was inside. But whatever spell the bag was supposed to break didn't go away, so George tried someone else.

An old man told George to drive a new nail into a can of lye each day for seven days. "After seven holes are in the can, bury it under the doorstep." Then Linda was to come out of the house each morning at dawn and walk up and down the steps.

The disease in her head was still there, but she couldn't explain it. So she let her father think she was cured.

No matter what, she wanted to please her father. Just being around him made her happy. He had a quiet sense of humor that could deflect a brewing argument. But he didn't do what Linda thought all fathers did: Linda couldn't remember him ever hugging or holding her.

Linda's uncle Wayne was a different sort. He lavished his attention on her. It was Wayne who had taught her how to ride a bicycle. And even though her brothers were around, Wayne would come by the house and say, "C'mon Linda, let's you and me go to the movies. There's a Saturday matinee." Other times, it was "Let's you and me go fishing." Whenever she drifted away into her own mind, Wayne didn't seem to notice.

One afternoon while they were dangling their fishing lines in a stream, she said to Wayne, "Sometimes, you meet people and say, 'Boy, they're crazy.' But you never think *you* are crazy."

Linda often wished she could talk to her own mother about what was happening to her. But she hadn't seen her mother since she was three years old. She remembered watching from a corner, and seeing her mother and father standing inside the front door, talking quietly. Probably they were saying good-bye, Linda decided. Each time she contemplated that scene, she came to the same conclusion: Her mother was leaving. It was the last memory she had of her.

When the voices got loud or other bad things happened, Linda would look out her window at night and repeat, "Star light, star bright, first star I see tonight. I wish I may, I wish I might, I wish I get my wish tonight."

She wished her mother would step through the door and rescue her.

After her mother left, Linda lived with her father's mother for a couple of years, a happy time when she was fussed over and maybe a little spoiled. Then her father remarried. Anne didn't like to be re-minded of the woman whose place she was taking, and Linda, who re-sembled her mother, was a constant, silent irritation.

Then Anne and George started having their own children and Linda, as she grew up, was often left in charge of them. Once when she was thirteen and George took off on what he said was a business trip, Anne went off with her sister. The refrigerator was empty and Linda's younger brothers were hungry. She knocked on the back door of their neighbor's house. Inside, a card game was going on.

"Miss Willa Mae, please give my brothers something to eat and I'll wash the dishes for you," said Linda. She thought this was a good plan. And she was confused when Willa Mae started crying. Then Willa Mae told her card-playing friends what Linda wanted, and they began sniffling too.

Willa Mae set places for the children and fed them big helpings of potatoes and meat.

"Can I wash the dishes now?" Linda asked.

"No, baby," Willa Mae sputtered and began crying again.

At first, Linda had the reputation in school of a conscientious student. She could concentrate in school and focus on her work, and she had appeared to be the bright, attentive achiever that her grade school teachers predicted she'd become. She won the local junior high school spelling bee and moved on to the regional bee. There she was successful, too, not even hesitating as she spelled out *diphtheria.*

But as the years went by, the triumphs began to dwindle and her strange behavior grew more noticeable. In the middle of algebra class, she'd have conversations with herself aloud. Sometimes she'd break out laughing. Sometimes she'd cry.

The teachers couldn't understand what was going on. Neither could her friends. Neither could she.

"I can't get a grip, sometimes, no matter how I try," she thought.

The kids in school shunned Linda because of her antics. Every day, she ate lunch by herself. Her marks fell. In eleventh grade, she dropped out. Neither her father nor stepmother tried to stop her.

For a while, being out of school and away from its rigid schedule of classes and deadlines seemed to be the right solution for Linda. She got a job taking tickets at a drive-in. Then she got hired as an elevator operator in Belk's, a fancy department store. She didn't wear a uniform. She just had to dress nicely.

But she didn't keep that job too long. Her strange behavior came back, more pronounced than before. She talked to herself at work. At home, she took walks at midnight and banged on the walls of her bedroom to hurt the voices, to make them stop. Eventually, her family had had enough. Her father told her to leave. Only one brother helped her pack.

"You embarrass me," he told her. "Why can't you stop this? Why can't you stop?"

Linda asked herself the same question.

She rented a small, one-story wooden house painted yellow. But she didn't live alone for long. A shy man from the neighborhood named Sam started coming around regularly. He liked it when Linda cooked dinner for him and he liked sitting next to her on the sofa watching TV. Three months after they started going together, Linda and Sam stood up in the living room before a justice of the peace and were married. Neither her father nor her brothers attended the ceremony. She had just turned nineteen.

At first, Sam didn't mind her moods. That's what he called them, her "moods." If she curled up into herself or talked funny, she always came out of it. But after the babies were born—a girl with curly dark hair followed by a boy thirteen months later—he got worried. Maybe she'd go off in one of her moods and forget she even had babies to look after.

One afternoon when Sam had taken the babies to the park, Linda decided she couldn't tolerate the confusion in her head any longer. She thought she was possessed by the devil. She couldn't find any peace and she wanted it all to end. Immediately. If she killed herself, she thought, she would be out of the pain. She stuffed rags under the back door, turned on the gas jets on the stove, and lay down on the kitchen floor.

A neighbor happened to come by. He smelled the gas, broke down the wooden door, and carried Linda outside. Someone called the fire department and within minutes, emergency personnel arrived, sirens howling. A technician with blond hair knelt down. He was giving Linda mouth-to-mouth resuscitation when she came to.

She looked at the technician and, for a dazzling moment, she thought, "He's an angel. I'm in heaven, thank God."

The suicide attempt landed her again in Clark Pavilion, the psychiatric wing of Memorial Hospital. For the first time, Linda learned there was a medical explanation for her condition, schizophrenia. Maybe it would be better to be possessed, she thought.

The nurses made sure she took her Haldol to control the voices she heard. Sam visited every Sunday. Linda talked to him pleasantly but dispassionately, as if he were another stranger waiting to get on the same bus. After three months in the hospital, the doctors told Linda she was being discharged. But they urged her to return each day to the hospital's day treatment program.

Linda expected the therapists there would talk to her about her problems. She didn't want to confide in strangers, but still she hoped that somehow this program might help her get through each day. What she discovered was something else.

She went to a room in the hospital with fifteen people looking just as withdrawn and unhappy as she and two perky women in pink smocks who were encouraging everyone to make ceramic ashtrays. After three weeks of gluing tiles onto a metal plate, they graduated to painting ceramic figurines.

Linda figured that the purpose of this program was to get the patients to talk to each other. But no one really talked except to ask each other for cigarettes.

Once a day, the patients gathered for a group session to discuss their problems. The therapist, a young woman named Bev, usually began the session by asking, "Any depression? Any anxiety?"

Linda almost wanted to laugh.

"Who wouldn't be depressed being here?" she thought. "Who wouldn't be anxious? You do the arts and crafts and the therapy groups and you paint by numbers. And each day, the patients stand in line while Bev passes out their medications. I hate every minute of it."

Eventually, Linda stopped attending the day treatment program. And she stopped taking her medication because she felt so much better. Then the slow slide from reality began all over again. Sometimes, she'd put the babies in the playpen and leave them there all day, just so they'd be safe. Within a year, she relapsed and returned to Clark Pavilion.

Several times, Linda went through the cycle—hospitalization, day treatment, a period of stability, deterioration, rehospitalization. Each time she left the hospital, she promised Sam she'd never have to return.

When she was twenty-four and showed the familiar, worrisome signs of an impending hospitalization, Sam emptied his bureau drawers into a suitcase and moved out. Linda spent the whole night pacing around her kitchen table, first clockwise and then counterclockwise, as her voices ordered her to do. At dawn, a neighbor noticed and called the police. Once again, she was taken to the hospital.

In group therapy, the other patients bad-mouthed Sam. What a worthless so-and-so, running out on you and your children. But Linda didn't blame him for leaving. She, too, was tired of the day program, tired of the psychiatric medications, tired of insanity.

The voices were now louder than ever. "Leave. Leave. You can't stay here. You don't deserve to be here. You're worthless." Her childhood neighbor, Willa Mae, agreed to take care of the children.

Linda went to the bus depot. Her money would take her as far as Jacksonville, Florida. She needed a job and because she knew how the mental health system operated, she knew there were always entry-level openings in that field. Within a week, she found a job as a nurse's aide in an alcohol detox center. Then she rented a two-room apartment in an old house. Sometimes her craziness erupted and she couldn't go to work. But her boss, who was attracted to her, forgave her periodic absences.

Then two years later, as abruptly as she had arrived, it was time to go. Linda just felt it. She got out on the road with a backpack and her thumb stuck out. She planned to hitchhike to California, the land of sunshine and happiness. Her first ride was with two college girls who took her to North Carolina. Then migrant workers brought her to Virginia. A man in a pick-up truck was driving to Philadelphia. And because she was in a hurry to see the ocean, she got another ride from Philadelphia with a man going to Atlantic City.

She applied for a job in the kitchen of a casino. When her fingerprints came back from state authorities showing she had no criminal record, she was hired. She telephoned Willa Mae and told her that she missed the children, but she wasn't coming home for a while.

"Alright, honey, I'll watch them. Sam comes by to see them every week. But they'll always be yours."

At work, the kitchen help ate at the end of each shift. At first, Linda sat with her co-workers around a big table and gossiped about the chef and the hostess. Then she stopped talking during their meal and looked at her co-workers suspiciously. Then she stopped eating. She knew somebody was putting something poisonous in her food.

Linda lived on one hot dog a day that she bought from a Boardwalk vendor. At the end of the month, when she got her paycheck, she quit her job. She checked out of her rooming house, walked to the bus station, and bought a one-way ticket to New York because there she could connect with a bus going to California.

Once she arrived at the Port Authority terminal in New York, she changed her mind. New York looked exciting. It looked like a fresh start. She found a job as a receptionist. She learned Spanish. She dated a man named Jimmy for a while. Once again, it looked like moving had been the right thing to do.

But the picture was deceiving. Jimmy stole the money she'd been saving in her bureau drawer. She had no friends, few acquaintances. Linda wore wigs all the time, attempting to look like anyone but herself. She lived in a world of her own creation. She drifted away from reality.

Then she started using cocaine. At first she thought it was so wonderful to be high, higher than all her problems. Then everything tumbled downhill. She couldn't afford her apartment and moved onto the streets.

When she needed to wash up, she'd sit down at a table in a coffee shop and order a cup of coffee. When the waiter went to fill her order, she'd head for the ladies room. One afternoon when she tried this ploy, the waiter stopped her and told her the ladies room was for real patrons, not her. "What are you talking about? What do you mean? Who do you think I am?" Linda spat out. Within minutes, the police were called. They dropped her off at Kings County Hospital in Brooklyn.

In the psychiatric unit of the city-owned hospital, patients gathered every morning in a large sunny room. "Now everybody, we're going to do ceramics," chirped the art therapist. Linda glared at her but dutifully painted little chipmunks with her brown and white paints. Once a day, medications were dispensed and Linda got in line with the other patients, holding out her hand to receive her pills and swallowing them under the aide's gaze. No one came to visit her.

She graduated to a day treatment program in a building near the decaying Coney Island amusement park where, in addition to paint-by-number art classes, she attended group sessions. Each evening, Linda returned by van to Kings County.

After six weeks, Linda was about to be discharged. But the hospital social worker wouldn't sign the discharge form until she knew Linda had a place to live.

Linda wanted to ask, "How can I find a place to live when I am locked up inside?" But she kept quiet. She went through a phone book, looked up Pierce, found a "Pierce, Dana," and wrote down that address. That satisfied the social worker, who signed the discharge forms.

Linda went back to living on the streets. She ate in soup kitchens and panhandled for money, sticking her cup out as commuters scurried past without looking her in the face. She found that the number 7 subway line going out to middle-class Queens carried the most generous riders. On the day she turned thirty, she spent her coins on a king-size chocolate bar.

She didn't take her medication. She knew she should if she wanted to feel good. But the voices in her head told her the medication was poison and the doctors were all against her and not to be trusted. Some nights, she slept in the sprawling New York Port Authority bus terminal. Then she and several other homeless women took over an abandoned building in Brooklyn. But on a cold night in January 1991, they were displaced by a band of young drug dealers.

Linda had no choice but to make her way to the shelter. A woman directed her to a cot. They had run out of sheets but she gave Linda a blanket.

In the Flushing Women's Shelter, a social worker named Maureen approached Linda about getting her life back together. She asked if Linda had ever been hospitalized for psychiatric problems.

"I got out of Kings County last year," she said.

Maureen asked her to meet with a counselor working with the

Community Support Team from New York University, a program designed for homeless mentally ill people. In some ways, it was like being back in the hospital. They got Linda back on her antipsychotic medication by treating her like a six-year-old. They gave her a pill and water, watched her swallow, and then made her open her mouth wide to make sure it was gone. Linda was furious, but she needed the bed and three meals a day that the shelter provided. Then, gradually, as the Haldol started taking hold, she began to feel better.

The team convinced Linda to move into a residence for people with mental illness near Columbia University in upper Manhattan. Linda resisted. "There's nothing wrong with me," she told them over and over. But the team was persistent. When another homeless woman told Linda she'd signed up to go to the residence, Linda said, "Okay, I'll try it too."

At the residence, a social work student from NYU named Serena suggested Linda look into the day program at a place called Fountain House.

It took one month to convince Linda to visit Fountain House. She was suspicious of any program described as rehabilitation. She had one reason after another why she wouldn't even waste her time to visit.

"I am not going to a place with crazy people because I am not crazy," Linda said.

"It is not like that," said Serena.

"I am not going to a place where they make ashtrays and color pictures by number."

"It's not like that, either."

Finally, she agreed to spend one morning there.

What she saw was nothing like what she expected. She saw wallpaper and carpeted floors, flowers and people smiling. She came back to the residence more talkative than she'd ever been with her roommates.

"I looked around and I was bowled over. It was like a home," she said. "I kept looking around. I never saw a doctor. I never saw a nurse.

I think someone was playing the piano. People were sitting around in the living room. People were walking around. No one was in a strait-jacket.

"There were no medication lines, no hypodermic needles. No clay pottery, no connecting by dots. There were just people. People doing people things."

Please Don't Knock. Walk Right In

Walking west on 47th Street between 9th and 10th Avenues, it's easy to pick out the complex of buildings that comprise Fountain House. A large American flag flies from a holder outside a second-floor window and waves over the sidewalk. And the complex's five buildings— a stately Georgian colonial brick house, three sandstone buildings, one brownstone guesthouse—are the best-maintained on the street.

This section of Manhattan runs from the old docks on the waterfront in the West 40s and 50s over to the theater district. It was once called Hell's Kitchen, so-named, as the story goes, by an 1890s policeman describing how hot it was in the summer on his beat. Later, Hell's Kitchen became known as the place where scruffy Irish gangs roamed dark, mean streets. When gentrification began in the 1980s, local civic groups referred to the section as Clinton, a less colorful but also less derogatory name.

The Clinton neighborhood has become home to aspiring actors and musicians, immigrant Latino families, and young professionals who wheel their infants in elaborate strollers along cracked sidewalks. They rent narrow apartments in the three- and four-story brownstone tenements, some of which still have fire escapes bolted to the facade. The apartments turn over quickly as the tenants' careers either take off or stumble, and there is often a string of rental trucks idling along the curb at the end of each month as tenants shuffle in and out.

Hollywood discovered the neighborhood too, and West 47th Street has held a prominent place on filmmakers' lists of "sleazy locations" for its authentic tenements directly across from Fountain House. The opening scene of *Raging Bull* was shot there. For *The Seventh Deadly Sin,* Frank Sinatra spent a day filming inside the Fountain House guesthouse. In the thriller *Marathon Man,* Dustin Hoffman was pursued down 47th Street to a phone booth outside Fountain House.

A few willowy trees with small flowers planted at their base grow in front of Fountain House. They're separated from the sidewalk by a waist-high iron fence painted black each spring. Except for several people on staff who have small apartments within the guesthouse, no one lives at Fountain House. It is open every day of the year and the activity level is high. A steady stream of people, usually 400 each weekday and about half as many on weekends, come and go, working to keep Fountain House functioning or attending lunchtime meetings of Alcoholics Anonymous, evening social activities, or weekend coffee klatches for people employed full-time.

These people are called "members" and Fountain House is their clubhouse.

There are 1,300 active members, all of whom have suffered from severe and persistent mental illness. The majority have schizophrenia like Linda, while the rest have bipolar disorder (or manic depression), major depression, or borderline personality disorder. More than 15,000 members have participated in Fountain House's program since the mid-1950s.

Anyone who comes in the large green front door is greeted by a person standing inside the foyer with a hearty "Hello, welcome to Fountain House." This tradition began shortly after Fountain House's first executive director, John Beard, was hired. He wanted visitors and members alike to be welcomed when they crossed the threshold and decided the greeter should be someone from the neighborhood. For many years, that role was held by affable Jack Daley, whose presence stifled whatever concerns the neighbors had about the increasing number of mentally ill people who came there each day.

Then, as the neighborhood changed to transient renters with less stake in what happened on West 47th Street, members were encouraged to serve as greeters. Their presence was a security measure to keep out people with no business at Fountain House. More important, their "Hello, how are you?" to fellow members served as a daily reminder that people with mental illness, one of the most shunned populations in society, were welcome here.

A member greeted Serena and Linda when they visited Fountain House in May 1991. Serena explained to the member they'd come to see what happened at Fountain House.

"We're just looking," Linda reminded Serena.

Inside, Fountain House didn't have an institutional look. It was intentionally decorated to look like a private club. The walls were covered with wallpaper, not tile. The furniture was upholstered, not vinyl. The lighting came from overhead chandeliers and table lamps, not bare fluorescent tubes.

Another member acted as their guide for a tour of the facility. In the living room, the guide explained that members can spend all day, if they like, sitting on the couches and easy chairs. However, most members choose to join one of the work units that help in the daily operation of Fountain House. Like all activities in the clubhouse, participation was voluntary.

Linda, Serena, and their guide climbed a graceful, curved staircase to the second floor, where administrative offices and a lending library were located. They went up two more floors to the clerical unit. Here, several men and women were working on computers, typing up stories for the daily, in-house newspaper called *Fountain House Today*. At a large table, people were stuffing envelopes for a fundraising appeal. Linda couldn't tell which were members and which were staff. Neither could Serena.

Throughout the tour, they couldn't distinguish members from staff. They saw people working together in small offices. Someone was answering the switchboard. In the horticulture unit, which tended the plants throughout Fountain House, people were making an arrangement of dried flowers. On another floor, a few men were preparing to broadcast an interview with a member over closed-circuit television. Everywhere she went, Linda was introduced to people who greeted her warmly.

In the dining room, Peter Wargo, a forty-year-old social worker with master's degrees in counseling and social work, was cutting cakes into sixteen equal pieces for lunch. He directed a crew of five staff and ninety members who comprise the dining room unit. Usually, he could expect thirty members to show up to help each day. Working together, the dining room unit prepares lunch for 200 members and staff, serves the food, works the cash register, and clears the tables.

Once he finished cutting the cake, Peter needed to plan the menus for the following week's lunches. He rolled out a blackboard at the far end of the dining room. Twenty members and staff pulled up chairs to form a large semicircle facing him.

"Okay. Next week, what will we have?" Peter asked, a piece of chalk in his poised hand.

"A Reuben with rye bread for Friday," someone suggested and Peter wrote it down.

"Sloppy Joes on Wednesday?" an older man proposed.

"Sloppy Joes. That's on bread," a woman said.

"Or it's on your lap," another woman said and everyone laughed.

"Maybe we should put it in pita bread?"

"No, let's get a real roll."

"How about spaghetti with cream sauce for Tuesday?"

"That's high in cholesterol. Maybe just tomato sauce?"

Around the group, suggestions flew and Peter gradually filled out the menus for each day. Now he'd have to determine how much food they'd need to buy, make up a shopping list, and decide which members would come along to the supermarket.

The more Linda saw, the more she was puzzled. She couldn't figure out what was happening at this place and, more importantly, what they might expect of her. Still, she had to find a day program to attend because the group home where she lived with ten other women required that they be out from 9 A.M. until 4 P.M. every day.

The following week, Linda returned to Fountain House for one more look. On the sidewalk, she passed Joanna Romano, a red-haired woman who headed the education unit that helped members earn their GEDs or attend college classes.

"Good morning, Linda. How are you?" Joanna said.

Linda was shocked that she remembered her name.

In the hallway, the same thing happened again. Tom Malamud, the associate director for program, said, "Hello, Linda." Someone else greeted her too. They'd only met her once and they knew her name! They remembered her! From a homeless person who was always in the way, someone who was stepped around or ignored, she became a person with a name. It convinced her to apply for membership to Fountain House.

Still, she was suspicious, looking for some kind of trick. After her application was approved, she wondered what the staff was going to make her do. They told her she didn't have to do anything she didn't want to do. Membership at Fountain House, they said, is voluntary. We'll see, Linda thought, trusting no one.

During the two weeks of orientation, she learned what the various units did and met the social workers in each unit. When asked which unit she wanted to be part of, she said horticulture. She chose it because she felt as though her life was dead and she wanted to bring something to life. And she was attracted to the serene nature of Clare Smith, a social worker from England in her early thirties who led the unit.

For the next few weeks, Linda went to the horticulture unit — and did nothing. She felt overwhelmed by the cheerful people around her. She sat at one of the round tables in the unit, surrounded by small potted plants and flowers drying overhead, staring angrily. Clare gently tried to draw Linda into the group.

"Would you like to repot this plant?"

"No."

"Would you like to make the tea?"

"No."

Linda wanted to say yes but she couldn't. She wanted someone to care about her, but she couldn't respond to Clare's overtures. Clare persisted. She knew how difficult it was for a member to break down the walls of isolation that mental illness built in the brain. Day after day, Linda returned to the horticulture unit. And that was all Clare needed to see: a member who kept returning was a member who would someday participate.

"Can you help us water the plants through the house?"

"No."

One day, a new freestanding set of open shelves had been delivered to the horticulture unit and Clare was transferring some plants onto a shelf. As she stood up with a potted plant in each hand, her left hand wobbled.

"Oh, Linda, grab this! It's going to topple over."

Instinctively, Linda reached out for the plant.

"Thank you. Thank you very much. Would you please put that on the top shelf? Thank you. And could you help me with this one too?"

Over the next few weeks, Linda still kept her distance from Clare but the invisible barrier between the two had been penetrated. Gradually, it opened up a bit more. Clare noticed whenever Linda styled her hair differently. She complimented Linda on her choice of sweaters, her eye for detail, the way she combined varieties of plants. One morning, Clare suggested that Linda and another member switch the dried floral arrangements throughout the house.

"Where do you want them?" Linda asked.

"You decide where they should be put," Clare said softly.

Some days, Linda didn't feel like going along with whatever Clare suggested. She didn't like being assigned to water plants. She didn't like being stuck in this "stupid horticulture area in this place for crazy people." "What am I doing in this place?" Linda asked herself angrily. She thought she needed to get away, get out of this city, get back on the road to California.

Once when Clare asked Linda to get down some wicker baskets stacked on a shelf, Linda spewed a stream of curses at her. Claire said nothing. This outburst wasn't significant enough to confront. Clare turned and focused on another member. Linda stomped out of the room.

Linda couldn't wait to tell her therapist that she'd decided to move on. But by the time their weekly session at the community mental health clinic arrived, Linda's anger had given way to embarrassment.

"Give Fountain House another chance," the therapist suggested.

By the winter, Linda was more comfortable coming to Fountain House; she came three or more days a week. The other days, she'd walk along Amsterdam Avenue in Manhattan, looking in store windows or going into churches. Sometimes, she'd buy a cup of coffee and nurse it for an hour. As the weather got colder, she had less desire to wander aimlessly. What was going on at Fountain House was more interesting.

She was walking along the sidewalk on her way to the horticulture unit one morning when a man across the street shouted out. He'd come out of a house and was walking down a small set of steps when he lost his footing on ice. Esther Montanez, the assistant director of Fountain House, was walking toward Linda and she heard the man's shout too.

Plop, plop, plop, the man bounced down the steps on his rear. When he hit the sidewalk, he stood up and dusted off his pants. Seeing he had an audience, he called out humorously, "It was a soft landing." Esther and Linda laughed and then caught each other's eye.

"Hi, my name is Esther."

"My name is Linda."

"Isn't it great to laugh?" Esther asked.

Linda said nothing.

Several weeks later, Linda was walking toward Esther in the crowded dining room. Even though Linda was wearing a wig of straight dark hair over her close-cropped hair, Esther recognized her.

"Hello, Linda."

"I remember your name. Your name is Esther."

"Thank you," said Esther. "Will you sit down and have a cup of coffee with me?"

Startled, Linda agreed.

At least once in the morning and again in the afternoon, Esther stood outside Fountain House to smoke a cigarette. Smoking was banned in all but two designated spots in the facility and although Esther would occasionally sneak a cigarette in her office, she stepped outside most of the time. It gave members a chance to come up and talk to her spontaneously, and it gave Esther an opportunity to see which members were lingering outside, too afraid or disconnected to come inside.

She saw Linda hurrying in her direction one day in early April 1992. Linda looked terrible. Her face was clouded in distress. Esther grabbed her and wrapped her in a hug. Linda started crying hard. Esther began crying too. It didn't matter what the problem was. What bothered Linda, bothered Esther.

The two women slowly became friends. Esther could be intimidating. As a girl, she'd been a star basketball player in youth leagues and she still had a no-nonsense, drive-to-the-hoop approach. But as Linda gradually became more confident, she began to seek out Esther.

Whenever Linda entered the main building, she rapped on the window of Esther's office, which overlooked the steps, and waved to her. Sometimes, she'd stop in and talk. In May, when Fountain House was preparing for its annual banquet to honor the employers who hire its members, Esther asked Linda to help her wash down the doors on the first floor. Together, they sang as they worked. In 1993, when Esther started the Connections Program to reach out to members who had stopped coming to Fountain House, the first person she asked to join was Linda.

This was the kind of social work that Esther knew how to do. She'd engage members in work, making them feel valuable as they accomplished a real task that needed to be done. Members felt they were a contributing part of society, just like everyone else. Most programs for the mentally ill, Esther felt, were too busy doing *to* people rather than doing *with* them.

"When a member says to me, 'I got lost on the subway,' I say, 'What happened?' I take that extra second and I am friends forever. I don't say,

'Can I help you?' or 'What are you going to do now?' She's telling me what happened. To listen and to make time, that is what I do.

"When I see a change in the way a member acts or looks, I say, 'Let's have a cigarette.' All I have to do is listen and be compassionate. I just tell people that I am sorry and I hold them. That's my job."

She didn't learn this technique inside a classroom. All of Esther's professional knowledge about dealing with mentally ill people came from John Beard, who served as executive director from 1955 until his death from lung cancer in 1982.

Beard hired Esther Montanez in 1961 to be a housekeeper at Fountain House. She was twenty-six years old, a former youth counselor with a high school diploma. She came with her family from Puerto Rico as a child and grew up on Manhattan's Lower East Side. Because her mother had bouts of depression, Esther had seen mental illness up close and it didn't scare her.

At Fountain House, she discovered her job description meant little as John Beard expected every employee to participate in creating a supportive environment for the members. Quickly, she grasped Beard's innovative concepts: people with mental illness needed a place to come where they were welcomed and needed; and these people could regain a place in society by performing valued work.

These concepts ultimately became known as the Fountain House model of psychiatric rehabilitation. But in the early years, Esther thought she was simply doing what needed to be done.

"We'd say, 'Let's have lunch' and two members and I would go around the corner. We got salami, Wonder bread, mayonnaise, and mustard. Someone got apples. And that was the start of our dining room unit.

"We started a housekeeping unit because the house was dirty. The clerical unit began because we needed money. Everyone got the telephone book and picked the first person on the page. We wrote a letter to them. 'Dear Mr. Jones, My name is Esther Montanez. I am a staff worker at Fountain House. This is a place for people with mental illness to come each day. We need a donation.' We made $722 on our first appeal. We kept a little chart. We'd open a letter and say, 'Ooh, we got another dollar.'"

At the time, Fountain House depended heavily on donations from private philanthropists, many of whom had a relative with mental illness. The program's beginnings traces back to a wealthy New Yorker whose intense interest in schizophrenia sparked a desire to meet people afflicted with the disease.

Elizabeth Ker Schermerhorn, who was born into one prominent family and married into another, had met Carl Jung in Switzerland in the late 1930s and began Jungian analysis with one of his students. With the outbreak of World War II, she returned to New York. Her interest in psychiatry expanded from a personal quest to an intellectual pursuit, with a special interest in the relationship between schizophrenia and society. To see firsthand how mental illness affects individuals, she took a job in 1942 as a psychiatric aide at Rockland State Hospital outside of New York City.

She was assigned to work with a staff psychiatrist, Dr. Hiram Johnson, who was attempting to apply the self-help principles of Alcoholics Anonymous to a small group of male patients who were soon to be discharged. Dr. Johnson was concerned about the high relapse rate among discharged patients. He hoped they would be better able to cope with life in the community if they had support from each other, if they remained friends with their fellow patients.

Elizabeth Schermerhorn got to know the men individually as they met regularly with Dr. Johnson in a hospital club room for discussion groups and social gatherings. However, her physical health was poor and she was forced to leave Rockland State in the summer of 1943. That fall, she was contacted at her home by a newly discharged patient who'd participated in Dr. Johnson's self-help group. He asked for her help in developing an informal association of former patients. She enthusiastically agreed. She was the only outsider and the only woman present when ten former patients met for the first time on March 15, 1944 in the boardroom of the Third Street YMCA in Manhattan. They decided to call themselves "We Are Not Alone," shortened to WANA.

Almost from the beginning, the WANA members talked about having their own building. They didn't always have access to the YMCA meeting room. Sometimes, they got together on the steps of the New York Public Library.

In 1948, Elizabeth Schermerhorn found a lovely, four-story brownstone for sale on the south side of West 47th Street and arranged for its purchase for $25,000. Behind the house was a small patio with a fountain built into a brick wall around the property. Schermerhorn and other supporters of WANA formed a board of directors and incorporated as the Fountain House Foundation. At the same time a patients-only body, called Fountain House Fellowship, formed and began to set house rules and organize activities for members.

Over the next few years, the program developed in fits and starts. Members wanted to run the clubhouse without staff supervision, but their lack of experience and their bouts of illness caused confusion, dissension, and financial problems. Fountain House needed a strong guiding hand. Elizabeth Schermerhorn had heard of John Beard's innovative work with psychiatric patients in the back ward of Wayne County General Hospital in Michigan, and she recruited him in 1955 as executive director.

John Beard was a bit awed by the opportunity presented by Schermerhorn, but he had no doubt about the validity of his theories for helping people with mental illness make the transition back to the normal world. A tall, thin man with a penetrating gaze, he made changes immediately upon his arrival at Fountain House.

The program had been operating only in the evening. Since most members were unemployed and had nowhere to go during the day, he began daytime hours too. He asked one member to work on the switchboard, another to deliver messages between floors. Soon, members and staff were rubbing elbows as they scurried up and down the narrow staircase.

Beard didn't use a desk because he didn't like its authoritarian implications—as if sitting across from a member, he had something marvelous to impart. So he sat at a long rounded table, frequently inviting members to sit down next to him and talk.

One of the three lavatories in the building could be reached only by walking through Beard's office. To make sure members knew they were permitted to use this bathroom, he hung a sign on his office door: "Please Don't Knock. Walk Right In."

Members who'd spent years in locked psychiatric wards were stunned by the sign. The invitation to walk into the director's office at any time clearly signaled that this place was vastly different from anything they'd experienced.

Beard developed his interest in mental illness while working toward a master's degree in social work at Wayne State University in Detroit, Michigan. After completing his field work as a graduate student, he was hired as a social worker at the Wayne County General Hospital in its Eloise mental health complex.

In a 1978 interview videotaped at Fountain House, he described how he and other staff workers related to patients in Eloise where his instinctive approach originated.

"We had crazy images like 'their hair at least was not schizophrenic, or their fingernails at least.' There has got to be some part of these [patients] that is not mentally ill," he said. "Then [we] try to find out what those pieces are, what are those parts of the person that can begin to function, and try to bypass what the obviously gross illness is."

Beard worked closely with a patient with schizophrenia named Arthur, a World War II refugee from Romania. He arranged for Arthur to get a part-time job stocking shelves in a supermarket.

"I had no interest in why he was sick," said Beard. "That was not my job. That was other people's jobs. I wasn't interested in trying to review his history or any psychopathology. I had no interest in it at all. I was terribly interested in how normal we might get him to function."

Beard brought his vision to Fountain House. Through the daily activities of normal people, he tried to engage the parts of a member's personality not consumed by mental illness. He expected other employees at Fountain House to adopt his approach.

Several social workers rebelled and quit. Others, who agreed with Beard's overall philosophy of psychiatric rehabilitation, eventually left Fountain House to develop their own programs, most notably in Chicago and Miami. Many employees, including Esther Montanez and Jim Schmidt, a social worker trained at Columbia University who ultimately succeeded John Beard as executive director, embraced Beard's ideas wholeheartedly.

In her own work, Esther imitated Beard's method of reaching out to members. When she cleaned the piano in the living room, she asked a member for help. "You clean the white keys and I'll do the black ones," she said. When it was time to clean the panes of glass in the French doors, she used the same approach. "You clean the left side and I'll clean the right side."

During the early years of Beard's tenure, there were no more than ten staff workers and a hundred members. By the early 1960s, what had once been a trickle of patients coming from Rockland State Hospital and other public psychiatric facilities became a steady outpouring because of a process that became known as deinstitutionalization.

Deinstitutionalization arose from the discovery in the late 1950s that a tranquilizer, Thorazine, could diminish psychotic symptoms such as hallucinations and delusions; patients were discharged in hopes their symptoms could be managed in a less restrictive environment. In 1963 Congress passed the Community Mental Health Centers Act which allocated federal funds for outpatient services intended to keep people from being readmitted to the hospital.

Fountain House was overwhelmed with membership requests from people newly discharged from state hospitals. The building couldn't accommodate them all. John Beard arranged to buy a vacant lot on the north side of the street and built a new clubhouse. When the hole for the foundation was dug, he walked around the dirt excavation with a tape measure and paced off where the living room and the staircase would be.

He selected the Georgian colonial facade. He picked out the furniture, nothing "motel modern." He insisted on the noninstitutional look. After the new, larger clubhouse was opened in 1965, Beard sold the original building.

For the next twenty years, Beard put his distinctive stamp on every aspect of the Fountain House program. While some mental health professionals advised patients to avoid other patients in their search for a normal life, Beard encouraged them to come together. Rather than face daily living alone and isolated, people with mental illness could find others sharing the same concerns in the clubhouse.

Looking back, Esther couldn't imagine Fountain House without John Beard. Without his dynamism and his genius, it wouldn't have happened. After his death, she felt responsible for keeping alive his memory. Invariably, when staff or members gathered in her office, she'd bring his name into the conversation as she tried to explain his influence.

"When you have an idea, you make a soup. You put the greens in and the salt, and you taste it. You create it," she said.

"Fountain House was a creation. It was a new way of living, a new way of breathing new air. He was working with an idea. It was a philosophy, a breath. And he was the wind."

John Beard showed Esther that reaching out to a member could happen in something as elementary as hanging a picture to improve the decor in the Fountain House living room.

"It would take two or three hours," she said. "John would get all the members. Then we'd get a frame. Then we'd talk about where the picture would go. Then we'd have to measure, from side to side, top to bottom. Make sure the measurements are right. Then someone would have to get the right nails. And the right hammer. Then we'd put up the picture and say, 'That's right.'

"And in that enjoyment, that process, we could say, 'Well done.' All of us, we all put up the picture together. We all said, 'That's right.' Now *that* is rehabilitation."

Because Esther was the Fountain House employee with the longest tenure and the strongest ties to the memory of Beard, some members called her the "spirit of Fountain House" or the "mother of Fountain House." Although many people suspected Esther secretly was pleased by this talk, she claimed to dislike it.

One day in her office, a friend suggested that Esther was "like a legend" in Fountain House. Esther spun away from her desk and glared across the room.

"I am not the mother of the house. I am not the spirit of Fountain House, not the character of Fountain House. For me, the spirit is this: I see men and women walk in here on their knees in pain. And their life changes a little bit."

The friend wondered if that was enough.

"Yes, it is. They're not lonely anymore. They have friends. They have a place to come to. Then there comes housing and schooling and getting back to work. But that first thing, 'Hey, there's a lot of other people like me here. And I won't be alone.' That's the spirit."

3

Too Young to Know Anything Could Go Wrong

Margie Staker, a social worker at Fountain House, beeped the horn of the dark blue van and Matthew Palmer jumped in on the passenger side.

"Are you okay driving?" he asked.

It was December 11, 1993, the start of what would prove to be one of the worst winters in East Coast history. The weather was daunting, with ice on the streets and more snow threatening. But this was the Saturday that Matthew needed to buy furniture because he was moving into his new apartment in four days.

He owned practically nothing. Not a bed. Not a chair. Not a television, although he did have a VCR. When he moved, he planned to bring his clothes, his typewriter, and his medications.

Matthew approached each new experience warily. This day, he was uneasy about the roads. After all, Margie was making this trip on his behalf and it was somewhat of an imposition. She lived in Brooklyn and didn't own a car. She'd borrowed Fountain House's van for the shopping trip.

"I'm fine. Just fine," Margie said warmly. "Don't you worry."

Margie, who pronounced her name "Mar-gee" with a hard g, was confident. A tall Englishwoman who learned how to drive on the left side of the road, she'd been living in America for the past dozen years. And driving the big, institutional van gave her a feeling of invincibility. If she hit anything, she'd worry more about the other vehicle.

Matthew, on the other hand, hadn't had a confident day for more than fifteen years, not since his world was turned upside down by schizophrenia. He'd probably have measured 6-foot-2 or 6-3 if he held himself erect, but he didn't. His shoulders were stooped. His clothes were dark, inconspicuous. He wore his house keys dogtag-style on a metal chain around his neck and slipped them over his head when he needed to unlock the door. He always looked overdue for a haircut. In the winter when he pulled off his black knit cap and hair strands flew around his head, he didn't smooth them into place. He figured no one noticed him.

Without incident, Margie and Matthew drove through the Lincoln Tunnel to northern New Jersey and arrived at a large warehouse-type store filled with easy-to-assemble Swedish furniture.

"Let's look at couches," Margie suggested. She led Matthew through the stick-on tile department and the kitchen cabinet displays to the area where two dozen sofas were arranged in small sitting areas.

"Try this one out," she urged him as she sat down on a red, upholstered couch.

"Too bright," he replied, still standing.

"Well, then, what about this one?" she asked, moving to a model with a pine frame and separate cushions covered in coarse, natural fabric.

"That'll do. It's a good deal, too," he said.

"Before you say that, sit down and try it. You're the one who has to live with it."

Matthew looked up sharply. The thought was astounding. The choice was truly his to make. And his to live with.

For the first time in years, Matthew would be on his own. He was moving into an apartment by himself in Long Island City, a polyglot, blue-collar neighborhood in Queens. The lease was in his name. He'd live there without roommates and without another adult checking on his whereabouts or his well-being.

In his new three-room apartment, a second-floor walk-up with a view of the street from the kitchen window, the superintendent had just slapped down a coat of flat white paint on the walls to cover up the fingerprints of previous tenants. After some coaxing from Margie, the super also agreed to tack down a new speckled linoleum floor in the bedroom to cover an ancient wooden floor that gave off splinters.

This apartment was not at all what Matthew Allen Palmer II would have envisioned when he was about to graduate from a New England prep school some years ago, a bright student who'd been accepted at an Ivy League college. He had plenty of friends and plenty of dreams. Some days, he thought he'd become a lawyer. Other days, he wanted to become a writer.

His father had owned a restaurant in Greenwich Village but went broke gambling on horse racing. His mother, Erica, was the daughter of a world-famous university professor and author who owned a villa in the Italian Alps. When he died, Erica and her two sisters inherited the villa. When her marriage collapsed, Erica and her children moved into the villa for several years. Matthew and his two sisters, Karen and Laura, learned how to speak Italian and German, and attended local grammar school.

The family returned to the United States when Erica married a successful corporate executive she'd met on holiday. Within a year, she had a baby, whom they named Thomas. They settled in fashionable Westport, Connecticut outside of New York. On weekends, Matthew would take the train into Manhattan to visit his father or attend a New York Rangers hockey game.

From prep school, where Matthew was a boarding student, Erica received glowing reports. He played soccer, a sport he'd learned in Italy, for the school team. He wore a wig and lipstick for his role in the school play, *The Importance of Being Earnest,* and he was an editor on the school newspaper. His marks were stellar and he was one of six boys in his class admitted to the University of Pennsylvania.

But in his senior year, Matthew abruptly withdrew from his friends. He stayed in his room. He dropped out of all extracurricular activities. He stopped handing in his homework assignments. The school mailed home an ominous report: "We don't know what is happening." Erica had no idea what could be the matter. Matthew had already been accepted at Penn, and she fervently hoped whatever was bothering him would disappear once he began college.

For a time at Penn, he did seem to do better. He found the schoolwork demanding but he could keep up with it. He made friends with his classmates, especially with three who lived in his dormitory. Midway through his freshman year, Matthew and a classmate from Oregon named Dan walked over to a party across the Quad on a Friday night. The party was boring—that is, few girls were in attendance—so they returned to their dormitory and met up with several other freshmen.

One said, "Let's go to New York City for the weekend."

Matthew suggested, "Let's go to Europe." He'd recently read an article in the *New Yorker* magazine about a new trend, especially popular among Ivy League students, of taking a year off from school.

Dan said, "Yeah, good idea."

Paul said, "I am going too."

Then Ted, a freshman from Chicago who was just sixteen years old, said, "Me too."

The next day, to strengthen their joint resolve to leave school, the friends—Matthew, Ted, Paul, and Dan—went to the Philadelphia International Airport to watch the planes take off. On Monday morning, the foursome went to the assistant dean's office to tell him their plan to take off a semester. He didn't offer resistance.

"Fine," he said. "Good luck."

Within days, Matthew and his friends were on their way to Europe—not flying but traveling tourist class. They had booked passage on an inexpensive Italian cruise ship called the *Volcania* and spent the journey across the Atlantic playing cards and drinking. When the ship docked in Barcelona, the friends disembarked and split up. Matthew hitchhiked to Paris, where he stayed with family friends for several weeks.

Eventually, he needed cash. Someone told him that work was plentiful in the shipyards of Bremen, Germany, so he hitchhiked to that seaport city. He'd forgotten how to speak German, but that made little difference. He found a job as a laborer in a shipyard and rented a room above a tavern, where young men and women gathered each night.

It was a heady time and, recalling the trip years later to a friend at Fountain House, Matthew said, "I could do anything I wanted. I was too young to know anything could go wrong."

After a few months of working all day and drinking beer all night, Matthew was ready to go back to school. He located a Scandinavian freighter that was headed to Kenosha, Wisconsin through the St. Lawrence Seaway. To pay his passage, he signed on as a crew member. He scarcely saw the Atlantic Ocean during the trip—his job was to paint the engine room. By the time he arrived home, he felt sad that his romantic escapade was over, but proud that he'd actually done something so adventurous.

After his European jaunt, Matthew returned to Penn. But back in school, his sense of accomplishment evaporated. He was very anxious about being back in school and drank heavily. After taking a course in group dynamics, he switched his major from English to sociology. Then he visited a psychiatrist at the school's mental health center and discussed his feelings during a few appointments.

Matthew convinced himself that his troubled emotions were caused by the confusion swirling on college campuses in this period of late 1960s. Some classmates were following the advice of ousted Harvard lecturer Timothy Leary to "turn on, tune in, drop out" with LSD. Other students organized angry protests against the war in Vietnam. Matthew's response to the turmoil was to withdraw from most of his friends. He studied hard but earned mostly Cs. On the weekends, he drank. He wasn't worried about being drafted after graduation—he had a medical deferment due to high blood pressure.

Following graduation, he moved to New York City intending to become a playwright but instead found steady work as a computer programmer. He had a girlfriend, Sandy, who wanted to become an artist but supported herself by waitressing. Eventually, she moved into his apartment.

During his first winter in New York, Laura, his younger sister, suffered a breakdown and was diagnosed with schizophrenia. Matthew was deeply saddened—and terrified. He knew he didn't always think rationally and he thought schizophrenia might be hereditary. Maybe he read it somewhere. His older sister, Karen, seemed fine. So did his half-brother, Thomas. He didn't ask his mother about the family history.

Erica, too, was privately worried. She thought there were European relatives on her father's side who had schizophrenia. However, her mother's and former husband's family tree were both free of mental illness. She hoped Matthew would be spared.

With his sister's diagnosis of schizophrenia, Matthew was pushed into acknowledging his own sporadic episodes of disturbed thought. He sought out a psychiatrist at St. Vincent's Hospital and met with him once a week for the next few years. Talking things over seemed to help.

After one session, he decided to visit the town in northern Italy where he'd lived as a boy. He took his vacation, traveled to Europe, and stayed in the villa owned by his mother and aunts. When he met up with his childhood buddies, they slapped him on the back and welcomed him home.

When he returned to New York, he decided to quit his daytime job so he could use the time for writing. He drove a taxi at night to make ends meet. One night in the fall of 1971, he was cruising down 2nd Avenue looking for a fare. At a red light, a fellow on a motorcycle drove up next to the driver's window and asked, "Want to take a trip?"

"Sure," said Matthew and held out his hand. The motorcyclist handed him a small piece of paper and sped off as the light changed. Matthew presumed the paper was laced with LSD. He swallowed it but nothing happened.

Several months later, Matthew was sitting in a bar at closing time. Another cab driver asked him, "Want to come to my place and keep on drinking?"

"Sure," Matthew said.

Out on the sidewalk, the man said, "Instead of beer, want to take a trip?"

"Sure," Matthew nodded. He pulled out his wallet and offered the man a five-dollar bill. The man shoved it in his jacket pocket and gave Matthew a tab.

When he returned to his one-room apartment, Matthew swallowed the tab. The walls started vibrating. Matthew saw colors. He rode the colors like ribbons of highway. The trip lasted forty-eight hours and when it was over, he felt exhilarated, enlightened.

He bought a few more tabs of LSD and took them over the next year. But the excitement of the drug gave way to a sense of dread. He went back to drinking beer and vodka. He stopped telling people he was writing a play.

He'd known Sandy for nearly four years, the longest relationship he'd ever had with a woman, when she abruptly moved out of their apartment in 1975 without really explaining why. Matthew was crushed. He couldn't discuss her leaving with anyone. He quit seeing his psychiatrist.

The voices started in 1976. Persistent, intrusive voices. *Go to the park,* they said. *Call your sister. Get a cup of coffee in this restaurant.* A running commentary of what he should do. Sometimes the voices talked to each other about his behavior. They didn't seem strange or frightening. They reminded Matthew of his LSD trips.

His earlier episodes of social withdrawal and strange thinking were probably signs of the insidious onset of schizophrenia. But once he began hearing voices, the disease swept him away with tidal wave fury.

He couldn't concentrate on driving a cab, and he was fired after a minor accident. Without income, he lost his apartment and began living on the streets in the Bowery section of lower Manhattan. He panhandled. He drank. The voices got louder.

Erica was stunned that her son had hit bottom like this. She couldn't help him financially because her own income was limited after her divorce from her second husband. She was living in a small apartment in Manhattan. She learned that for Matthew to receive public assistance, he had to be declared mentally disabled by a physician. She urged him to contact his former psychiatrist.

"No! No!" Matthew shouted.

"Just make one appointment. Ask him to help you," she implored.

Eventually Matthew contacted his former psychiatrist. With the physician's help, Matthew was approved by the Social Security Administration to receive Social Security Disability Insurance (SSDI) monthly payments. He fit the federal qualification guidelines because of his "inability to engage in any substantial gainful activity by reason of . . . mental impairment which . . . can be expected to last for a continuous period of not less than twelve months."

Receiving a monthly disability check didn't keep Matthew off the streets and in decent housing because he used the money as a passport to indulge his voices. When he received is first SSDI check, he cashed it and bought a bus ticket to the West Coast. Once he went to Reno, another time to Tijuana.

In 1977, he received a $3,500 lump-sum SSDI check that covered the months when his application was being reviewed. He bought a plane ticket and flew to Europe by himself for a two-week trip. He bought a Eurorail pass to travel on the trains.

"Where did you go? What countries did you see?" Erica asked upon his return.

"I don't remember," Matthew said.

Back in New York, he was arrested several times, usually for yelling in public or loitering. One night, standing in a doorway of a boarded-up factory building, he wrote notes about the voices he was hearing. He lit a match to burn up the piece of paper. A patrol car was driving by and Matthew was arrested for attempted arson. After a night in jail, a judge released him.

Periodically, Matthew would appear unexpectedly at Erica's apartment, usually holding a scrap of paper that he'd picked up in the street.

"This is very valuable. Put it away," he'd tell her.

She desperately tried to convince Matthew to admit himself to a hospital for psychiatric evaluation. But he refused.

When Matthew called her from a police station, she begged the police officer, "He should be in a hospital. Not with the criminals on Rikers Island." But a hospital would only keep him overnight. Then he would return to the streets. She watched helplessly as the down-ward spiral continued.

Erica's other schizophrenic child, Laura, was taking a different route to reach rock bottom. Even when her psychosis was raging, Laura would listen to her mother's insistent plea and voluntarily go into the hospital. She'd be stabilized on medication, attend group therapy sessions, and agree to continue therapy after being discharged to an outpatient program.

Within weeks of discharge from the hospital, however, she'd stop taking her medication. And her auditory hallucinations would resume. Once she and her mother met for lunch in a restaurant. While waiting for a table, they sat at the bar and ordered drinks.

"See those people at their tables," said Laura to her mother. "Those people know what I am thinking, and they are talking about me."

Matthew, however, had no rational periods that interrupted his psychotic state. He stayed on the streets. He came to his mother's apartment to take showers, then he'd drift back onto the streets for a few more weeks. His voices got louder, angrier, more insistent.

One day in March 1981, he did something that changed the rest of his life.

He was drinking in a Greenwich Village bar. Usually he drank beer, but it was the first week of the month and he had extra money from his disability check. He'd been drinking screwdrivers for a couple of hours. The voices told him to go to another bar that he'd been tossed out of the previous week. *Go there. Go there.* He had a grudge against the bar. *Stab, stab, stab, stab,* the voices thundered.

By then it was evening. *Stab, stab, stab, stab.* First, he went into a restaurant. Silverware was in an open drawer. He walked by, reached in, and picked up a steak knife.

Then he went into that restaurant's bar and ordered another beer. He was hearing powerful voices, louder than ever before.

"They were thundering," he later said. "It was like a stampede of buffaloes."

After finishing his beer, he walked a block into the bar that had thrown him out. He ordered another beer. He took a sip, then another. A woman sat down next to him. He'd never seen her before.

He took out the knife and stabbed her in the back. The woman screamed. Blood gushed out onto her pink blouse. Matthew ran outside. Some men chased after him, tackled him, and held him until the police came and arrested him. He spent the next seven months awaiting his court hearing, locked up in the Rikers Island prison, where inmates beat him up several times.

"When will I get out on bail?" Matthew asked a prison guard.

In return, the guard gave him an incredulous look.

For legal representation, Matthew contacted a childhood friend, now an attorney with a prestigious Manhattan firm. The friend had heard that Matthew had "gone off the deep end," but assumed it was because of drug use. Matthew, too, held his drug use responsible but for a different reason. "When the voices first started," he told his friend later, "I might have sought help then. But because the voices reminded me of LSD, they didn't seem strange."

His victim's wounds required a few stitches but were not serious. She wasn't in the court room when Matthew stood before a judge and pleaded "not guilty by reason of mental disease or defect." The judge deemed him too mentally disturbed to stand trial.

Matthew was sent to Mid-Hudson Psychiatric Institute, a 280-bed hospital for the dangerously criminally insane in upstate New York, where he received treatment for paranoid schizophrenia and alcoholism.

Immediately, he was placed on Haldol, an antipsychotic medication. As a side effect, the muscles in his neck and jaw stiffened. He couldn't talk because his tongue was rigid. He was given an antidote to reverse the rigidity, but the side effects still seemed to last for weeks.

When his active psychotic symptoms ebbed with the Haldol, he was horrified by what he had done. He had committed a crime. In fact, he was in a facility for the criminally insane. Both words, *criminally* and *insane,* sickened him.

He was also stunned by his lack of freedom. The windows were sealed shut. The doors were locked. He wasn't allowed to bring a cup of coffee from the cafeteria back to his room. He needed permission to eat, permission to bathe and to use the toilet.

He wanted to get better and he was desperate to find a way out. He realized he had to cooperate with the therapist whom he saw daily. Eventually, the head psychiatrist asked him if he wanted to transfer to Manhattan Psychiatric Center (MPC), the public facility on Wards Island. Anywhere would be better than Mid-Hudson, he said.

He was sent to Kirby, the forensic unit at Manhattan Psychiatric Center, in 1982. Despite barbed wire on its rooftop perimeter, the approach at Kirby was more therapeutic than punitive. He was treated by a female psychiatrist who'd survived a concentration camp. He wanted to cooperate with her and began to attend Alcoholics Anonymous meetings.

In the beginning, Matthew had no privacy and attended the group sessions and occupational therapy on the ward. Then he received an honor card and went to the rehabilitation building where he could draw or learn how to cook. At night, he smoked cigarettes. The days went by.

Erica and his half-brother, Thomas, came to visit once a week but his older sister, Karen, never did.

"She is very busy all the time," Erica told him.

As for his younger sister, no one knew where Laura was for months at a time. And when she did telephone her mother, she said she was too busy taking college courses to visit Matthew.

After three years, the hospital staff determined that Matthew's illness was under control. They transferred him out of the forensic unit and into an open psychiatric ward. He began job training and left the hospital for several hours each day.

By now the social workers were trying to locate a halfway house for him. But they didn't know that in the meantime Matthew had stopped taking his medication. The voices returned. He stopped attending AA. The anticipation of freedom was overwhelming for Matthew. He ran away from MPC.

Friends found him drinking in a bar in Greenwich Village and brought him back. He had to start over. Back on medication, back on supervised wards.

"I learned it is impossible to run away," he later told a social worker. "It just doesn't work. I learned my lesson."

Matthew spent the next two years in the hospital, working his way back to the outside world. In 1987, he received his first outside pass to attend the funeral of his younger sister, Laura. Erica had found her dead in the kitchen with the gas oven on. Matthew cried at the funeral, but he wasn't surprised by her death.

The next time Matthew was allowed out, he went with an MPC counselor to visit Fountain House for a day. Several patients from MPC were attending during the day and Matthew was enthusiastic about becoming a member because it represented another step toward getting out of the hospital.

The intake committee at Fountain House was composed of six staff workers, including Margie Staker, and several members. Over several meetings, they carefully weighed Matthew's membership application. He would be one of the first members to come from a forensic ward. Was he still prone to violence? Could he adjust to the program?

The MPC social worker, Robin Green, who'd placed former patients at Fountain House before, spoke movingly about Matthew's improvement. The only violent incident in his life had happened six years ago, when Matthew's schizophrenia was florid and untreated. Since Robin had accurately assessed MPC patients in the past, Fountain House was persuaded to accept Matthew.

"It's obvious he needs a break," said a committee member.

"And he's still a resident of MPC," someone else pointed out, "so if he acts bizarre, we can say he's not appropriate."

After completing his two-week orientation to Fountain House, Matthew chose to work in the clerical unit with Margie. At first, she didn't realize that this tall, quiet man was the forensic patient over whom the intake committee had debated.

Because Matthew was determined to be released from MPC, he agreed to whatever Margie asked him to do. He didn't want to be labeled as difficult, so he never said no to her. She had to teach him no was acceptable: From 10 A.M. until 2 P.M., while he was at Fountain House, he could say no.

He could choose what time to eat his lunch and whether to have a sandwich or a hot entree in the dining room. He could walk out the Fountain House door and down 47th Street. No one kept close track of his movements. But he chose not to. He could even have gone out to a bar and had a beer, but since his runaway episode he had remained sober and had resumed going to AA meetings.

The MPC van picked him up every afternoon at 2:30 P.M. Matthew was always waiting outside at 2:15, just to be sure he wouldn't miss it and break a rule. Margie took her lunch break about that time and on her way to the corner coffee shop, she would stop and talk briefly each day with Matthew. They'd joke how the bus was always late and Matthew was always early.

It was obvious to Margie that Matthew was extremely intelligent. But how to draw Matthew out? How to get him to see he had a future outside of MPC? Each time he showed interest in a project or acknowledged another member, Margie was there to support him. She treated him just like any other member.

A year later, the state forensic treatment team recommended that Matthew be released from MPC, and the district attorney's office agreed to release him under court supervision. Finding an MPC psychiatrist to sign the release papers was difficult, however. There's always a worry that if the patient commits a violent act, the press and the public will blame the person whose signature is on the release. One more time, Robin Green, the MPC social worker, spoke on Matthew's behalf. And the Fountain House staff supported her, expressing confidence in Matthew's rehabilitation. A psychiatrist was found and he was released on Labor Day weekend.

Now he was free to travel anywhere in New York City, but he decided to continue to come to Fountain House each day. What he needed was a place to live — Erica had no room for him — so Fountain House director of housing Bonnie Bean arranged for him to move into a small, four-story residence on East 100th Street.

In this group home owned by Fountain House, twenty members had private bedrooms but shared a modern, communal kitchen and dining room with four round wooden tables with chairs. On each floor, there was a living room area with a TV. Matthew was assigned one task a week, vacuuming the rugs one week and setting the table the next. At least one staff worker was present twenty-four hours a day, but members were encouraged to take responsibility for the smooth running of the residence. Members managed their own medications, and each day Matthew made sure to take 550 milligrams of Mellaril, an antipsychotic, and 30 milligrams of BuSpar, an anti-anxiety medication.

After eight months, Matthew moved to a staff-supervised building in which he had his own apartment. A year later, he graduated to an unsupervised apartment on the Upper West Side that he shared with three other Fountain House members. One of his roommates, a man in his early thirties named Glenn, hit it off with Matthew. Each night, they'd watch TV together. Nothing special, just whatever was on. Sometimes, he and Glenn would go to the movies.

His mother never came to visit him. He said it would have been too hard for her to climb the steps from the subway. She said he never invited her. He went to visit her every Sunday.

"Do you take your medication?" Erica asked him.

"Mom, if I didn't, I'd be out on the street again."

Shortly after his release from MPC, and with Margie's encouragement, Matthew went to work on a Transitional Employment (TE) placement, one of some 150 part-time jobs that Fountain House sets up with local employers. Each member's stint on a TE lasts about six months.

Matthew joined a crew of ten members and a staff person working as indoor messengers at D'Arcy Masius Benton & Bowles, one of the world's largest advertising agencies. He wore a shirt and tie each day and a pair of dark pants. He had to arrive at nine each morning, something that was hard for him to do. To avoid being late for work, he set his alarm for 6 A.M.

At work, his principal responsibility was photocopying. He took the elevator to four different floors occupied by the ad agency, picked up printed material that needed to be copied, made the copies, and distributed them. Occasionally, he'd say hello to a secretary as they passed in the hallway. But most of the day, his conversations were with other Fountain House members working on this TE placement.

Over the next few years, he worked on a variety of TEs: as an indoor messenger in a law firm and at the *Wall Street Journal* offices, as a clerk in a hardware store, and as a clerk in city hall filing time sheets of municipal employees. He generally worked four hours a day, Monday through Friday, sharing the job with another Fountain House member.

Most of his co-workers at these jobs didn't know he spent the rest of his day at a psychiatric rehabilitation program. He didn't talk much to them and they weren't overly friendly. Just friendly enough.

To Margie, Matthew explained how meaningful this work was to him. "When I am working, I feel more productive, more responsible, more in demand. It helps my self-esteem to fill a role where you're useful and can be an integral part of the situation. People at work are nice. If you do something for them, they say, 'Thank you.' It makes you feel they are a little dependent on you."

Still, he often passed unnoticed through others' lives. One day, he and a friend stopped in the hardware store on 9th Avenue where he'd worked on a TE four years earlier. The friend showed the store manager an old doorknob that wouldn't stay on its spindle. While the manager looked through a drawer for a small screw, they had a spirited conversation about the merits of old brass doorknobs. Meanwhile, Matthew stood by silently. Finally, the manager found the proper screw and Matthew and his friend left the shop.

On the sidewalk, Matthew said quietly, "I worked for that man."

Matthew is well aware of what he has lost to mental illness. He calls it a lack of confidence. "It's quite difficult to make a full recovery from mental illness, especially schizophrenia," he said. "You're never 100 percent together as you were when you were young. You don't have the full confidence that you had before you became mentally ill."

These days, Matthew continues to visit his mother once a week, usually Sundays. Sometimes he brings his laundry and uses the washer and dryer in her building's basement. He doesn't stay for dinner because it's a long subway ride back to his apartment and he doesn't like to travel after dark.

Occasionally, he visits his half-brother, Thomas, a high school teacher who lives nearby with his wife and two-year-old son, Brent. Matthew enjoys reading to his nephew and spends hours choosing picture books to buy for him. Every once in a while, Thomas asks Matthew to babysit Brent for an hour. Matthew is honored.

"It's a big responsibility," Matthew said to his mother.

At least once a week, he attends Alcoholics Anonymous meetings. He tries to speak out about his experiences, but it never comes out the right way.

"At AA, I can't stop talking about my past, about the hospitalizations," he told Thomas one afternoon. "I can't break into the mainstream. Other people at AA talk about the past and the present. They say, 'I had a good day today.' I wish I could think more about today. But I am caught up by the hospitalizations and by the fact I committed a crime."

Erica hopes that when she dies, Thomas will take responsibility for Matthew. But she has never asked Thomas point-blank if he would fill this role. Instead, she talks to her younger son about her worries for Matthew's present well-being.

"My concerns for Matthew are that he manages to have a roof over his head and enough to eat and a decent life," she said. "I wish he had friends. But that doesn't seem to be possible. He is still very withdrawn."

Social isolation is one of the characteristics of Matthew's illness, one of the "negative" symptoms of schizophrenia, along with depression, loss of spontaneity, and slowness of thought. Most days, he seems plodding, void of emotion. As Erica noted in both her schizo-phrenic children, the disease didn't affect their intellect but it certainly affected their mind. Intelligence was intact but without imagination to spark it.

"I wish I had some of the ability I had when I was younger," Matthew admitted to a friend. "I wish I could live that way. The dif-ference between then and now is apparent. I didn't have any hang-ups. I was drinking but I was quite independent. I had no trouble making friends. I got along with people. Now it's difficult to make friends. So I come to Fountain House to provide structure and mean-ingful contact with the staff and some members.

"Being in a hospital has an effect on you. It just makes it more dif-ficult to relate to people in a relaxed, comfortable way. I don't know why, but that's my observation. I still feel that way a little bit, even though I've been out of the hospital for a while. I sure hope that feel-ing will go away."

The last time Matthew had a social relationship with a woman was several years ago, when he and a fellow patient at MPC got together every day for coffee. He continued seeing her after he was discharged, whenever she could get a day pass, but eventually he broke up with her. He just couldn't see the relationship working out. "It's not your fault," he told her. Still, Matthew knew he had hurt her feelings and he felt guilty.

Now he'd like to find another girlfriend. "I look around Fountain House and there are quite a few women I like quite a bit. But I am not sure I have the self-confidence. This is a big admission to make, but I am not sure I can handle it exactly the way it has to be handled. I just find it hard to take the steps you have to take to meet a girl. You have to take concrete steps. You have to ask her for her telephone number. Or ask her to go out to get coffee or something. I guess I'm afraid that she'll say no."

In early December 1993, when he was returning from giving his rent deposit to his new landlord in Long Island City, Matthew met a woman on the subway. She struck up a conversation with him. He was startled but managed to respond. She said her name was Marie.

"I'm Matthew," he said.

He told her he was buying furniture for his new apartment. That he was moving into a place by himself after sharing an apartment with three men. He mentioned Fountain House.

"What's that? A drug program?" Marie asked.

"No. Psychiatric," Matthew answered.

"Oh."

Marie didn't turn away. But her tone of voice changed. At least Matthew thought it did. He'd been thinking about asking her for her phone number, but let it pass.

After Matthew bought the furniture for his new apartment, Margie and a friend came over on a midweek afternoon. The corrugated boxes of furniture lay on the living room floor, waiting to be assembled. Matthew went across the street to a Mexican deli—the three chuckled at the ethnic incongruity—and he bought sodas and sandwiches while the others tried to decipher the instructions. It took nearly three hours, but together they managed to assemble a sofa, a chair, and an end table. They set up the bed frame and plunked a box spring and mattress on top. Matthew moved it around in the bedroom, trying to find the best place for it to fit. The next day, he would officially move in.

"The three guys I've been living with have been good guys. But it's hard to have guests. In my own apartment, I could bring friends over. And I could say, 'I live by myself in Queens.' I feel ready to live by myself. I just feel ready to make the move. I have no doubts about it."

It Can Change Your Life

Several weeks after Matthew was settled into his apartment, Margie began to "dance" with another member named James. That's what she calls what she does with a member who appears to be slipping back into active psychosis—the "dance." Usually it means the member has stopped taking his or her medication. But sometimes it means that, even though the member is compliant and swallowing the medication that controls his illness—and may make him obese, sluggish, and impotent at the same time—the drug loses its effectiveness. Because Fountain House is not a clinical treatment center for mental illness and no medications are dispensed there, a staff worker doesn't come right out and immediately ask, "Are you taking your medication?" Instead, the "dance" begins.

Margie noticed James wasn't acting like himself. A thin young man with a boyish face and singsong voice, James lived with his parents in Queens and took the ninety-minute subway ride to Fountain House by himself each day. When he was a teenager, he seldom left his family's apartment because his older brother was there to watch out for him. But when his brother got married and moved away, James was alone at home whenever his parents went out. Twice, neighborhood kids came in and attacked him. Worried about his safety, his parents desperately searched for a place for James to go each day. A friend of a friend had suggested Fountain House.

James was one of the best typists in the clerical unit and he'd learned how to use a word processor in high school before he became sick. Almost every day, he volunteered to type up an article or two submitted for publication to *Fountain House Today,* the in-house newspaper that appeared Monday through Friday. Each morning, Margie cheerfully greeted him, "Hello, James. How are you today?" and he answered with a raised hand and a sound that was part hiccup, part giggle. He knew most of the fifty members of the clerical unit who came in regularly and acknowledged them in the same manner. Very seldom did he speak.

But one Tuesday morning, James didn't even raise his hand in greeting. He kept his hands jammed in his pockets. He stalked around the large, carpeted room and sat down far away from his usual terminal under a window. "What do you want?" he snapped at a member who sat near him.

Maybe he'd had a fight with his parents, Margie thought. It was highly possible. The strain of three adults living in one small apartment could cause friction even without the stress of mental illness. Or maybe he'd had a bad incident on the subway. A nasty remark by another passenger. A surly employee in the token booth. These things happened.

But people with mental illness don't have the luxury of getting angry. Any emotional outburst is always attributed to the mental illness. Margie and the members sometimes joked that she was the only one who could act out—slam down a phone, shout at a co-worker, even cry in frustration—because she wasn't labeled mentally ill. "If I did something like that," a member asked, "would you all be looking at me like I'm losing it?" Ruefully, the others nodded.

After lunch, James put his coat on early and walked toward the door.

"James, are you leaving?" Margie called after him. He didn't turn around.

She didn't want to jump to conclusions. James was entitled to his privacy, his dignity. Maybe he was simply having a bad day, she thought, trying to convince herself. The next few days, he came in but was unusually quiet. Margie noticed but said nothing.

A new member came into the clerical unit and Margie introduced her to James. "You two live near each other."

"I take two trains to get here," said James. "I was in the evening/weekend program for two years before I got into the day program. They said that in my case, I had to come to the clerical unit every day for three weeks in a row before I can go out on Transitional Employment. The alarm went off but I didn't hear it. Someone was moving my books in my bedroom. Someone was in there. They were looking for secret writing. I know. I used to share my bedroom with my brother but now I have it to myself."

Margie was shocked to hear him so talkative. At his mention of "secret writing," she winced.

Two weeks later, James came in wearing a shirt with stains down the front. Margie and Paula Barthel, another social worker in the clerical unit, exchanged glances. A member's suddenly slovenly dress or hygiene was a sign of deterioration. They also worried when members would suddenly show up wearing sunglasses or headphones to block out stimulation. Or when out of the blue, members began talking about religion.

The clerical unit had been asked to mail out a fundraising campaign and there were 1,000 brochures to be stapled and folded. James pulled up a chair but didn't help out. The new member was sitting next to Margie and asked her, "What happens here if you don't take your medication?"

Bless you, Margie thought.

"Nothing *happens*," Margie said, careful not to look at James. "You can still come here even if you stop taking your meds as long as you're no bother to anyone else. But it seems that the longer people stay off their meds, the longer it takes for them to come around again."

Several members nodded.

"I remember what it was like without meds," said a member named Richard. "I used to think the TV antenna was talking to me. Wherever I went, the antennae told me what to do."

Richard looked down, and others looked away from him.

"I got into this feeling that I wanted to share with everybody and I gave away all my money," said Mary Helena.

"I take my meds because I don't want to go back to the hospital," said Michael.

James looked at them blankly.

To what extent Margie or any social worker at Fountain House could intervene was a blurry line. Staff must have the member's permission to call his or her psychiatrist. Sometimes, staff could sit down with a member and say frankly but kindly, "I am really concerned as to what I see. Is there something bothering you? Would you mind if I talked to your doctor?"

When Margie finally asked James these questions, she got nowhere. No, nothing was bothering him. No, don't call the doctor.

The next few weeks were difficult for everyone in the clerical unit as they watched James get worse. His face became clouded. His cheerful personality was being swallowed by grimness. He looked like he was suffering. It was painful for everyone, including Margie, to watch James deteriorate. But he couldn't be forced into treatment.

In her ten years working at Fountain House, Margie had seen many people lose their ability to function normally because they went off their medication. Sometimes the descent was gradual because it could take months for all traces of psychotropic medication to ebb from a person's system. In other people, the change happened within twenty-four hours. Almost all the time, Margie could tell when it was beginning. It all came down to knowing the member and developing a relationship, just like you notice mood changes in a close friend.

*

Margie came to Fountain House when she was twenty-three years old, a recent British college graduate participating in the Winant Clayton international exchange summer program. The program began in 1948 for the immediate purpose of sending young American volunteers to help rebuild bomb-shattered London and, in a larger sense, to con-

tinue the wartime spirit of friendship and understanding between the
United States and Britain.

Rev. Dr. P. B. Clayton, an energetic British chaplain during both
World War I and II who everyone called "Tubby," came to America in
1947 looking for help. His plea was heard by Matthew Gilbert
Winant, a former New Hampshire governor and the U.S. ambassador
to Great Britain from 1941 to 1946. Since Winant died shortly after
he'd agreed to help Tubby Clayton recruit young American adults,
Clayton called the program the "Winant Volunteers" to honor him
and to help attract students in New England prep schools.

Twelve years after the first Winant volunteers traveled from their
American homes to England, the exchange program became two-way.
The first group of British young people, who were called Clayton volunteers, came to New York in 1959. They were assigned to work in social service agencies for eight weeks in the summer, and then spent
August traveling through the United States. The program remained
deliberately small with just twenty volunteers traveling in either direction across the Atlantic each year.

Shortly after Margie's arrival in 1975, she was introduced to Nick
Robertshaw, a former Clayton volunteer who was on staff at Fountain House. "It can change your life," Nick told her. (Years later, Nick
said the same thing to Clare Smith when she arrived as a Clayton
Volunteer.)

When Nick was a child in Hampshire, England, Tubby Clayton
visited his family on Christmas and Easter. Nick waited until 1970
when he was twenty-five years old to sign on with the Clayton volunteers for a summer. He'd just passed his final exams as a chartered (or
public) accountant and wanted a break in routine. Nick wasn't sure
where he'd be assigned in America. Most of the Clayton volunteers
were placed with agencies that helped children, but Nick had never
worked with children.

At that time, Rivington Winant, the son of the late ambassador,
was serving as a member of the Fountain House board of directors.
With Winant's support of the volunteer exchange program, John

Beard approved Nick's joining the staff for the summer and set him to work in the kitchen and the thrift shop.

When his three-month summer visa expired, Nick reluctantly returned home. But he was captivated by the caring clubhouse atmosphere and Beard's approach to creating change in the members' lives, and decided to come back to Fountain House permanently. Beard put him back to work ringing up sales in the thrift shop.

Several years later, when Fountain House's bookkeeper quit, Nick took over that role. Eventually, he studied at Columbia University for a degree in social work and also passed the examination for a certified public accountant. When he married a co-worker, the ceremony took place in the Fountain House living room.

Nick had been a Fountain House staffer for four years when Margie Staker came for her summer as a Clayton volunteer. She spent June and July working in Fountain House's dining room. Following a short sightseeing trip to the West Coast, she returned to Britain and began her career as a social worker, although not as she had originally planned. Before volunteering at Fountain House, she'd expected to work with families and children, but after her summer, she chose psychiatric social work.

In Britain, however, she found the approach to mental illness paternalistic and dissatisfying. The emphasis was on getting mental patients into treatment programs where psychiatrists could evaluate their progress. She compared everything she did to how it was done at Fountain House. Whenever she explained the clubhouse approach to co-workers, they said, "Gosh, that makes an awful lot of sense. But how do you *do* it?"

Sometimes, Margie thought she was fantasizing about her two-month Fountain House experience. Then she'd go to her desk drawer, pull out a Fountain House brochure, and reread it, just to verify that it did exist.

Six years later, Margie found a way to return. She had married and her husband received a visa to work for a computer company in New York. Shortly after they found an apartment in Brooklyn, Margie called Nick Robertshaw. He arranged for her to begin as a volunteer in the thrift shop, sorting donations of used clothes and old books, working side by side with members. Immediately, she thought "Yes, this is what I remembered." In February 1983, she and her husband received their green cards and she was brought on staff as a social worker.

Although she had no written job description, she knew exactly what was expected of her. The social workers in a clubhouse were generalists, not specialists assigned to one department. The staff's role was to be "talent scouts," drawing out members and helping them find a way to be comfortable and productive. When a member felt comfortable enough going to a particular staffer for help with housing or entitlement problems, that staffer was designated for the purpose of record-keeping as the member's social worker.

Margie had learned the basics of this approach to mental illness when she was a Clayton volunteer. On her return to Fountain House in 1981, she was looking forward to practicing this approach and to working with the people who made it so successful. She was saddened to learn that John Beard was suffering from lung cancer and was away from Fountain House much of the time. But she was pleased to discover that his influence was still strong within the clubhouse.

Following Beard's death in December 1982, his longtime assistant, Jim Schmidt, was appointed executive director and there was no break in philosophic continuity.

Schmidt liked to tell the story about the day a prospective member, an Ivy League graduate in his twenties, came to look over Fountain House. The man had just been released after several years at Creedmore, the state psychiatric facility in Queens. "I heard about this place," he said to Schmidt. "I want a friend and a job. I don't want anyone screwing around with my head."

To Schmidt, providing "a friend and a job" summed up Fountain House's role. He looked for staff who would help members function normally, who would help them make friends and prepare them to join the work force, if possible.

When asked if Fountain House was appropriate for everyone with mental illness, he quickly said, "Of course not," and then clarified his answer.

"However, should everyone have friends? Of course. Should everyone have a chance to go to work? Of course. Should everyone have a chance to be appreciated even when they are crazy and unstable? Of course."

By 1985, when Schmidt appointed Margie to head up the clerical unit, she had a clear understanding of the significance of her role. She was reminded in so many ways that members counted on her as their lifeline.

Even when Fountain House served as the springboard and members went on to full-time work or school, they didn't forget the program or a special social worker. Occasionally, when Margie worked at Fountain House on a Sunday, she'd answer the phone and hear the person on the line say, "I was a member in the 1980s. I'm doing fine. I just called up to say 'hi.' Tell Esther that I said hello."

The power to touch someone's life so dramatically, Margie felt, could be sobering.

In late December 1993, Margie was preparing to go skiing for a long weekend. She planned to leave early on a Thursday morning. That meant Matthew Palmer, who had just settled into his new apartment, would be on his own to do one of his weekly tasks in the clerical unit. Matthew and another member, Richard, distributed checks to members from the state office of Vocational and Educational Services for Individuals with Disabilities (VESID). The checks, which reimbursed members for subway tokens they bought to travel to and from Transitional Employment placements, were issued on Thursdays.

All Matthew could focus on was that Margie wouldn't be around on Thursday. Richard would be there as usual. Other social workers would be available, in case Matthew had any questions. But not Margie.

On Monday, Matthew questioned her about the VESID check distribution procedure. "What if a member comes in without identification? Do they get a check? What if I know their name anyway?

What if they couldn't work because they were sick. Do they still get a check?" Margie answered each question. On Tuesday and Wednesday, he asked the same questions. "I'm sorry, Margie. I just have to get this straight. Tell me again," he said.

Margie understood. Any change in routine was scary. Matthew had lost his self-confidence years ago when he emerged from his psychotic haze and realized he was a patient in a facility for the criminally insane. His ability to trust in anything—his thoughts, his emotions, his world—was shattered. Even now, when he had come so far, he still couldn't be sure that the procedure he followed the previous week would still hold true when Margie was gone.

"Don't worry. Everything will be fine," Margie said.

"How do you *know* everything will be fine?" Matthew answered. "How do you *know* that?"

Matthew recognized how important Margie was to him. He tried to explain her significance to him when he and a friend took a mid-afternoon break at the fifth-floor snack bar. It is a beautiful room with a wall of glass that offers a panoramic view of the midtown Manhattan skyline. Matthew took a sip from a can of Diet Coke and talked about his relationship with Margie and other social workers on staff.

"Margie represents 75 to 80 percent of what Fountain House offers. It does have cheap food. That's good. But I realize my limitations and I am quite dependent on Margie.

"Other staff people are nice. But when I go into Fountain House, the person I think about seeing is Margie. Other members think the same. One of my old roommates who didn't like elevators or public transportation was dependent on Riva. Dennis liked several people who left and he stopped going to the clubhouse."

Sometimes the members' dependence got to be too overwhelming and Margie felt they were all climbing on top of her and she was going to suffocate under their weight. What she tried to do was to get members to depend on each other for a least a fraction of the support she provided. She tried to weave a fabric of caring from one member to the next as they relearned how to have a relationship.

Sometimes she was asked by friends if she could ever quit Fountain

House. Yes, she always responded. If she left this job, she'd miss the members. But she was certain they'd survive, especially when she knew the horrors and hard times they'd already survived. But she wasn't planning on leaving, so she did what she could to reassure the members of her presence. Whenever she and her husband returned to England for a family visit, she gladly told the members that, yes, she did have a return ticket.

Before Margie left to go skiing for the weekend, she asked a member to keep an eye on Matthew. Rebecca Blake, a waif-like woman in her thirties with shaggy blonde hair, had joined Fountain House in 1989. Now she came by the house infrequently because she worked on a Transitional Employment job at the Wall Street Journal. But because Margie called, Rebecca was happy to stop in.

Before she went to work on Thursday, Rebecca came to Fountain House. She climbed the stairs to the clerical unit on the fourth floor because the six-person elevator was too pokey. She set her green backpack down on the floor and walked over to the large table where Matthew and Richard were sorting through the VESID checks. "How's it going, Matthew?"

"Fine," he answered, not looking up.

"When's Margie getting back?"

"Monday," he said.

"Okay, see you then."

Later, Matthew said to a friend, "Rebecca is a very nice person. I like her a lot. I talk to her once a week or once every two weeks."

On Monday morning, Matthew was waiting for Margie in the clerical unit when she arrived for work.

"Matthew, how good to see you," she said heartily as she took off her coat.

"Good to see you, too," he mumbled, glancing away from her.

That morning, Margie didn't have time to draw Matthew into conversation because she had another duty to add to her usual assignments. She was scheduled to participate in a program called "Colleague Training."

Fountain House regularly hosted mental health professionals from around the country and occasionally from foreign countries who wanted to see how the clubhouse operated. Also, staff and members from other clubhouses came to Fountain House, the "mother house," to get a fresh understanding of the clubhouse culture.

In keeping with the Fountain House philosophy that staff and members contributed equally to the clubhouse community, every visitor was called a colleague. So when a member or staff saw a stranger in the hallway or elevator at Fountain House, they asked, "Are you a colleague?"

Each Colleague Training session lasted three weeks and was led by two staff workers and two members from Fountain House. For this session, Margie was one of the leaders along with Rebecca Blake and Ralph Bilby, who headed the employment unit. The fourth was a member named Keith Hunter.

The dozen colleagues, who were staying in the Fountain House guest house, came from South Carolina, Utah, Virginia, and Pennsylvania. Their exhausting schedule included working in the various units, touring several Transitional Employment placements, and attending hour-long discussion sessions. Margie enjoyed participating in Colleague Training because it forced her to articulate how she felt about her work.

During the final week of the training session, the topic for one discussion was "The staff, my friend; or the friendly staff." The visiting colleagues sat in chairs that fanned out from Ralph and Margie. Keith sat at the end of the table. Almost everyone held a cup of take-out coffee from the corner deli. Rebecca couldn't attend because she was working.

"Friendship is a murky area," Margie commented. "If you go out to do something socially, members say, 'You're only doing this because it is your job.' And that's not true. Anything I do socially, it's because I enjoy being with those particular people. Some members, I like to go to the movies with. And some staff. But some not.

"From a member's point of view, I'm sure it's a question of 'Is it real?' So many people are relearning 'What is friendship?' and 'What are the boundaries? If you're friends, can you disagree? Is that okay?'"

A young woman from a South Carolina clubhouse looks per-plexed. "Margie, you probably have lots of friends. Some are Fountain House members but I'd guess that most are not. But most of the members have no friends outside the clubhouse. So is the relationship between member and staff intrinsically, fundamentally unbalanced?"

"But what's the alternative?" another colleague asked. "Keeping a distance from members? Keeping it strictly professional? Doesn't that go against the clubhouse standards that members and staff are equal?"

"No," someone interjected, "the standards only applied to rela-tionships *within* the clubhouse."

"But how can you regulate feelings?" someone wondered aloud.

"People at other jobs become friends with co-workers," said Keith Hunter. His brother and sisters all had jobs and, from listening to them, he knew their work friendships were almost as important as their family relationships.

"Do you ever give out staff phone numbers to members?" another South Carolina colleague asked.

"I have an answering machine to screen calls from members who just want to talk," answered a staff worker from the Virginia clubhouse.

"I've given mine to some members," said Margie, thinking of Matthew and Rebecca.

The colleagues from Utah worked at a clubhouse located on the grounds of a state hospital. "The Utah Mental Health Department encourages us not to list our phone numbers," said a staff worker named Ron, "in case people on the criminal unit get released and come find you."

Margie gasped but no one said anything about that frightening image. Within the clubhouse movement, the possibility of people with mental illness becoming violent was a sensitive issue, blown out of proportion by the media. Still, staffers and members weren't un-aware of the potential for danger. None of the colleagues followed up on Ron's comment.

Several days later, Margie was working in the clerical unit. Three older members seated at a large, laminated table were collating *Foun-*

tain House Today. Belle, a small, frail grandmother, was in the middle.
She was handed pages 1 and 2 from Theresa and her job was to add
pages 3, 4, and 5. Each time she was handed 1 and 2, she checked to
make sure they were in order. Of course, this delayed the process but
Mary, waiting to add 6 and 7, didn't display the slightest grimace of
annoyance.

Suddenly, an argument broke out between two male members,
Roberto and Scott, who were standing next to the work table. Both
were large men and their shouting could be heard out at the elevator
thirty feet away. Roberto was holding a pair of large scissors. He
seemed unaware he was holding them. But everyone else in the room
saw them. Belle, Theresa, and Mary froze.

Quickly, Margie and a male staff worker intervened. "Put the scissors down, Roberto. Put them down. We don't have that in here."

Roberto glared and set them on the table. The male staffer walked
him out of the room.

Belle whispered to Margie, "That was scary."

Some mental health agencies don't allow scissors or sharp instru-
ments to be in plain view. Fountain House's approach is different. If
scissors are needed for work, then scissors are available. Usually there
were no second thoughts about it. Once at a going-away party for a
staff worker, a member picked up a large carving knife on the food
table. Margie watched him closely while a shiver of fear passed
through her. He walked over to the cheese tray, cut off a massive
chunk, and put down the knife.

Margie won't initiate talk about the specter of violence. If asked,
she discusses it haltingly. "Violence in the clubhouse has happened,"
she said in response to a friend's question. "I've been boxed on the side
of the head once by a member whom I didn't know. I was shocked, the
members were shocked. I bawled my eyes out.

"I honestly believe that if you know the people you're working
with, you can anticipate problems. The easiest thing for me to do is to
ignore anger but it will boil over. Usually, it's verbal. People are going
'aaaargh' at each other. There are moments when someone is in your

face. The first thought that goes through my mind is, 'I know this person and this behavior is different.'"

Because she knew James so well, Margie quickly recognized that he was behaving aberrantly. Instead of the mousy, friendly fellow she enjoyed seeing each day because of his even disposition as well as his typing skills, he was sullen and sounded paranoid. She was increasingly worried about him. Not that she feared he'd become violent, but she knew that when a person with schizophrenia stops taking medication and the voices start up, he might do anything to appease them.

She hoped that because James knew her and trusted her when he was well, he would trust her even as his mind was losing the ability to relate to her. But she firmly believed that she couldn't force him into treatment. If an individual at Fountain House had the right to choose, then he could choose to deteriorate too.

For several days, James didn't come in. Finally, he shuffled in looking worse than anyone had ever seen him.

"James, is something up? I am concerned," said Margie.

"Yes. Yes. Jesus is looking at me. I can hear Him talking to me. I know I am a sinner. I am going to hell. Jesus is on the cross and He is looking at me."

Margie took James's hand. "Why do you think Jesus is looking at you?"

"He knows that I am bad. I am a bad person. I have bad thoughts."

"James, maybe we need to talk to your doctor."

This time, he nodded. Margie reached into her desk drawer and found the name of James's psychiatrist at a mental health clinic. But when she telephoned the clinic, the receptionist said, "He missed three appointments. His case is closed."

"That's the point," Margie argued. "He is sick. He has stopped taking his medications, so he is missing his appointments. That's why he needs to be seen."

Grudgingly, the receptionist agreed to reopen James's case and schedule an emergency appointment for that afternoon.

"Guess what, James? I'll take the train with you to the doctor. I'm going uptown now anyway. I have an errand."

The two of them left the clerical unit. The dance was over.

The next day, Margie and a friend headed for a late lunch at the Galaxy, a coffee shop on the corner of 46th Street and 9th Avenue whose regular clientele included a number of people from Fountain House. Margie and her friend slid into a booth with red vinyl seats. Tacked up overhead were glossy publicity photographs, autographed by actors who were also Galaxy regulars. When the waiter approached, Margie ordered without looking at the menu.

"You did a good job with James," the friend said.

"Um, well, yes, it did work," she said. "But, you know, you never can count on the same thing working the next time.

"That's why being a staff worker here is such a challenge. I think we always need to be looking at ourselves. We shouldn't ever be able to say, 'We know it all. We are doing fine.' You can never stop improving.

"That's why it's helpful having Tom Malamud as the associate director for program. You do things a certain way on instinct. Then he'll stop and throw in a totally different way of doing something. Next time, you have a whole new way of looking at things.

"And that's what visitors and colleagues provide too. They'll ask, 'Why do you do things this way?' It makes us think. And that's so good for us.

"Without beating ourselves up, we should always be striving to be the very best. After all, we're asking the members to strive against enormous odds."

I Was Standing On My Self-Esteem

Early on the morning Governor Mario M. Cuomo was expected to come to Fountain House, even before the New York Police Department set up wooden barricades to block off the sidewalk for him, Esther Montanez was sweeping the steps to the main entrance.

It was December 30, 1993, cold, but no snow on the ground. The winter air was no deterrent to Esther's clean-up. Nor did she care that she was wearing a good woolen suit with a narrow skirt, not her usual baggy black trousers. This was a big day and Esther, the assistant director of Fountain House, wanted the place she cared about most to look its best.

Already she had checked that the people who work in the dining room, where the governor would sign a major piece of legislation, had converted it into an auditorium. Folding chairs had been placed on the small stage in front of a dark curtain. New dried-flower arrangements were on display over the brick fireplace.

"Let's get this place picked up," Esther urged a few members waiting outside for the house to open. She handed a dustpan to a young man who then stooped over and held it as she swept a few cigarette butts into it.

"C'mon, everybody. Let's get to work. The governor is coming."

He was coming down from Albany to sign the 1993 Community Mental Health Reinvestment Act. Under this legislation, five state hospitals would be closed and $180 million in savings from these clo-

sures transferred to community programs. Also, the state was ear-
marking money from the general fund for the homeless mentally ill.
Altogether, $210 million was expected to be made available over the
next five years for community programs.

It was a big day of celebration for the mental health advocacy community which had put aside its individual agendas and called for the
reinvestment bill with one voice. People with mental illness, their
family members, and professionals in the field had lobbied vigorously
for the bill's passage. Each group was sending representatives to Fountain House to greet Governor Cuomo.

It was also a significant moment for Fountain House. Some of the
reinvestment money for New York City would go toward opening sixteen new clubhouses, each one operated independently but affiliated
in spirit with Fountain House. And the choice of Fountain House as
the site for the signing of such historic legislation affirmed its stature
as a leader in the contemporary mental health movement.

The night before Governor Cuomo was due to arrive, Esther invited Linda Pierce to her three-room apartment within the Fountain
House guest house. Linda, who had blossomed from the sullen new
member of the horticulture unit into a valuable Connections partici-
pant, had been asked to speak at the signing ceremony. Esther wanted
to discuss what Linda would say.

For a long time, Esther had believed most people shun the mentally ill because they know the randomness with which this disability
strikes. "Everyone in politics knows, every police captain knows he is
just as close to becoming crazy as the next guy," said Esther. "That's
why they can't deal with their uncle who's a little crazy."

Having the governor of New York as a visitor to Fountain House,
even for an hour, was an opportunity to make him see the needs of
people with mental illness. Esther wanted Linda to spell out to Governor Cuomo the devastation of living with mental illness. Esther urged
Linda, "Tell him you lived in an abandoned building. Say, 'That was
hell, governor.' Tell him."

Linda listened to Esther but kept her thoughts to herself. She wasn't sure exactly what she wanted to say.

Over the past eighteen months, Linda felt she had been reborn. Maybe it was because of Clare Smith's constant gentle coaxing for her to become involved in the horticulture unit's work at Fountain House. Or Esther Montanez's encouragement to do more, look at this, try that. Or a combination of both of these women, so different in education and temperament, convincing Linda that she could take steps forward instead of watching her life spiral out of control again.

Esther was the one who had pushed Linda to look into Fountain House's Transitional Employment (TE) program. In the dining room one day, Esther called Ralph Bilby over to the table where she and Linda were finishing their lunch. Ralph, a lanky six-footer born and raised in Arizona, was in charge of the TE program.

"This is Linda Pierce," Esther said to him. "She's ready for a TE. She's been working in the horticulture unit with Clare. What do you have for her?"

Ralph smiled at Linda and shook her hand. She was wearing a bouffant wig and a blue mohair sweater with rhinestones, but her flamboyant appearance didn't put him off. After thirteen years at Fountain House, he knew not to dwell on what a member was wearing. What mattered was that a member wanted to go to work and was ready to do what it took to keep a job—show up on time, listen to the boss, act pleasant with co-workers. The rest would take care of itself.

"I'll look into it," Ralph said. "Gotta go now."

A few weeks later, Ralph spoke to Linda about a TE placement that had opened up at a nursing home in lower Manhattan. Another member had been working there for six months and now it was time for him to move on to a different TE placement. The nursing home job involved caring for the plants and helping the aides with the elderly patients. Linda was due on the job at 9 A.M. Monday and was supposed to work until 1 P.M. This schedule suited her. She always had been a morning person. She could even eat in the patients' dining room if she wanted, Ralph told her.

This opportunity sounded exciting to Linda, but it was a big step. What she really wanted to do was run home. She was afraid she would make a mistake. She kept telling herself, "It's just plants. It's just plants, for goodness sake." She was terrified to walk in the door on her first day. But the nursing home supervisor, who had worked for several years with Fountain House members, was expecting Linda.

As soon as she came in, the supervisor said, "Hang your coat in that closet and come with me. Are we happy to see you today!"

Linda's first two months on the TE placement were filled with fear and uncertainty. Each day, she had to force herself to go to work. As soon as her four-hour shift was finished, she grabbed her coat and caught an uptown bus to Fountain House. Then slowly, her feelings about her job changed as she became more confident. She began to push the patients' wheelchairs into the game room and sat down to play cards with them. She brushed the women's hair and listened to them talk about the old days. The supervisor and the other employees made Linda feel like she was part of their team. Before she knew it, her six months were up and she was asking Ralph about another TE placement.

He sent her to do data entry at the National Resource Defense Council, an organization that was liberal in its politics and its dress code. Linda dressed like the other employees—jeans in cooler weather, sandals and shorts in the summer. She even went to one of the company softball games in Central Park.

After completing that placement, she moved to a TE opening at Chemical Bank, doing data entry. She was taught how to use four different types of software, working in a room with thirty-two other people.

Looking back over her TE experiences, Linda thought most warmly of the nursing home. "I was scared witless. I was standing on my self-esteem. I had no self-confidence. But they took me under their wing."

The work experience bolstered Linda's confidence and she began to think that maybe, someday, she could get a full-time job. Something with a future. She knew a few members were taking college courses and some others were studying for their General Equivalency Diploma (GED). She'd heard them talking about schoolwork when she went into the education unit to tend to the plants. What she really wanted to do was what Clare and Esther did. Linda was afraid Clare would laugh at this idea, but late one afternoon, she confided that she'd like to go to college and study to become a social worker.

"What a marvelous idea," Clare said immediately. "You know, you need to talk to Joanna Romano. She runs the education unit. She knows how to talk with the people from New York State."

The education unit was on the fourth floor of the Van Ameringen building next to Fountain House. There were architectural plans somewhere that depicted an interior connection between the two buildings, but for now, everyone scurried outside to go from one building to another. Although Clare had just signed out for the day, she went over to the Van Am building with Linda and took the elevator up to meet Joanna.

"It's not easy," said Joanna. "But our members have done it. I don't see why you can't, too."

Joanna arranged for Linda to be tested by the state office of Vocational and Educational Services for Individuals with Disabilities (VESID). She qualified for her GED, and VESID agreed to fund her college studies at LaGuardia Community College. Steve Polizzi, a member in the education unit, helped Linda fill out the application to LaGuardia, which was located in Queens.

Steve had studied photography when he was a student at New York University. Even after his mental illness developed, he clung to his dream of becoming a professional photographer. He lived alone and had rigged a darkroom in the bathroom of his small apartment. There he developed his black-and-white photographs of people waiting for the bus and neon restaurant signs hanging above the sidewalks. Most mornings, Steve arrived in the educational unit even before Joanna. He spent his time printing his photographs and mounting them in well-used wooden frames with gray mats.

Linda listened closely to what Steve told her about being a college student. Because he was a member, she trusted him. He'd been in her shoes. He'd had the same fears she had now.

"There'll be all kinds of people in the classroom," Steve said. "People who are quote-unquote normal. Kids who are just out of high school. Maybe even some of the professors will be younger than you."

On her first morning of classes, Linda woke up at 6:30, even before her alarm went off. Joanna Romano called her fifteen minutes later to ask if she could accompany Linda on her first day. At 7:00, Steve called, asking the same question. "No, I'm going to try it by myself," Linda said.

She was pleased with how she looked in her jeans and baggy sweater with a backpack for her books. She blended in with the other students rushing through the hallways. But on the inside, she was a woman in her mid-thirties who'd never before tried to find a college classroom and didn't know where to go to buy the books and couldn't take notes fast enough when the psychology professor spoke. And what could this class called Principles of Human Relations be about, anyway?

"Excuse me, can you tell me where I am supposed to be now. I can't read this schedule," Linda said, stopping a young woman in the hallway. The woman looked friendly, almost familiar.

"Do you go to Fountain House?" the woman asked.

Linda stiffened. How did she know? Did it show somehow? Do only mentally ill people take Principles of Human Relations?

"Why do you want to know?" Linda countered.

"I am a member too," the woman said.

Linda smiled and nodded her head. It was good to know other members were around.

Other members were looking up to Linda as a role model too. When she was working with Esther in the Connections program to reach out to lapsed members, she typed on the computer in Esther's office. That's how she got to know dozens of members who poked their heads in each day to say hello. One of them, Keith Hunter, spent mornings out on a TE and afternoons working in the financial services unit, where members could cash and deposit checks from their TE employers or from Social Security.

"You got your GED?" Keith asked Linda.

"Yes."

"Was it hard?"

"No."

"Think I could do it?"

Before long, Keith was stopping by every day to chat with Linda. She sensed he had a romantic interest in her, and Esther sometimes teased her about him. But Linda put a quick stop to that. She didn't want a boyfriend who needed her as much as Keith needed someone. Yet Linda didn't hesitate to help him prepare for the GED. She went out for coffee with him at least once a week. Occasionally, it was pizza. And she invited him to her apartment for Christmas dinner in 1993.

"I have a lot of respect for Keith," she told a friend. "He is very fragile when it comes to emotions and I have to set these boundaries. He is searching for something he has to find in himself. He still struggles with that. But he is trying to make things better for himself. I like that."

Linda knew how hard it was to have mental illness and still hope for a better tomorrow. Because of the cyclical nature of this disease, a person can never be completely certain that it is truly beaten. To persevere, to continue trying to make it back to the normal world is an accomplishment in its own right. Fountain House's policy that membership has no time limit means the door is always open for members to continue trying. Some accept the outstretched hand of the Connections program and return to Fountain House after they'd been away for months or even years. All they'd been waiting for, it seemed, was someone to ask them to come back.

Others did not return but stayed in contact. John Connelly, for instance, resisted all efforts by social workers to get him to come to Fountain House or to a day treatment program. He said no to attempts to get him into permanent housing or even a homeless shelter. But once a month, or so, John telephoned Esther and arranged to meet her for breakfast at the Galaxy coffee shop. Aside from asking, "How are you doing?" Esther let John talk about what was on his mind.

Linda's personal goal was to get an associate's degree from

LaGuardia Community College and then a bachelor's degree in social work. But she knew there were no guarantees that she could set a timetable for herself and stick to it. One afternoon as she sat in Esther's office, updating the Connections outreach list, she pushed her chair back from the computer keyboard and tried to explain.

"The thing is about mental illness, it's not a disease that you can pinpoint. You can be doing so well today and then tomorrow you are back at the starting gate. If that happens to me, I have to be able to say to myself, 'Okay. Now what?' I'll take a deep breath, and I'll wait a little bit and then I'll start over. I believe that won't happen, but you never know. When you try and don't succeed, it's not failure. It's re-grouping, I like to call it.

"Mental illness is something that is not a stable disease. It's controllable but it is always there. We have been damaged somehow — biological or psychological. And it is never gone. When I was in the hospital the last time, they said to me, 'Do you think you'll ever try to kill yourself?' I thought it was an absurd question. It's like my saying, 'I will never breathe again.' I never know."

*

Over the years, Fountain House has received a small degree of public recognition. Various government dignitaries have come to West 47th Street to tour Fountain House. The New York newspapers — the *Times* and *Daily News,* and *Newsday* on Long Island — have written complimentary feature stories about this program that helps people with mental illness lead productive lives. But the lobbying campaign that led to passage of the 1993 Community Mental Health Reinvestment Act, and the governor's decision to sign it at Fountain House, represented a new level of visibility and activism for the clubhouse.

From its beginning, Fountain House had avoided high-profile public advocacy for the mentally ill. As a private, nonprofit organization with a board of directors chosen from New York's business and philanthropic communities, Fountain House preferred to work behind the scenes to influence public policy.

Also, John Beard and his successor, Jim Schmidt, who served as executive director from 1982 until 1992, concentrated primarily on developing and sustaining the Fountain House program. Their style was hands-on help for the membership, whose active roll reached capacity at 1,300 people.

Still, according to state estimates in the early 1990s, New York City had 95,000 people with severe mental illness, nearly a tenth of whom were homeless. Their needs were heartbreakingly basic.

Soon after Kenn Dudek was selected to succeed Schmidt as executive director in 1992, he decided to commit Fountain House's reputation, its members and staff to work for passage of the Community Mental Health Reinvestment bill. Kenn, formerly an official with the Massachusetts state office of mental health, didn't expect the bill to benefit Fountain House financially. But he fervently supported legislation that would create other community programs to serve the needs of so many mentally ill people. Also, working for passage of the reinvestment bill was an opportunity for Fountain House to gain heightened visibility in the field it helped pioneer.

Members and staff wrote letters to state legislators. They participated in a rally that culminated with advocates of the bill marching down Broadway to Fountain House. As part of Fountain House's contribution to the public relations battle over the reinvestment bill, Kenn Dudek wrote a letter to the editor of the *New York Times* that was published in September 1992. In it, he laid out the economic case for community programs:

> Programs like Fountain House can provide necessary support at costs far below those of institutions: $42,000 annually for housing and support and vocational programs versus $120,000 for an institution. We receive more than 100 referrals a month, but we only have the ability to welcome fifteen to twenty new members a month.
>
> Some of those we cannot accept may enter another program, but others will remain in shelters, on the street or in hospitals. This situation is unfair, unwise and inhumane.

Meanwhile, advocates and supportive legislators looked for successful community programs to hold out as examples of the kinds of services the new legislation would fund. Fountain House was a great example. Its methodology was so down-to-earth that people outside the psychiatric community could understand how it worked.

Staff and members from Fountain House were interviewed on nightly news programs in New York City and Albany. The clubhouse was featured in articles about the reinvestment bill published in the *Times* and other New York newspapers. Linda was one of the members interviewed most often. She expressed herself with a quiet dignity and her story of overcoming homelessness was compelling, particularly to Manhattanites who often felt overwhelmed by the magnitude of the city's homeless population.

In the fall of 1993, it became apparent that the legislature and Governor Cuomo finally concurred on a bill. That's when Kenn Dudek pushed hard to have the bill-signing take place at Fountain House.

The city's commissioner of mental health, Dr. Luis Marcos, was a Fountain House booster. Assemblyman Steven Sanders, who represented the East Side of Manhattan and was chair of the assembly's mental health committee, backed the idea. So did officials in the state Department of Human Services that oversaw the state Office of Mental Health.

In its bid to host the signing, Fountain House also appealed to the governor's office through another channel. A member had held a responsible position on Dianne Feinstien's campaign for United States senator in California. At Kenn Dudek's request, the member called Senator Feinstein's office to solicit support, and a request went through Democratic channels in Washington to Governor Cuomo's office.

As recently as two decades ago, Fountain House might have been the only psychiatric facility in the nation where a professional would ask a patient for help in contacting the governor. The traditional view was that patients weren't expected to take a proprietary role in their treatment program. Professionals ran the program, administered therapeutic help, and determined when someone improved.

Under the leadership of John Beard, Fountain House offered people with severe mental illness a revolutionary option. Here was a chance to form friendships, to contribute to the functioning of the program, and to go to work through the Transitional Employment program that could be a stepping stone to full-time employment.

Beard's views about the capabilities of people with mental illness were initially shared by only a few mental health professionals. They set up similar programs, including Horizon House in Philadelphia, Thresholds in Chicago, and Fellowship House in Miami. These psychiatric rehabilitation programs were enlightened oases in the 1960s and 1970s for the relatively few mentally ill individuals who could access them.

Most people with mental illness received no treatment at all beyond medication, and while these medications proved effective to some degree, they were nowhere near the miracle cure anticipated when they were introduced. What treatment was available almost always took place either in a partial hospitalization program held for outpatients on the grounds of a mental hospital, or a day treatment program that operated in a community mental health center. In theory, these programs provided a bridge between the rigid structure of inpatient care and the free fall of living independently. They were designed as a crutch that an individual would eventually throw away once he or she learned how to cope with dysfunctional thoughts, feelings, and behavior.

The partial hospitalization and day treatment programs' emphasis was therapeutic. Counselors, psychiatrists, or other professionals identified a patient's emotional problems and deficits, described the strategy for addressing these problems in a treatment plan, and worked on them through regularly scheduled periods of therapy. By offering a variety of interconnected therapeutic experiences, including activity therapy like arts and crafts or dance, and individual or group talk therapy, therapists evaluated and hoped to improve a patient's functioning.

For a small percentage of patients, day treatment worked—that is, some people progressed to another program devoted exclusively to vocational rehabilitation, while others returned to school or caring for their family.

But for most patients, these programs were marginally effective and a cruel disappointment. Patients rotated in and out of hospitals. When released, they first came to a partial hospitalization program and later to day treatment, often because they had no other place to go each day.

Roberta Vorspan, who became a social worker after spending time as a patient in psychiatric hospitals and intensive therapy, chillingly described the disillusionment with day treatment in a 1988 article in the *Psychosocial Rehabilitation Journal:*

> What we have been offering is a synthetic life, and we wonder why patients don't improve.
>
> We offer ample opportunity for patients, or clients, to engage in "meaningful activity" by gluing tiles on a trivet, and we label them chronic because they don't get better. Does it enter our minds to question the usefulness of a trivet in the life of a person who has no one to whom to give a gift, and who is probably served his meals in some institutional dining room?
>
> We structure hour after hour of class time, where we teach clients the precepts of budgeting, when there is nothing in the world that this client can envision budgeting for. Don't we understand that there is no reason to save to buy new clothes when there is no place to go in them, or [save] for a vacation when there is no one with whom to go and nothing from which to take a vacation?

Patients and their family members began to ask the same questions and convinced mental health professionals to rethink what it means to have mental illness and what kind of a limitation this disability places on a person's life. As part of the reevaluation, professionals and family members looked to the experience of Fountain House and similar programs.

Could people with schizophrenia make friends? Yes. Could they work? Yes. Could people with major depression be in charge of their own medication? Yes. Could they live without twenty-four-hour supervision? Yes.

The answer was not yes for every person in every circumstance. But day treatment offered few yes answers, and patients and their families were fed up with no after no.

What happened in the late 1970s was nothing short of revolutionary. Instead of trying to fix what was wrong with a patient, new theories developed around teaching patients, *regardless* of their specific psychiatric diagnosis, how to navigate the real world. This groundbreaking shift in treatment for the mentally ill became known as psychiatric or psychosocial rehabilitation.

Psychologists and other professionals with advanced training in behavioral sciences developed theories and structured programs to address these rehabilitation needs. Boston University, the University of Wisconsin, and UCLA each developed a signature approach. State mental health offices funded community programs implementing one approach or another.

Meanwhile, Fountain House received a National Institute of Mental Health grant in 1976 to teach mental health professionals about its program and the Clubhouse Philosophies. By 1988 more than two hundred clubhouses based on the Fountain House model were opened. And each year, the number has increased.

In the last two decades, psychiatric rehabilitation has grown dramatically from a few isolated programs into a major and integral part of the American mental health service system.

Today more than two thousand agencies, including public mental health centers, freestanding clinics, and religious social service programs, provide psychiatric rehabilitation services to people in the communities where they live.

On the morning Governor Cuomo came to Fountain House to sign the Community Mental Health Reinvestment bill, the dining room was jammed with four hundred people. Linda Pierce sat in the first row of chairs, waiting for her turn to speak. State and city political dignitaries, people with mental illness, and parents active in the National Alliance for the Mentally Ill and other family-support organizations filled up the chairs. Those who couldn't find a seat, including Margie Staker and several members from the clerical unit, were standing along the wood-paneled walls.

Executive Director Kenn Dudek stepped to the podium set up on the small stage at the north end of the room. He opened his remarks by explaining what happens at Fountain House.

"Fountain House," he said, "is a settlement house for people with mental illness. A place to come for jobs, housing, education, and for whatever else it takes for someone to survive in the community.

"Like the settlement houses of the past, it's a place for people with common ground to come together and help one another. We are friends. We are peers. We are brothers and sisters. We have been a community and a partnership between members and staff for more than forty years."

Then Kenn introduced Governor Cuomo to enthusiastic applause. The governor began his remarks by talking about the "anger, concern, confusion, the divisiveness, the uncertainty about what we are as a people" that he had observed around the state. "We are fundamentally rattled in this country, fundamentally confused about our values."

Passing a law that promises to make a dramatic difference in the lives of the mentally ill aids not only that group of people, said Governor Cuomo; it aids every citizen.

"What this bill says is: We are not all wrong. There is a sweetness here. There is an intelligence. There is a love. We do have feelings for one another.

"What [the bill says] about the mentally ill: We've got to love them. These are our brothers and sisters. They need something from us. We owe them. We have an obligation to believe in something larger than ourselves. . . . You are supposed to love one another. You're not supposed to hurt one another. You are supposed to take care of one another."

Then he addressed the mental health advocates who worked so hard to make the reinvestment bill become law. "I congratulate the advocates because you prod the system. But let's be honest about it.

There aren't enough of you to get anything done politically. No one is going to respond to the mentally ill because it's so many votes. There aren't that many votes in that community . . . to make a person a winner. Certainly not enough votes to justify purely politically all the money that is being spent here.

"What you appeal to is not just the political sense. You appeal to people's conscience, people's sensitivities, and people's sensibilities.

"That makes this bill all the more beautiful. For what it does for the mentally ill . . . But it goes way beyond that. This is good for all people of the state. It instructs them as to what really counts: Believing in one another, loving one another, doing for one another."

Governor Cuomo's warm words touched the right chords and as he moved away from the podium, he received a standing ovation. He sat down at a table to sign the bill. Looking over his shoulder and framing him for photographers were the bill's sponsors, Assemblyman Sanders and State Senator Nicholas Spano of Westchester County, and Kenn Dudek.

After the signing Kenn motioned to Linda Pierce, who rose from her seat, smoothed her skirt down, and stepped up to the podium. She wore a mustard-colored business suit and oversized glasses. For once, she wasn't wearing one of her wigs. Instead with her close-cropped dark hair, she looked like the social worker she hoped to become one day.

At the podium, she spread out her notes. She looked out over the audience. When she saw Esther sitting up front, she smiled. She glanced at Governor Cuomo, who was sitting to her left on the small stage.

She looked down at her notes and then back at Governor Cuomo.

"I have been a member of Fountain House for two years. And it saved my life," Linda said in measured tones.

"I have been in and out of psychiatric hospitals. I tried to end my life many, many, many times. I lived in abandoned buildings, the Port Authority, and women's shelters.

"I am here today because community-based programs work."

The audience burst into applause.

"Today, I have my own apartment. I attend LaGuardia Community College and work as a data entry clerk at Chemical Bank."

The applause was louder.

"My dream is to become a social worker to help other people like myself.

"Governor Cuomo, we thank you for turning our dream into law. Thank you for making it possible for more people like me to have the opportunities I've had."

Linda stepped back from the podium. The audience stood and applauded heartily. Governor Cuomo came up to her and took her hand.

"I wish you the best of luck," he said. "I am proud of you."

6

How Can I Escape?

Uptown, on West 56th Street near 6th Avenue at 11:30 A.M., Keith Hunter was delivering his last package of the day. He worked as a part-time outdoor messenger for *Newsweek* magazine, one of a half-dozen Transitional Employment placements Keith had held since he came to Fountain House in 1982.

Since this was a place Keith hadn't been before, he carefully checked the building's address. If he let his mind wander he could have easily walked into the wrong building. On a windy February day like this, when the air was too cold to snow, you didn't want to make a lot of mistakes and stay outside any longer than necessary.

Once through the revolving door and in the lobby, he took a few seconds to orient himself and find the directory of the tenants. Keith had learned that some buildings had security officers who could tell you where to go, but in the smaller buildings you had to take the time to look for yourself.

Waiting for the elevator, Keith took a look at himself in the mirrors around the elevator doors. Not too bad for a fellow almost forty, but he wasn't happy because he'd gained more weight. He looked puffy.

But maybe that was better than the alternative. For a while he was scared because he was losing so much weight. He lost nearly fifty pounds before the doctor told him his thyroid was causing the problem. Thank God it wasn't something horrible like AIDS, he thought. But he'd had an AIDS test twice, just to be sure.

Dressed in a pair of pressed chinos and a plaid shirt with a solid colored tie under his coat, Keith kept up a neat appearance even while struggling with his recent weight gain. He satisfied his taste in clothes modestly by buying sports jackets, sweaters, and shirts in bargain shops. Despite being fashion conscious, he had to wear comfortable shoes with thick rubber soles as a concession to his job. Messengers spend a lot of time on their feet.

As the elevator opened, several young, nicely dressed women emerged on their way to lunch. Keith noticed them with a shy glance. This was definitely one of the perks of the job, Keith thought, getting to see a lot of good-looking women while making his rounds.

At his next stop, a few flights up, he dropped off a package and extended a clipboard for the receptionist's signature. She was another very pretty young woman and Keith admired her elaborate hairstyle. She signed his receipt, smiled up at him, and turned back to her telephone board where all the phone lights seemed to be blinking at once.

Going back to the elevators, Keith felt relieved. This was the last delivery of the morning and it was Friday. This placement at *Newsweek* definitely had its good points. Like getting a lot of time outside alone to think, walking down the canyons of office buildings lost among the crowds.

*

Throughout his twenties, Keith had been possessed by his illness. He heard voices. The actors he saw on television were out to get him—he was certain of it. He ran around the house, pulling down the shades and shouting about the Mafia.

Each time his illness surfaced, his mother frantically called the police and they sent emergency medical technicians who restrained Keith and took him to Creedmore Psychiatric Center, the public facility in Queens. Six or eight weeks later when he was stabilized on medication, he'd be discharged to his mother. Sometime within the next four to six months, Keith would go crazy again. Finally, his mother couldn't stand the uproar anymore and she found Keith a one-room apartment with a kitchenette in a building two blocks away.

In one of the more acute episodes of his illness, Keith became convinced that actress Pam Grier was coming to his apartment. Grier, the macho woman of action films, appeared in the movie *Fort Apache, the Bronx* as a razorblade-wielding prostitute. Keith was expecting her to arrive at dinnertime. He cooked an elaborate meal for two. He changed into clean clothes. Later that night both plates were empty.

Keith wasn't sure whether she had really been in his house or if he had imagined it. When he visited his mother, he told her that Pam Grier had visited with him and they had eaten dinner together.

His mother looked at him suspiciously.

"Well it must be true," Keith said, "because by the end of the night, both table settings had been used and the food was gone."

His mother looked at him, laughed, and said, "She wasn't there. You ate all the food yourself."

When Keith was not hospitalized, he spent his days either attending day treatment programs or trying to find work. The day treatment programs didn't offer much more than learning the hustle or playing bingo. If he did get hired at a factory, he didn't keep the job for more than a week or two. Either he'd show up late for work or he'd take too many cigarette breaks.

Once, a social worker sent him from Queens to a sheltered workshop in Manhattan where he spent forty hours putting toy soldiers into plastic bags. When he opened his first pay envelope, he found a total of five dollars.

Keith looked down at the envelope and then at his supervisor and said, "You're jiving me. Where's the rest of the money?" The supervisor explained how all of this was rehabilitation, not a way to make much money.

Now, more than ten years later, walking the crowded streets of midtown Manhattan, it felt good to be living on his own and getting paid for what he was doing. Keith liked the exercise he got from walking all over the city, but most of all there was plenty of time to let his thoughts wander.

Sometimes he could do a little window shopping as he went along. Or when he was running ahead of schedule, he'd pop into a store and check out some clothing. If he wasn't careful, though, he could walk right past the building where he was supposed to make a delivery, or get into the Up elevator when he was supposed to be going down.

The pay was $5.40 an hour, which amounted to $97 a week. Not bad for this kind of work, Keith thought. For every $2 he earned above $85 each month, $1 was deducted from his Supplemental Security Income check. Still, the combination was better than if he was just on SSI. After he paid his rent and bought food, he still had enough money to take a martial arts class at the YMCA.

There wasn't much money left over for a girlfriend but, at the moment, this wasn't a concern. His former girlfriend, Toni, had left him broke and disillusioned.

Toni, a Fountain House member, was going to divorce her husband. She said she wanted to be with Keith. Keith remembered that she wanted him to take her out on the weekend, and she expected him to foot the entire bill. Toni wasn't into no Dutch nothing. She'd say, "You pay for it all or we don't go."

Then came the phone call. Toni was returning to her husband, she told Keith.

"It was a good experience," Keith figured. "It was fun while it lasted."

Since the break-up, he was looking for someone else. Someone single. No more of these women saying they're separated or divorced, he concluded. He met another member, Joan, who showed an interest in him. Joan wanted to take it slow because she had just ended a relationship.

She said they could go out Dutch treat. But Keith insisted that he would pay both for himself and Joan, because he wasn't a cheapskate. However, it was good to know they could split the bill if he was a little short.

Joan had a ten-year-old son and Keith bought him a toy for Christmas. Sometimes when Keith went to visit, he and the boy would play-wrestle in the living room. Keith wasn't sure where the relationship with Joan was headed, but he was patient. He learned from his experience with Toni that you just don't jump into an intimate relationship.

Maybe he'd buy Joan a present. Maybe he shouldn't. He didn't want her to think he was too serious. Even thinking about his options made Keith feel confident.

It felt good just to be a part of the world again, moving through the streets with other people who are being paid for what they are doing. Not like the years of roaming around without a job, afraid that people would ask, "What do you do?" and not wanting to say "Nothing," always trying to make up a good answer.

It felt good to have proven the doctors wrong, like the psychiatrists at Creedmore who said he would never work. He had to admit, though, he had often believed he would never work. That's probably what his family thought, too, when he was so sick for so many years.

When he was a kid, it looked like he might grow up to have a decent life, if he could live through his childhood. As the oldest of seven brothers and sisters, he was the one everyone looked up to. He taught all the younger ones how to shoot a basketball. And Keith did his best to protect the other kids from their father.

Looking back, Keith thought his father must have been mentally ill. That's what he and his siblings decided when they had grown up. By then, Pop was dead from a heart condition. He died alone in a basement apartment with a cold floor. But when the kids were little, they just thought Pop was real mean.

Keith remembers, you weren't allowed to change the TV station or Pop would beat you. It was wrong to rest your chin in your hand. You could get a beating. You never knew what to expect when he came home from work or came out of his room after taking a nap. One second he'd be loving and caring. The next, he'd be like a madman.

Pop wouldn't allow the children to go out and play. All they could do was walk to school or the store. All of the neighborhood kids thought Keith's family had just moved in, even though they lived in the same building for years.

When Keith was twelve, he thought it was strange that his father told nine-year-old Renee to come in and take a nap with him. She seemed too big to be taking a nap with him. Keith saw his father lying on a bed with his arm around Renee. Then his father closed the door. It all seemed really weird.

Ma used to tell the kids that one day, she'd gather them all up and leave Pop. "When he comes home, he'll just see furniture," she promised. But then she'd read in the newspaper about a man who killed his whole family. That scared the living daylights out of her. So she stayed.

Pop used to hit her and the girls. When Keith was fifteen, Pop punched one of the girls in the face and her nose started to bleed.

"No more, no more," Keith shouted, jumping on his father's back.

Pop swung around, picked up a kitchen knife and slashed Keith's left hand. It took twenty stitches to close the gash. The doctor told Keith he was lucky to still be able to use the hand.

Keith used to wish that one of their neighbors would intercede. Pop knocked the kids up against the wall, so the neighbor in the adjoining apartment had to hear the commotion. But maybe they decided to mind their own business.

As the abuse escalated, Keith had one thought, "How can I escape?"

He had plenty of time to remember those terrorized years as he went up and down in the elevators of all those anonymous and nearly identical office buildings delivering packages to mail rooms and receptionists. Plenty of time to think and plenty of things to not think about, like the real hard times when he was only fifteen and getting addicted to heroin.

It wasn't hard to do. Drugs were on every corner, very cheap. And the obliterating bliss was worth any price. He started with marijuana. Soon, he dropped out of high school. He got lost in a heroin haze. A couple of times, he used LSD.

When he was eighteen, he heard the voices for the first time. Ma called her brother. When he heard Keith ranting, he called the police and arranged for Keith to be taken to Creedmore. But a nurse there said, "You're not mentally ill. You're a drug addict."

Keith was admitted to Phoenix House, a residential drug treatment program in nearby Far Rockaway that usually takes a year to complete. But after nine months, Keith got clean and was ready to begin the reentry phase and look for a job. Instead, the paranoid thoughts returned; he started hearing voices again. This time, there was no doubt that their origin was psychiatric, not pharmacologic.

Keith left Phoenix House and went to see a psychiatrist at a community mental health center, who prescribed medication. The doctor told him that if Pop hadn't abused him, maybe he wouldn't have gotten sick. But none of his brothers and sisters were mentally ill, so Keith didn't completely believe the doctor. He blamed his mental illness on his drug use, had to have been that.

"What I believe is, by me getting high off of so many different drugs, I had the mental illness but it hadn't come to a head. Or the head hadn't busted open. Maybe I would have gotten sick when I was twenty-four or twenty-five. Maybe I never would have gotten sick. But drugs had a place in it. That's why my mental illness went to a full explosion."

At Phoenix House, the counselors had talked about ex-users being rehabilitated and entering the working world. That was still Keith's goal. But the psychiatrist told him, "As long as you take your medication, you'll be all right. But if you go to work, you're going to get sick. You're never going to be able to work for the rest of your life."

Keith initially took Stelazine, which tamed his psychotic symptoms but caused stiffness of his neck muscles, and Cogentin, to reverse these side effects. Sometimes, it seemed he needed to double or even triple his dose of Cogentin to eliminate the side effects. Then, he'd run out of Cogentin before it was time to renew the prescription. He didn't want to take the Stelazine without it, so he'd stop the antipsychotic medication. Without it, his symptoms would erupt and he'd be hospitalized again.

After he left Phoenix House, he never used heroin again. But he didn't think there was anything wrong with marijuana. If he had some money, he would buy cheap wine and a nickel bag of marijuana. It made him feel better for a while.

He could have spent his whole life going through the revolving door between hospitalizations and day treatments and sheltered workshops. But on a Sunday in June 1982 his mother picked up the *New York Daily News* and read an article about Fountain House. She showed it to Keith.

"These people are just like me," he said.

The next day, Keith telephoned.

"Is this the same Fountain House that was in the *Daily News*?"

"Yes," said a woman.

"I want to join this program. Can I?"

"Wait a minute. Why don't you first come here and take a tour and see if it's what you want."

Keith told a social worker at his day treatment center that he was going to visit Fountain House. The social worker was familiar with Fountain House, but never considered Keith an appropriate referral.

Fountain House was just what Keith wanted. Yet becoming a member didn't lead to immediate improvements; in the beginning, he acted the only way he knew how to act. For the first four months, he sat in the living room every day and smoked cigarettes. No one could persuade him to even empty an ashtray. Then one day he emptied one, then two, then all of them. Eventually, he was sweeping up around the place.

Some people move on their own time, Keith thought. Then it comes to you. It's an awakening. He turned down the first person who asked him to help out. But then another person asked, not demanding that he work but encouraging him to pitch in. One of the staff workers, Ray Stridiron, said Keith had great potential. Keith almost believed him.

Then Keith began to backslide. He jumbled his medication schedule and landed back in Creedmore. But just for two weeks this time. When he came out, Ray helped him make arrangements to see another psychiatrist, who changed Keith's medication from Stelazine to Prolixin, an antipsychotic that could be administered as a long-acting injection.

Another social worker, a woman named Donny Lee, taught Keith how to concentrate when he was working in the financial services unit. No more running back and forth for cigarette breaks or wandering around for fifteen minutes. He learned how to stay in one spot. And because of all the female members and staff working in that unit, he pressed his pants every morning before he came to Fountain House.

Then Donny suggested that Keith try a Transitional Employment placement. She told him about an opening in the mailroom of an insurance company. She said the job involved lifting heavy packages, but Keith said physical labor didn't bother him. Donny took him to the mailroom several days and explained the routine. And on the day he was to start by himself, she came with him.

"I'm scared. My stomach is flipping," he said.

"Mine too," Donny said.

Her words made Keith feel better. If she's normal and she's scared, then it must be okay to be scared, he thought. When he walked in the door to the mail room and left Donny standing in the hallway, it felt like the first day of school when he left his mother behind.

His first week at work was hard. One day, he was late. But he made it through until Friday. After getting his first paycheck, Keith took the subway out to Far Rockaway, Queens, to tell his good news to Ma and his younger sisters and brothers still living at home.

As soon as he got in the door, he shouted, "I'm working, I'm working, I've got a job." The family erupted in joy. Ma thought it was his salvation. To the youngsters, it meant Keith now had money to take them to the movies.

Many professionals in the mental health field think that what determines whether someone can work is what kind of diagnosis they have. But Keith noticed that the members who succeeded with TE placements and got their own jobs were not necessarily the ones you'd think would succeed. It's not always the members with college educations—who look and dress and talk nicely—who take the placements and go on to full-time work.

Sometimes, he realized, members who have had really bad periods of illness and who look like they have serious problems actually are more successful at work. So, he concluded, maybe it's not so much what the doctors think about you or write about you, or how bad or good you look, but how much you want to work.

Keith wanted to work really badly. His pent-up frustration and feelings of hopelessness fueled his longing to succeed. But he wasn't ready to commit all his time to work. He wanted to keep some time for fun — for drinking and smoking dope.

He wondered if he could get high on marijuana while taking Prolixin. Yes, he could. And the side effects he used to get from smoking a joint when he was on Stelazine — spasms, when his body twitched and his mouth opened and he couldn't close it, part of his body going one way and part of his body going another way, against his will — he didn't get any of that. However, the voices would come back if he smoked enough. Then he'd try to drown them out with more Prolixin and run out of medication before it was time for renewal.

It was crazy. Crazy. Crazy. He and a buddy would be walking down the street with a marijuana joint in one hand and a cigarette in the other so that if the police rolled by, it looked as if they were only smoking cigarettes.

He couldn't visualize himself totally sober. But maybe he could give up marijuana and just drink. Finally, he decided to do something else. He prayed. He told his marijuana-smoking partner, Sandy, that he had to quit the pot and the alcohol.

"Go to 125th Street and Morningside. There's a church with an AA meeting," Sandy said.

Keith found out the meeting was on Tuesday nights. He got there at seven and a knot of people were waiting outside for the parish hall doors to be unlocked. When they were opened, Keith sat in the back. "Move up closer to the front," an older woman suggested as she walked in. Keith took a seat in the middle of the room. There were thirty people there, mostly men.

A guy in his twenties wearing a T-shirt and jeans stood up. "I don't know where I'd be without you people and this program," he said. "I used to be out drinking every night. My mom asked me to stop. I had a girlfriend; she begged me to stop. I thought they were wrong. I couldn't think of not drinking. But I did it."

Another man stood up. He had been a drug user and drinker. "I have been clean for fourteen months."

Keith raised his hand timidly. "I have one day clean," he said.

The people clapped warmly.

Then the man leading the discussion asked, "Are there any newcomers here tonight?"

Keith stood up. Again, people were clapping and cheering and the sounds echoed off of the stone walls. He couldn't believe it. All you had to do was stand up and say a few things about your sobriety, even if it was just one day's worth, and you had all this immediate love and approval.

After the group stood, held hands, and said the Serenity Prayer—something Keith had never heard before—so many people came up to him and hugged him and congratulated him on his first day of sobriety.

I feel like a movie star, Keith thought.

*

Standing at the bus stop at West 57th Street and Broadway, Keith looked impatiently up the street for a sight of the bus. He was headed downtown to West 49th Street to get the crosstown bus. He didn't want to be late for his AA meeting at the storefront near Fountain House.

Pacing back and forth in front of the Plexiglas bus shelter designed to keep people out of the rain and protected from the wind, Keith glanced around at the people dressed in business clothes and topcoats also waiting for the bus. It was good to feel a part of humanity, being out working, but he kept thinking, "I'm only halfway there."

When he met new people, particularly outside of Fountain House, he wondered what they thought about the part-time jobs he talked about. Now that he was nearly forty, he felt pressure building inside him to take the next step. He wanted a full-time job.

He hadn't been hospitalized for twelve years. He thought he was ready for full-time work. Any rough stuff spots he could iron out on the job. On his TE placements, the full-time employees had given him pointers, such as to stop talking so much. He liked to talk. Sometimes after his deliveries, he'd be making his rounds and talking to secretaries. But he knew the boss was looking for him. So he stopped this talking and hurried back to work.

The bus finally pulled up. Keith stepped up inside, dropped his quarters into the change receptacle, and took a seat on the driver's side. Most passengers preferred this side because it had only single seats that faced forward, giving people a greater sense of privacy. Keith looked out the window and began to prepare himself for the AA meeting.

In the beginning, it hadn't been easy. He found out that AA meant sobriety both from drugs and drinking. Sometimes what AA calls "stinking thinking" took over and he'd slip and have a beer. Or smoke a joint.

Eventually, he enrolled in an outpatient dual diagnosis program at St. Luke's Hospital for people with mental illness and addiction problems. He got back on track. Then an AA meeting started on Friday nights in the group home where he was living. That helped immensely because the weekends were when temptation was strongest. He'd be in his room by himself, bored, and getting high sounded good. But for the past year, he'd been completely sober. He couldn't wait to say "clean and sober for one year" at the meeting.

Keith got off the bus at 9th Avenue and 49th Street and immediately pulled his coat more tightly across his chest. Brrr, this was a chilly day. Looking at his watch he noticed it was already 12:05. He hurried down the street. He hated arriving late to a meeting. Pushing open the door of the small storefront, Keith sank into an open chair just as the leader of the meeting stood up in front of the group.

"Hi, my name is Riva, and I'm an alcoholic and an addict."

"Hi, Riva!" replied a dozen people, including Keith.

I Think I Am an Alcoholic

Sweat was dripping down Riva K.'s face as she neared the end of her daily jog. After running for twenty minutes, Riva felt good. The runner's high was starting to click in. Years before, the high of running had replaced the high of alcohol and diet pills in her life.

It was a summer morning and the humidity and heat were building. Riva, wearing green running shorts, a yellow T-shirt, and running shoes, breezed by men and women dressed in business suits, already wilting on their way to work. She was in good shape for a woman in her early fifties, tall and broad shouldered, with a handsome face and short blond hair. The jogging helped keep her weight down.

As Riva pounded the pavement, she barely noticed the little, colored crack cocaine vials that littered the streets. In this part of Manhattan, pimps and hookers, men and women down and out on alcohol and drugs, all inhabited these streets, coming out after midnight and drifting away before sunrise. At 7:30 A.M., only the devices of their vices were left behind to document their presence.

Riva's route took her down 10th Avenue to 43rd Street. There, she turned east to avoid the crowds pouring out of buses and subways at the Port Authority building on 42nd Street.

"Ooops. Sorry," Riva called out as she sidestepped around a man with a briefcase. She ran one block on 43rd before heading north. Now she was on the home stretch. Coming up 9th Avenue, she recognized several members and staff headed to Fountain House.

"Hi, Riva," a woman named Alice called out.

Riva waved in response.

She ran down 46th Street, heading to her apartment in the middle of the block. A couple of men in jeans and undershirts standing in front of a deli mumbled something, the only understandable phrase, "Hey, baby." Riva barely noticed, she'd heard it all before. She walked through the front door of the tenement building that contained eight apartments, including hers. Bounding up the steps, she started to think about the day ahead.

After a shower and change of clothes, Riva walked briskly toward Fountain House, joining a steady stream of people converging on its large green front door. She thought, as she did most mornings on her way to work, about the member who told her that when he first came to Fountain House, deeply depressed, he just focused on making it to the "big green one." If he could drag himself out of bed, get on a bus, and make it through Fountain House's front door, he considered that an accomplishment. Funny thing, after all these years of sobriety, Riva felt the same way about making it to the big green one.

"Hi, Riva." "Good morning, Riva."

Warm greetings from members and staff interrupted her thoughts. She'd known most of these people for years. And over those years, she celebrated their accomplishments—completing a TE placement, reconciling with a sibling, taking a vacation. And Riva mourned with them over their disappointments, particularly when their mental illness flared and they had to be hospitalized. The Fountain House community reminded her of a small town, right here a few blocks away from Times Square, the pulsating center of Manhattan.

"How are you doing?" Riva answered.

"Can't wait to get inside," a young man piped up.

Everyone chuckled in agreement. Fountain House was air-conditioned.

Once inside, Riva reached for a ringing telephone in her first-floor office. One of the four members who worked with her was calling to say she wouldn't be coming in.

"Stay out of this heat," Riva agreed. "We'll look for you tomorrow if it's cooler. Thanks for calling."

Riva looked at her watch, grabbed a notepad, and hurried off to the conference room on the second floor. She didn't want to be late for a meeting of the Intake Committee.

The conference room had an elegant, old-world look. Along one wall was a mahogany breakfront containing the china and glassware for board meetings. Formal photographs of founders and former presidents of the board hung in heavy frames on another wall.

The committee met weekly to review applications for admission to Fountain House. Because of the liberal eligibility criteria—a diagnosis of severe mental illness and no recent history of violence or drug or alcohol abuse—the committee's input was critical. Because membership was for life and because progress through the program was measured in years, not months, there were few openings. Fountain House received six times as many applications as it could accept.

Having members involved in this decision-making process was a highly unusual practice in the field of mental health. However, for Fountain House, members' presence on the Intake Committee represented the evolutionary changes in their roles over the years.

Since Fountain House opened, members had been involved in welcoming and orienting newcomers. After Jim Schmidt became executive director in 1982, he encouraged members to participate in administrative duties. Members joined the Intake Committee in the late 1980s and also worked in the intake unit that managed the applicants' paperwork. To maintain the confidentiality of applicants, their names were seldom mentioned in intake meetings.

Riva was thoroughly at ease working and sharing decision-making responsibilities with members. Ever since she came to Fountain House in the mid-1960s, she had embraced the egalitarian atmosphere.

"Hello, Margie. Good morning, Matthew," Riva said as she took a seat next to Margie Staker and Matthew Palmer from the clerical unit. Several other staff workers and members were sitting at the table too.

Riva spread her breakfast in front of her, opening a bottle of spring water and smearing cream cheese on her bagel as the meeting began.

Donny Lee, the social worker who was head of the intake unit, was chairing the meeting along with Tom Malamud, the associate director for program.

"I want to continue a bit with a presentation which I put on the table last week, a referral of somebody with a chemical abuse history," said Donny. "We collectively felt good about approving him."

Looking down at papers that she removed from a manila folder, Donny read, "This is a thirty-nine-year-old man who is being referred to us by St. Luke's Dual Diagnosis Program. He's been with the program for two years."

St. Luke's Hospital operated a service for mentally ill chemical abusers, often called a MICA program.

"Diagnosis: schizophrenia and substance abuse. Medication: Clozaril.

"He has had multiple hospitalizations, beginning in 1977. Each hospitalization has been identified with substance abuse."

Very seldom was such clinical jargon employed at Fountain House, but this was the language of most mental health professionals as they described patients.

"There is a statement in the original referral note that this man has been chemical-free for several years," said Donny.

She had requested more information from St. Luke's to verify the applicant's abstinence from drugs and alcohol. She knew that, because it was so difficult to enroll dual diagnosis patients in rehabilitation programs, social workers anxious to graduate a patient to rehab might gloss over slips off the wagon. Now a more accurate picture of this man's situation was emerging.

"The more detailed piece of information that I just got states that he continued to use alcohol with periods of sobriety for three to four months. When falling off, if you will, binges would last three to four days," Donny said. "He just moved to Project Renewal, a very supportive residence, and they are asking for his admission to our day program."

"Shouldn't they be referring him to a MICA program," a member asked, "if he has been actively abusing as recent as two months?"

"That's what strikes me," said Donny thoughtfully. "This guy is trying. He's stuck with the program. It's just been a very long history."

Donny looked at Riva.

"It sounds like even though he's been in a MICA program, he still has relapses every few months," said Riva. "It sounds like he needs something at least as structured as what he's been having rather than jumping into our program, which is less structured."

Around the table, the committee nodded. The man's application would be turned down, at least for now. Donny made a notation on the man's chart and put it aside.

Nobody else at Fountain House could approach Riva's credibility on this subject. Her expertise on drug and alcohol addiction, learned the hard way and supported by studies in graduate school, made her the in-house expert on substance abuse. But few sitting around the table realized how close Riva had come to destroying herself with alcohol.

*

Riva was a survivor. Born in Estonia on a farm before World War II, she was a little girl when, with her parents and baby sister, she was caught up in the chaos and destruction caused by the Nazis in eastern Europe. By September 1944, the war was clearly coming to an end. To avoid the advance of the Soviet army—their ethnic enemy—as the Nazis retreated from Estonia, Riva's parents wanted to escape to Sweden. Riva left her dog and her dolls behind as her family boarded a boat headed across the Baltic Sea.

But the boat traveled too far south and was captured by Germans, who forced it to land near the German-Polish border. Nazi soldiers forced the passengers to board empty freight cars near the docks. Riva's family was told that these trains were taking refugees to a place where there would be food.

They were transported to what looked like a work camp, a facility with many windowless buildings surrounded by barbed wire. Along with other Estonians and people speaking languages that Riva couldn't understand, her family slept outdoors for two weeks inside the barbed wire perimeter. Nazi guards brought huge vats of hot water with small bits of potatoes in them.

The guards told Riva's parents, along with the other refugees, that they would be processed for jobs. In the distance, they could see people snaking single-file past a desk where an official-looking man sat at a chair. Two guards stood behind him. Beyond them were the barracks. Riva's father and a few other Estonian men crept up near the front of the line where people were being processed. They saw guards branding numbers into the upper arms of men and women. They smelled the singed flesh.

Terrified, the Estonians suspected they would be sent to a slave labor camp or worse. It was clear they were being lied to. They had to escape.

They moved at night, digging a hole under the barbed wire at a minimally guarded spot. Although she was ill, six-year-old Riva and her baby sister were passed under the barbed wire by her father.

"I'm scared," Riva whimpered. Her father held her closer to his chest. Her mother followed, as did a handful of other refugees. They crept in the darkness toward the train tracks, near a freight car with its door open. The freight car was empty. They climbed inside and waited. Riva fell asleep. In the morning, the car started rolling as the train pulled out. Riva's family had escaped the infamous Dachau death camp.

When the train came to the outskirts of a small town and slowed down, they jumped off. A road sign told them they were still inside Germany. They walked along the road, encountering no one. They found an abandoned house in the countryside and survived the rest of the war hiding in that house.

After the war, Riva and her family were identified as refugees. She was hospitalized with tuberculosis for a year. Her parents, who were forbidden to visit, stood in a courtyard under her window and waved to her.

When Riva was eleven, the family emigrated to the United States and settled on Long Island. Riva had grown up fast amidst the falling bombs and insecurity of war-torn Europe. But her teenage years in America were, in a way, even more difficult. By the age of twelve, she'd grown to her adult height of 5 feet 8 inches and looked like a mature woman. She towered over her mother and her schoolmates, many of whom initially thought she was the student teacher.

Her mother couldn't cope with her daughter's physical development. She belittled Riva's shape, her behavior, her appearance. Meanwhile, as Riva moved into high school, the students ridiculed her pronounced eastern European accent.

Riva rebelled. She began smoking her father's Camels. Obsessed with a boy in her class, she created a homemade tattoo, carving his name on her knee with straight pins she sterilized with a match.

When she was thirteen, her parents went to visit friends in Delaware for the weekend. They took her sister but left Riva home alone. Her sadness was overwhelming. She swallowed one hundred aspirins, turned on the radio, and went to sleep, hoping not to wake up. When she did wake up, the radio was still playing and no one had discovered her.

Still longing to escape, she spent the next three years working in the darkness of a movie theater as an usher. She ate popcorn all night. She had no friends, just some of the older ushers. It was a difficult time of her life, so painful that as an adult she detested hearing songs popular in the fifties.

Riva was increasingly distressed about her weight. When she was seventeen, someone told her about these new prescription diet pills. Her mother happily paid for a doctor's appointment to get a prescription for Dexedrine. The pills worked. Riva got thinner, happier, more energetic—and hooked on amphetamines.

After graduating from high school, Riva moved to Manhattan. Because of her mature appearance and serious demeanor, she was hired by a social service agency to work with emotionally disturbed teenage girls. Sometimes when a girl needed acute treatment, she was admitted to Bellevue Hospital, the large city hospital known for its psychiatric wing, and Riva visited her charges there. Then Riva was hired by the Society of Friends, or Quakers, and spent three years working with women recently released from prison.

About this time she had her first drink. She went to a bar that her co-workers frequented. Too insecure to approach them directly, she first ordered a drink. She didn't particularly like the taste but, by the time her glass was empty, her inhibitions were gone. "I feel great, this is fantastic," she thought. "A vodka martini straight up, with an olive." For her, alcohol was love at first sip. She no longer had trouble talking to anyone.

In 1966, Riva left her job due to internal labor strife. She went to the New York State Employment Service and asked for a different sort of social work. After she rejected several job openings, the employment counselor had one last suggestion.

"There's a place called Fountain House. Call them up. We're not sure what it does. Something with the mentally ill. All we know is that the people we send to work there either leave immediately or they stay for a very long period of time."

Carrying the address on an index card, Riva walked over to West 47th Street. It was December and a crowd of a hundred people were huddled close together on the sidewalk, spilling over the curb onto the street, in front of a stately brick building.

"What's happening?" Riva asked.

"It's a fire drill," a young man explained.

"Is this Fountain House?"

"Yes."

Riva was confused. She couldn't tell which people were the staff and which were the patients.

All she knew about psychiatric care was the gray, dingy corridors of Bellevue, the restraints and straitjackets that were used to keep patients subdued, and the lack of dignity and care. Fountain House looked different. What she observed on her tour of the building and heard in her job interview convinced her she had to be a part of this place. She was willing to do any job, anything, just so she could be a part of it.

Riva was hired in January 1967. She had an instinctive and intuitive ability for seeing the good and talented parts of even the most disabled members. Her smile and extroverted ways were contagious to many shy and withdrawn members.

A man named Phillip who had spent thirty years in Pilgrim State Hospital on Long Island was brought to Fountain House by his parents. When Riva asked him what he'd like to do at Fountain House, he said he couldn't do anything. Riva took out a piece of stationery and folded it in half.

"Do you think you could fold a piece of paper like this?" she asked.

"I think so," said Phillip. He folded the paper she handed to him.

"Good. You can fold the napkins at lunch for us. Because we need them folded."

That became Phillip's job. He progressed in the dining room to setting the tables, then taking the lunch orders. Eventually, he took a TE placement as a messenger at a law firm. His parents never forgot Riva's kindness. Neither did Phillip.

But Riva's success in her professional life did not carry over into her personal life. During her first fifteen years working at Fountain House, Riva became increasingly and desperately alcoholic.

At Sunny's, a local bar at the corner of 9th Avenue and West 47th Street, some staff workers would hang out after work, drinking whiskey at fifty cents a shot and sharing stories about working at Fountain House. Riva fit right in.

After a few drinks, she'd sometimes teach her friends how to tango. At least once, she instructed them while dancing on the top of a table. But during the day, Riva decided this behavior would be outlandish for a staff worker at Fountain House. She didn't want to embarrass herself around John Beard or his assistant, Jim Schmidt, two men whom she admired greatly.

She knew she had to do something about her drinking. In her heart, she was scared about how out of control she got. But rather than cutting down on her consumption, she switched from drinking martinis to sipping scotch.

And she continued to take her diet pills—one a day, just like a vitamin.

Her work seemed unaffected by her drinking. After several years, John Beard asked her to take over running the Fountain House thrift shop on 9th Avenue. At first she was reluctant.

"Riva, you of all people can work in any unit of Fountain House and you will be smashing," said Beard. "I need you to do the thrift shop. I need to know what you think should be done with it. It's a mess."

That much was true. The space was overrun with stray cats. The stench of their urine was overwhelming. Nevertheless, Riva couldn't resist Beard's request.

She closed down the thrift shop for a month. Tossed out every bit of used clothing. Commandeered members with bleach, ammonia, and mops. They scrubbed and painted. Divided the shop into eight departments—including men's wear, women's wear, bric-a-brac.

For the grand re-opening, Riva ordered sixteen sales coats from Bloomingdale's for the members to wear while working and had Fountain House Thrift Shop embroidered on the pocket. Nick Robertshaw, the Clayton volunteer from England who'd just returned to Fountain House, picked them up.

Riva developed the thrift shop into a unit, with thirty to forty members assigned to it. They were salesclerks, sorters, cashiers, or part of Nick's heavy-lifting crew for donated furniture. Apartments above the thrift shop were assigned to a few members. Riva was given an apartment there too.

After a time, John Beard wanted Riva to move into an apartment within the guest house and serve as a residential manager. Riva rejected the request. She wouldn't have any privacy, she told him.

What she really feared was that living in the guesthouse—with Fountain House staff and visiting colleagues coming and going—would interfere with her drinking. Someone would discover her habits: because she didn't want to stop drinking when the after-work get-togethers broke up and the other Fountain House staffers went home, she continued alone in her apartment.

She tried to analyze why she drank so much. She was sure the cause wasn't stress from working with mentally ill people. Not at all. She genuinely loved her job and got tremendous satisfaction from helping people. But that feeling wasn't enough. She needed the high and then the oblivion of alcohol.

She decided to move out of the thrift shop apartment and found a place around the corner on West 46th Street. Once she moved, she stopped spending time with the Fountain House crowd and their after-work socializing. She isolated herself in her new apartment. She drank alone and no one knew.

Occasionally, someone asked her at work, "Why are your hands shaking?" But Riva always had an excuse and no one pressed her. Nevertheless, it was becoming increasingly obvious to Riva that she had a problem, although she couldn't quite admit to herself what it was.

On a Monday morning, she woke up and rolled toward the telephone. She had to call in sick.

"This is the eighth Monday I've missed," she thought. "I wonder what I said last Monday, why I can't go in."

"I'm too sick. I'm too hungover. I need a drink. I can't go in. There's liquor on my breath. I can't go into work with liquor on my breath. I can't go in today. I don't care if it's the eighth Monday. What did I tell them last Monday? I can't remember.

"I better not call. I better say that my phone was not working. The liquor store opens at ten. I don't have anything in the house. I'm shaking, I need a drink to straighten myself out. To think clearly. Maybe I'll remember what I said last Monday."

No one called her on the carpet for missing those Mondays. Despite the fact that Riva was a critical component of this innovative psychiatric rehabilitation program, many years went by without the staff confronting her. The Fountain House staff had little knowledge about people with alcohol and drug problems, and they had a fear of working with them. At the same time, some staff members regularly drank, sometimes heavily, when they met after work.

One Monday, when Riva did manage to drag herself to work, she began shaking uncontrollably by midmorning. "I have to go to the bank," she announced, got up, and darted out of Fountain House. She didn't dare go to Sunny's Bar, so she ran one block to her apartment and poured herself a shot of vodka.

She told herself, "I'm working too hard. I'm too anxious. That's why I need this drink."

It was a member who first confronted Riva. "Riva, I hear you have a drinking problem," the member said. Fuming, she ignored him.

"You can't prove that," she thought defiantly. "If you don't have a photograph of me actually taking a drink, you can't say I'm drinking. If I close my apartment door at 5:30 and drink there all night, that's my business. You can't say I have a drinking problem. You're not here."

Riva decided the diet pills were to blame for her problems. She had been taking them every day for years. Her latest prescription was for a drug that acted as an amphetamine and a tranquilizer.

So in the summer of 1977, when she went to California to visit her sister who was going through a divorce, Riva left her diet pills behind in New York and went cold turkey, sleeping during the day and walking around in a daze. She telegrammed John Beard that she was quitting Fountain House and staying in California.

However after several months, she decided to return to New York, her apartment, and her belongings. She would soon be out of money. Her rent was due. She called John Beard and asked for her job back.

"It's good to hear from you," Beard said. "Yes, I want you to come back to Fountain House."

"Thank you," Riva said, trying to hide her relief.

Freed from her addiction to diet pills, Riva felt like a new person. But soon she looked worse than ever. Without the amphetamine boost in the diet pills, she began to more openly show the effects of her drinking. She would stumble or even fall in the street after a night of drinking.

Still, the Fountain House staff didn't seemed to notice. Beard even gave her a new assignment. She was to go into the West Side welfare hotels, which often housed severely isolated mentally ill people, and invite them to come to Fountain House.

Riva loved this job. She marched fearlessly into the seedy hotels, sometimes dressed in a cowboy hat and boots, and ferreted out potential members. After a few visits, all the strange, lonely men and women recognized her, and more than a few responded to her outreach effort. People at Fountain House praised her for her accomplishment.

She tried to tell herself she deserved their attention, that she was a success. She tried to act like a success. Looking through the *New York Times* in the evenings in her apartment, she made lists of the Broadway plays and the movies that she would like to see. But she never bought a ticket. She couldn't imagine sitting three hours in a darkened theater without a drink.

In 1980 a staff worker went on a year's sabbatical and Riva was assigned to do his job of reaching out to psychiatric patients at Bellevue Hospital. Riva was supposed to visit the hospital once a week and record the patients' names and their interest in Fountain House in a logbook. Instead, she found herself lingering over glasses of wine in restaurants near Fountain House, or downtown near Bellevue, pretending to do paperwork.

"Gee I could really go to Bellevue a little later," she said to herself. "Actually I could skip seeing wards six and seven today, and I could just catch ward three and see that guy there because I told him I would be back."

Inevitably, one glass of wine led to another and often to a drink of scotch. After the first sip of scotch, she was never sure where she would end up. She would either rationalize away the need for her to be at Bellevue or begin to shake so badly she would have to take a taxi home and then collapse into bed.

When her co-worker returned and asked to see the logbook, she said she had lost it.

John Beard, pacing back and forth in his office, confronted Riva about the loss of the logbook.

"I'm wondering how much you've been drinking," he said, "because, you see, you've begun to lie to us."

Riva began crying.

"This is a sign of alcoholism," Beard said. "I never thought it would come to this with you, that you would lie to us. We'll have to monitor you now."

Riva knew what this meant. They would smell her breath; they would watch where she went to lunch and how long she took for lunch.

Still, her drinking intensified. And perhaps because her co-workers were distracted by John Beard's diagnosis with cancer at this time, her behavior wasn't closely monitored. She came to work less and less. She was so physically sick that she couldn't even keep down a sip of coffee in the morning. She didn't have the energy to get undressed at night, so she would just pass out on her sofa and go to work the same way the next day, hiding herself with a hat, sunglasses, and dirty trench coat.

Riva had never thought she would descend to hanging out with the likes of the drunks who loitered endlessly on the corners in her neighborhood. But she found herself beginning to talk to them and even invited one man into her apartment to drink. Often, he brought his little dog, Moneka.

On a Tuesday in February 1982, Riva forced herself to go into work. She'd been out for a week, too drunk to come in. It was cold and raining. She was wearing her trench coat. Her sunglasses were held together by a bent safety pin. When Riva arrived at Fountain House, she was shaking. She went to the snack bar for a cup of coffee. A female staff worker looked up casually from her newspaper as Riva stumbled into the room.

"Riva, if you don't stop drinking, you are either going to wind up in an institution, wind up in jail, or kill yourself." Then the woman turned back to her paper.

Riva ran out of Fountain House and ended up in a place called Rudy's. No one else was at the bar.

"Yes?" said the bartender.

"Vodka martini, straight up."

When the bartender set down the drink, Riva looked at it. "I'm going to drink this drink," she told herself, "and then I'm going to go home and quit drinking. I'll just drink this to stop the shakes and I'll go home. I'm going to show them all."

Riva had always thought if she really needed to, she could quit drinking just like she had quit the diet pills. Cold turkey. She finished the drink and walked home.

Three hours later, she was reaching for the vodka bottle on her refrigerator and pouring herself a drink. She was defeated. She felt like a rat in a corner. Trapped. She thought she could never stop drinking. The one thing she knew about herself—that she could quit if she had to—was not true.

"I can't stop drinking," she thought. "Now what? I'll be homeless, I'll be without a job. And without that, I don't have a life."

In the afternoon, she went up to the roof of her apartment building and leaned over the edge, just to take a look. It was a rainy, gray day, and the sky blended with the pavement like soft velvet.

She thought, "I have been a fool not to come up here sooner. This is so comforting. This is so warm and gentle. This is where I can lie down."

Suddenly, the little dog, Moneka, was around her feet.

"Riva, you don't have to do that. You're an alcoholic. You can get help." It was her friend from the street corner, sitting against the chimney, drinking a beer out of a paper bag.

Riva was so shocked to see him that she turned away from the roof's edge, as if in a trance, and walked back across the roof to the stairwell. She went down to her apartment and called Fountain House.

She asked for Jim Schmidt and said, "I think I'm an alcoholic and I need help. I'm going to go and get help. I won't be into work today."

Schmidt grabbed another staffer and immediately came to Riva's apartment. They took Riva to Roosevelt Hospital.

An hour later, sitting on an examining table, she watched a young doctor approach with a nurse.

"Enlarged liver," the doctor murmured to the nurse.

"What do you mean?" Riva demanded.

"It's enlarged. But all you have to do is stop drinking and it will be fine."

"Completely?"

"Yes. Completely stop drinking. You are in detox for alcoholism."

"Well, I *have* been drinking a little too much lately," Riva said.

"You're in detox for alcoholism," the doctor said softly. "Your diagnosis is chronic alcoholism."

Riva looked down. She started to cry.

"Go to an AA meeting. There's one starting here in five minutes."

She put on her trench coat and hat over her hospital gown. She put on her sunglasses. Wearing the slippers supplied by the hospital, she shuffled off to the meeting.

Five days later, when she was detoxified from all the alcohol in her system, she was transferred from the hospital to its Smithers Alcoholism Rehabilitation unit, one of the premier—and most luxurious—residential recovery programs in Manhattan.

The program began in 1973 with a $10 million donation from R. Brinkley Smithers, the son of one of the co-founders of IBM who himself battled alcoholism. Celebrities and socialites, as well as regular working people, passed discretely through Smithers, located on the Upper East Side in a 40,000-square-foot mansion formerly owned by the showman Billy Rose.

Brinkley Smithers's philosophy, interestingly, matched John Beard's approach. Just as Beard believed people with mental illness deserved the handsome furnishing and atmosphere of Fountain House, Smithers felt substance abusers needed beautiful, comfortable surroundings to build their self-esteem and grow strong.

At Smithers, Riva was one of forty-three people seeking treatment. She didn't recognize anyone else who was there, and no one revealed more than their first names. Riva spent her twenty-eight-day stay going through a rigorous process of self-examination. She had to write detailed examples of powerlessness and unmanageability in her life caused by alcohol. Eventually, she filled up sixty-nine pages confronting her demons, all the while hoping she would find some loophole and be able to drink again.

On the twenty-seventh day of her stay, she realized there was no loophole. She was alone in an elevator when she dissolved into tears.

"I think I am an alcoholic," she said aloud, her pitiful voice echoing in the elevator. "My life has become totally unmanageable because of my drinking."

She realized she had just uttered the first step of the Twelve Steps of Alcoholics Anonymous.

When Riva left Smithers the next morning, it was Sunday, the quietest day of the week in New York City. Her counselor opened the front door, handed her the sixty-nine pages of self-analysis, and said, "Here is your life. Good luck."

Riva came down the steps of the beautiful building, looked back for just a second, took a deep breath and walked into her new life of sobriety.

*

After treatment, Riva returned to Fountain House shaken and humbled. No longer outgoing and animated, she was given work that allowed her to stay in the background. Members, even if they didn't know all the details, knew that Riva needed to be treated gently. If they had a personal emergency, they found another staff worker to take it to.

Riva did what Smithers had told her to do. Each day, she made sure she didn't pick up a drink. She focused on attending AA meetings every day and taking care of herself. She withdrew from the staff get-togethers after work because invariably they involved alcohol. Riva knew she had no business near alcohol. She had only her life to save by not being around it.

After several years, Riva became more and more secure in her recovery and her support from AA. She began to assert herself. When she looked around Fountain House, she saw how serious the problems of alcohol and drug abuse were among some members and how little was being done about it.

In the early days of Fountain House, very few members struggled with both mental illness and substance abuse. But since the late 1970s, as people were coming to Fountain House from the streets, shelters, or short-term hospitalizations, the number of members with "double trouble" increased. Members, like the population at large, now had greater access to illicit drugs; and like many people with serious mental illness, they tried to eradicate their symptoms with these substances.

Yet for a long time, Riva saw that the Fountain House staff wasn't even able to distinguish between a member's psychotic breakdown and someone high on crack. Sometimes a staff worker would slip a member ten dollars and say, "Get yourself a nice meal. Go to the movies. You look like you could really use a good meal and a little entertainment." But what the member really needed was a fix.

"We must educate ourselves," Riva insisted repeatedly to staff workers. In 1992, with the approval of the new executive director, Kenn Dudek, Riva established a series of seminars at Fountain House given by experts on alcohol and drug abuse rehabilitation and treatment. The meetings were held at lunchtime and were open to both members and staff.

A group of members who attended the educational seminars approached Riva in 1993 about forming their own Twelve Step group. She enthusiastically embraced the idea of starting an AA meeting at Fountain House to provide the support that members needed.

Certainly, plenty of AA groups met in the Fountain House vicinity at all hours of the day and night. But these groups did not necessarily sympathize with the special problems of people with mental illness. Although the official AA policy finally acknowledged the necessity of psychiatric drugs for people with emotional problems and mental illness, many AA and Narcotics Anonymous (NA) members continued to believe all "mind-altering" drugs should be avoided regardless of the reason. Also, it was difficult for members to talk about their struggles with delusions, hallucinations, or other upsetting thoughts in front of a group of people unfamiliar with the symptoms of severe mental illness.

Riva began the internal administrative work on establishing an AA meeting at Fountain House. But it was not easy. Fountain House's long-established tradition and practice was to ban such meetings at the clubhouse itself because they were too much like therapy or treatment. Fountain House believed therapy was important but thought it should happen elsewhere.

Fountain House had the same dilemma with several public psychiatrists who had been hired to reach out to members in several Fountain House residences. To avoid the conflict of a psychiatrist seeing members at Fountain House, a storefront on West 49th Street was rented and converted into a carpeted office partitioned for privacy. This allowed members who had difficulty keeping appointments in the traditional mental health system to still meet with a psychiatrist.

The storefront also proved to be a good place for Riva to nurture an AA meeting for Fountain House members. Beginning in April 1994, a small group met there every Friday at noon. Eventually, enough participants volunteered to be officers so the group could become a formal meeting listed in the AA directory for metropolitan New York.

For Riva, participation in the Fountain House AA meeting was as much for herself as for members. "I want to keep clean for myself," she said to another staffer. "I never want to forget. There are times when we can become complacent. It's like members saying, 'I'm working and I feel fine. I am well. I don't think I need to take my medication anymore.' *My* medication is my involvement in AA."

8

What Do I Do Next?

Just as Linda Pierce had decided she needed to go back to school, Rebecca Blake reached the same conclusion. Like Linda, Rebecca had come to Fountain House after bouncing around in other outpatient programs for the mentally ill and had been surprised and delighted to find how different this program was. The difference between the two women's lives was that Linda had come through the public health system, while Rebecca was treated in the finest private psychiatric facilities on the East Coast.

When she became a Fountain House member in 1989, Rebecca slowly immersed herself in the life of the clerical unit, taking a shift on the switchboard and helping social worker Margie Staker put out *Fountain House Today.* She and Margie became friends. Often she joined Margie and a group from the clubhouse going to the movies on Sunday afternoons.

Whenever Rebecca worked on Transitional Employment placements, she was so dependable and obviously intelligent that the employers wanted to hire her. It happened at a major advertising agency and at Dow Jones, publisher of the *Wall Street Journal.* She declined their offers because one of the stipulations of the TE program was that a Fountain House member couldn't convert the placement into a full-time job. If that happened, there'd be no placement available for the next member. And besides, Rebecca wasn't sure a clerical job was what she wanted.

She wasn't sure what she wanted. But after five years as a Fountain House member, Rebecca knew she was ready for something else. For several months after her thirty-fourth birthday, this is what she discussed at the weekly session with her psychiatrist, Dr. Peters.

"I've outgrown a lot of what Fountain House has to offer for me," she said. "I cannot spend a whole day there anymore. That's why I have been doing one TE placement after another. I'm in a quandary.

"I still have this dream of having children. But I have this chronic feeling, this suicidal feeling. I have my TE at Dow Jones and Fountain House. What kind of life is this? Fountain House is not making me unhappy. But I'm tired of delivering faxes. Now I'm really scared. What do I do next?"

She thought about going to college, but she had started college once before.

More than a dozen years ago, she had enrolled in Barnard College following her graduation from the fashionable Spence School in Manhattan. But she didn't last through the first year.

Instead, she found part-time jobs as a babysitter for several families and, although she didn't tell her employers, she dropped out of college. She watched one child every morning, a two-year-old girl while her divorced mother went to graduate school. Rebecca got the little girl dressed, fed, and out in the stroller to Carl Schurz Park along the East River. When a briefcase-toting mother arrived home and asked, "How's school going for you?" Rebecca answered, "Fine."

She spent alternate afternoons with two other children whose parents worked. Sometimes, the parents would schedule a weekend getaway and ask Rebecca to stay overnight with their children.

Rebecca was thrilled. She loved to be with children and watch them play with their toys. She never had a chance to be a real kid herself. She never had been in a real family that did such ordinary things. Her own family was always in crisis.

But in these families, everyone seemed happy. And Rebecca liked being a part of that.

When she had been a little girl, she used to walk her dog at her family's summer home on Fire Island and look in other people's windows. She watched those families having normal dinners and wondered what it was like.

Rebecca and her twin brother, Randy, grew up on the Upper East Side of Manhattan just off Park Avenue. Her playground was Central Park. Her father was a physician and her mother was a Wellesley graduate but never worked. Instead, she drank. Also, Rebecca's parents fought. Mostly it was verbal, sometimes physical, and Rebecca and Randy watched it happen blow by blow. Sometimes Mother turned on *her,* hitting her legs and back with a hairbrush over and over until the bristles pierced her skin and opened little holes that filled with blood.

The fighting was what scared off the live-in help. Just when Rebecca and Randy would grow attached to a nanny, she'd quit. At school, other mothers tried to arrange playdates with Rebecca but she never wanted anyone to come to her house. She wasn't sure what would be going on when she opened the door.

When she was twelve, Father dropped dead of a heart attack. Actually, he didn't drop. He was sitting at the kitchen table and he stopped talking, right in the middle of an argument with Rebecca. Rebecca knew something was very wrong. She ran in the back room and hid. Next thing she knew, she heard the sirens. But she refused to come out of the back room.

"I was angry with my father about my mother," Rebecca remembered. "They were planning a divorce, and I didn't want to live with her anymore because I couldn't stand her craziness. He wouldn't listen. He disagreed."

Rebecca's mother blamed her for her father's death. Rebecca already was feeling guilty and accepted her mother's verdict. "Maybe I did send him right over," Rebecca thought.

After Rebecca's father died, her mother drank more furiously. She'd go into rages, spewing all sorts of accusations, and neighbors would call the police. Randy escaped by moving in with friends for periods of several weeks. But Rebecca, acutely ashamed that everyone knew what was happening inside her abnormal home, stayed behind. Her mother spent most of her days in her bedroom. Rebecca came home from school and stayed in her room. Usually, she ate cereal for dinner.

Once, her mother was sent to a sanitarium and Rebecca thought this could be the cure. She threw out all the liquor bottles in the kitchen cabinet. But three days later, her mother climbed out of a taxi and cheerfully said, "I didn't belong there."

When Rebecca was fourteen, she swallowed nine straight pins. She thought, "This will get me in the hospital." And it did, for a six-week stay in Hall-Brooke, a Connecticut private psychiatric hospital where she was diagnosed with depression. At one point, she thought she was going to be sent to the long-term adolescent unit at New York Hospital-Cornell Medical Center's Payne Whitney Clinic in New York City. She was actually looking forward to being admitted, but her mother wouldn't permit her to go there.

Instead, her mother took her to one psychiatrist after another. Yet the antidepressants and lithium they prescribed had little effect on her depression. And they had no effect on her "self-destructive behavior"; that's what one psychiatrist told her mother. What he meant was that Rebecca had started cutting herself.

She would take a razor blade from the bathroom cabinet, cut lightly into the skin of her forearm, and watch little spots of blood appear on the tile floor. She wore long-sleeved shirts to school and no one noticed the scabs. And no one knew how good it made her feel to hurt. To feel *anything*.

Several days before Rebecca was to graduate from high school, her mother killed herself; it was her fiftieth birthday. She took an overdose of Rebecca's medication. Randy found her lying on her bed. She didn't leave a note. Rebecca's psychiatrist was the one who told her that her mother had died.

Rebecca was relieved. (Later on, she felt guilty about that reaction.) When she got the news of her mother's death, she didn't cry. She couldn't imagine her mother's life continuing the way it had been.

After the funeral, Rebecca thought she could begin to rebuild her own life. She and Randy got an apartment together. She dropped out of Barnard and worked as a babysitter. She tried to pull her life to-gether. Instead, it plummeted.

For the next four years, she saw a psychoanalyst weekly. The sessions didn't seem helpful, but Rebecca was incapable of making a change. Each week, she opened her wallet, paid the receptionist, and confirmed her appointment for the following week. Her depression was overwhelming. She hated herself so much. She just wanted the pain to end. She just wanted someone to take it away.

Meanwhile, Randy turned to alcohol and then cocaine, spending what was left of the money from selling their parent's vacation home on Fire Island. Rebecca moved out and got her own small apartment.

One night when she was watching television, her buzzer rang. It was Randy. She buzzed him in. As he came through the door, she realized he was drunk and backed away. A hammer, used earlier in the evening to hang a print on the wall, was lying on the coffee table. Randy grabbed it and flung it through the television screen. Shards of glass flew everywhere.

"You killed Father," he screamed. "You drove Mother to suicide." "You are to blame for everything."

Then he stormed out of her apartment.

Rebecca thought she was responsible for his rage and was certainly to blame for her mother's death. She was terrified of Randy and thought he might kill her.

One day she confided this to a babysitting employer, who arranged for her to see a lawyer. With the lawyer's help, Rebecca got a protection order against Randy. Still, he careened in and out of her life until finally, he was admitted with severe drug and alcohol addiction to Bronx State Hospital followed by a six-month stint in a halfway house.

Because she'd isolated herself caring for children, Rebecca knew only a few people who, like her, were in their early twenties. One of them, a former classmate of Randy's, had an apartment in Greenwich Village and he gave Rebecca the key so she'd have a place to hang out downtown. He traveled for business every week, leaving early Monday mornings and returning Friday evenings.

One Thursday afternoon, Rebecca went to the apartment in the Village with a plan. For weeks, she had been taking only half the anti-depressant pills she'd been prescribed. Now, she swallowed all the pills she'd hoarded and lay down on the couch.

Only a canceled business meeting saved her life. Randy's friend came home a day early and found her ashen-colored and barely breathing. When she woke up in the intensive care unit at St. Vincent's Hospital in the Village, she was furious. How could she still be alive? What did it take to escape this life?

She spent the next six months in the psychiatric wing at St. Vincent's. She was placed in a unit with adolescents since her behavior was closer to theirs than to the psychotic behavior of patients in the adult unit. To relieve her depression, doctors prescribed shock treatments, but they made no lasting change.

Upon discharge, Rebecca was assigned to Dr. Peters, a psychiatrist who accepted the Medicaid reimbursement as payment in full. Sometimes talking to him made her feel better. Sometimes worse. Most of the time, he took her problems seriously. When he didn't seem to be listening, Rebecca had to get his attention in other ways.

"I'm sorry. I don't want to bother you," she said, speaking into Dr. Peters's answering machine. "But I can't take it anymore. This is the end. I have enough pills." Then she hung up the phone and waited for Dr. Peters to call her back and ask if she was all right.

She stopped eating. Her face took on a sunken, pinched look that he couldn't help but notice.

She sat in her bedroom and calmly burned herself with a cigarette. Then she allowed the burn to fester for two days without telling anyone.

"What's wrong with your arm?" Dr. Peters asked her just before their hour was finished.

"Oh, nothing. Well, not much of anything," Rebecca said.

She sat silently when he came around his desk.

"Roll up your sleeve," he said gently.

The burn, perfectly circular, was fiery red around the circumference and oozing yellowish, viscous fluid. Dr. Peters called the emergency room, asked for an attending physician, and told him to be looking for Rebecca Blake to come in within thirty minutes.

Rebecca's behavior, what she called "playing games," was typical of someone with borderline personality disorder. The cigarette incident got her readmitted to St. Vincent's, but she was only allowed to stay there for two months. What she needed was long-term psychiatric care and Dr. Peters miraculously persuaded New York Hospital-Cornell Medical Center's Westchester County division to accept her on Medicaid.

"I'll see you when you come back, no matter how long that is," Dr. Peters promised Rebecca. She was hospitalized for two years.

Rebecca was housed in a section that looked like a college dormitory with nineteen other patients, all people in their twenties with borderline personality disorder. They each had a private bedroom. Only two were men. One woman was paralyzed from the waist down because she had jumped out a window in a failed suicide attempt. Another had terrible scars from burns.

Three times a week, Rebecca met with a therapist who wanted her to talk about what she was feeling. She wanted to call it emptiness but thought that wasn't the right answer. "I am going to kill myself," she said.

The therapist wouldn't permit Rebecca to consider suicide as the answer. She tried. She said to the therapist, "What can you expect, after all I have been through?" But she was challenged on that remark in session after session. Gradually, she began to see that her childhood was over, never to be replayed, and it was up to her to take personal responsibility of her future.

During her two-year stay at the hospital, she never left on weekends like the other patients who got forty-eight-hour passes to go home. Sometimes Randy came to visit her on Sunday afternoons.

Toward the end of her second year at the hospital, the staff was preparing her for discharge. But she had no place to go. No parents, no income. She couldn't qualify for public housing nearby because she wasn't a Westchester County resident. However, a hospital social worker found her a place with the Bridge, a community program for the mentally ill in Manhattan which included housing and day treatment.

Rebecca telephoned Dr. Peters, who sounded like he'd been expecting her call. He agreed to schedule her for two sessions each week, Tuesday and Friday afternoons.

Rebecca was assigned to an apartment in a residence. Her roommate, Pamela, had graduated from Teachers College, Columbia University. Rebecca thought they were extremely compatible. But she soon discovered that Pamela was content with the day treatment, while it infuriated her.

"All we do is sit and talk," Rebecca complained to Pamela. "The staff doesn't encourage us to do anything. If we spent the rest of our lives here, that would be just fine with them."

One afternoon when she was leaving Dr. Peters's office, Rebecca ran into Judy, a young woman she knew from her stay at St. Vincent's. Rebecca told her about the dreadful day program she was attending, and Judy said she was going to Fountain House.

"Don't you need a diagnosis of schizophrenia?" Rebecca asked. She'd heard about Fountain House two years before from another St. Vincent's patient and when she had asked Dr. Peters about the program, he told her it was only for people with schizophrenia.

"Not necessarily," said Judy. "Some people have schizophrenia. Others are like me, they're manic-depressive. It doesn't matter what you are."

Rebecca was suspicious when she came to Fountain House—the beautiful building, the plants, the nice furniture. Riva K. led her orientation sessions in the living room. Rebecca thought that since everyone was so cheerful, so positive, it must be a scam.

Nevertheless, Rebecca was immediately drawn to Margie Staker and the other social workers in the clerical unit. But for the first six months, unless someone talked to her, she said nothing. She stapled the in-house newspaper together. She answered phones at the switchboard.

"The only thing that bothers me about Fountain House," she told Dr. Peters, "is some of the other members. These people are obviously ill and I'm afraid I'll end up in their state. I'll go down."

"It's not contagious," he said. "Give it a try."

The clubhouse environment was different from anything Rebecca had ever experienced. In high school, she was surrounded by people and no one knew she was sick. In the hospital, everyone knew she was sick. Sometimes the patients actually competed to see who was the sickest. But most of the time, they ignored each other and focused on their personal misery.

At Fountain House, she knew all the members had some form of mental illness. But the staff expected her and the other members to act normally. Rebecca didn't really know how to do that. She couldn't remember the last time she had an ordinary, nontherapeutic conversation with someone. All she could talk about was her illness, her problems, her medications.

Margie took her aside. "Don't forget to greet people when you come in the door. Say 'Hello' and 'Good-bye.' You must learn to say good-bye. It hurts people if you don't say good-bye."

Before long, Rebecca was introduced to the Transitional Employment program. Another social worker in the clerical unit, Tom Whalen, was in charge of TE placements in the mailroom at the D'Arcy Masius Benton & Bowles advertising agency. Fountain House members worked as indoor and outdoor messengers there, carrying advertising tapes to ABC, NBC, and CBS or to the clients' offices. Within DMB&B's mauve and gray corridors, a member made the rounds several times a day to see if the account executives had anything to be picked up.

In December 1989, DMB&B asked Fountain House if a member would take over the job of dispatcher, logging in all the packages that were dropped off for delivery, assigning a member to transport them, and then verifying that the package arrived at its destination. Tom asked Rebecca and another member, Viola, to share the dispatcher's job.

Rebecca was terrified of the responsibility; she had been at Fountain House less than a year. But because Tom believed she could do it, she said yes. Every day she worked felt like torture. She thought everyone at DMB&B knew she was from Fountain House. She couldn't look them in the eye. Even in the employee cafeteria, she kept her head down. Some days, she called in sick so that she didn't have to face these strangers.

One day, a manager came to her dispatcher's desk in the windowless room where the Fountain House members waited until they were needed. Rebecca looked up.

"I just wanted you to know I think you're doing a great job," the manager said.

"Thank you," Rebecca answered. She couldn't recall a better compliment.

*

Rebecca stayed on this placement for two years, much longer than most members' six-month stint. Eventually, DMB&B offered her a full-time job. She turned it down but was very flattered. Even when Tom Whalen left Fountain House and moved to Boston, Rebecca didn't falter. She turned to Margie more frequently for support in the clubhouse. And for confirmation on a TE placement, she looked to Ralph Bilby, who headed Fountain House's employment unit.

After DMB&B, Rebecca moved on to work on a TE placement in the wire room at the Wall Street Journal. The office was in a sleek World Financial Center building two blocks from the World Trade Towers at the lower end of Manhattan.

The term "wire room" was an anachronism, referring to the time when black Teletype machines clattered away, typing out news from United Press International (UPI) and Associated Press (AP) wire services on scrolls of yellow paper. Then clerks would rip off the news and run it over to an editor. When a news flash came over the wire — when a war started or ended or a president was assassinated — ten

bells inside the ticker rang out, alerting everyone to the critical break-
ing news.

Now UPI was almost out of business and each *Wall Street Journal*
editor and reporter could call up the AP wire on their own cool green
computer screen. The wire room was filled with fax machines.
Rebecca's job was to fax copy to the Journal's bureaus around the
world and to deliver the letters to the editor that had been faxed to
the Journal.

Being on this TE placement meant working at the newspaper's
pressure-cooker pace. Not many Fountain House members could
handle it, but Rebecca thrived. Each afternoon, she arrived at 4 P.M.,
only hours from the Journal's deadline. Working side by side with several full-time employees, she assembled the faxes, stapled them together, and moved through the narrow carpeted hallways to place
them on the correct editor's desk. Many nights she was asked to work
late. She came home in a cab paid for by the Journal.

Sometimes when coming or going, she would bump into a Fountain House member named Stanley Jacobs, who worked full-time at
Dow Jones. Stanley had come to Fountain House in 1982 after he'd
been hospitalized for his second breakdown. Esther Montanez got him
started working TEs. He worked on a placement at Dow Jones in 1983
before moving on to a placement at the Bank of Japan. Several months
later, his Dow Jones supervisor called him to say there was a full-time
opening in the mailroom. Stanley applied and three weeks later was
hired. Eventually he was promoted to assistant supervisor of the mailroom, where several members work alongside full-time employees.

Aside from supervising these members and an occasional telephone call from Esther, Stanley had no contact with Fountain House.
But he still considered himself a member.

"At first, being from Fountain House was a stigma, but now it's
not," Stanley said. "I have proved myself at work. I was promoted not
because of Fountain House but because I could do the job.

"In a way, I feel responsible for the members who work here. I
watch out to see if anyone is getting ill. I let people know I am from
Fountain House. That's how I protect the members."

Whenever visiting mental health professionals came to Fountain House for Colleague Training, Ralph Bilby took them down to Dow Jones. He introduced them to Stanley. He proudly pointed out the members working on TE placements, especially Rebecca. This was one of his most prestigious employers, and Rebecca was one of TE's shining stars. But the more competent Rebecca became at her job and the more praise she received only made her more painfully aware of what was missing in her life.

She voiced her bitter feelings to Dr. Peters at their weekly session.

"If it weren't because of circumstances, I'd be on the other side of the desk," Rebecca said. "There's this one woman—I feel like taking the faxes and throwing them at her.

"I don't mean to sound like I'm above it all, that's not what TEs are for. But when I leave there, I don't feel good about myself. I see these people—women and men who are my age—and they have pictures of their children on their desks."

Rebecca started to cry. She grabbed for a tissue from the box on Dr. Peters's desk.

"I can't help it. Being there is just one more notch of rage."

Dr. Peters waited until she wiped her eyes and her sobs had dissolved into silent tears.

"You're destroying yourself by comparing. Think of what you can do. Think of what will make you happy," he said. "Look, you haven't been hospitalized since you came to Fountain House. That is good."

Almost reluctantly, Rebecca nodded.

"I can't help but be a little jealous," she said.

Maybe the sense of failure would never go away. Maybe the emptiness never would. Rebecca had done enough reading and talking to other patients to know that these were the symptoms of borderline personality disorder. So were her sporadic lashings out at Margie or Ralph when they slighted or disappointed her.

Sometimes she criticized Fountain House too. She felt the clubhouse offered little help to members who could move on to independent employment, or at least a life outside of the clubhouse world.

Stanley Jacobs had done it on his own, but Rebecca seemingly could not.

Rebecca was correct. The Fountain House staff doesn't consider helping members become less dependent on Fountain House a high priority. The staff is fully engaged in the daily crises that demand their attention: getting people off the streets, out of the state hospitals, into treatment, onto federal SSI and SSDI entitlements.

The purpose of the clubhouse is to give people with mental illness somewhere to come, not somewhere to leave. The employment unit does help members develop helpful strategies for finding full-time work, but the staff doesn't push members in this direction. The impetus has to come from the member, in part because working full-time means losing eligibility for government subsidies. It is a big gamble.

Rebecca wasn't ready for that drastic step just yet. But she did know that earning a college degree was a big step toward independence. She started off slowly at Queens College, signing up for two classes—anthropology and a remedial math course in algebra.

On August 31, 1994, a rainy and unseasonably raw day, Rebecca was waiting on the first floor of the Kiely Hall at Queens College. It was the first day of classes and students were hurrying around, looking for their classrooms. Rebecca had taken two buses to arrive at school on time. In fact, she'd been nearly an hour early for Understanding Elementary Algebra, but that was all right. At least she wasn't late. She hated being late. She took her place with 120 other students, taking notes as the professor lectured into a microphone.

After the bell rang and the algebra professor had assigned homework for the following day, it was time to buy books. Rebecca spotted Margie Staker making her way through the throng. Since the state VESID office had agreed to pay for Rebecca's tuition and books and the check hadn't arrived yet, Margie was lending Rebecca $100 so she could buy books. She had borrowed a Fountain House station wagon and driven forty-five minutes on the daunting Long Island Expressway to meet Rebecca as her class ended.

"Do you believe how young these students are?" Rebecca asked.

"They're like babies. I feel like their mother. Do you think I look like their mother?"

In her oversized blue-and-white print dress that billowed below her knees, Rebecca looked more like their little sister. But her look of apprehension matched the worried frown of most other students.

"You look fine," Margie answered. "I'm the one who looks like their mother."

Rebecca laughed. Some days, like today, she truly appreciated Margie's friendship. Other days, her emotions were all tangled up.

She liked Margie and the way Margie cared about her, listening to her complaints and remembering her accomplishments, noticing when she got her hair cut or caught a cold.

But then, Rebecca sometimes thought that Margie really didn't see her pain or understand how hard it was for her to get up each morning and face the day. And, thought Rebecca, Margie had such a cheery disposition. And a great career. And a loving husband. Rebecca had always thought she'd be married with a family some day and, yes, live in a house with a white picket fence.

And yet here she was back in college. She'd forgotten what it was like to study each night. For a while, she thought her brain had forgotten how to learn. She worried that she couldn't do the work. She almost dropped out.

"Do you understand the work?" Dr. Peters asked her.

"Yes, if I take my time."

"So you can do it?" he pressed on.

"Yes, but I'm afraid it'll get too difficult."

"Listen, I'd be worried if you weren't nervous," Dr. Peters said.

Rebecca laughed. He was right. She had good reason to be apprehensive.

"That's typical of what I do," she said. "I sabotage things without giving them a chance."

Rebecca had another reason for persevering in her studies. She was hoping to meet a man at Queens College and broaden her social life. She had dated a few men at Fountain House, one of whom had crushed her feelings. After they had spent every weekend together for six months, he told her they had to stop dating because he was grappling with his sexuality.

Shocked, hurt, Rebecca retreated. Then she learned he was seeing another woman.

After a year, Rebecca and another member began to go to the movies together regularly, but then he was hospitalized because of manic depression.

As Rebecca looked around the college campus, it seemed the men were either teenagers or married professors.

In anthropology, she became friendly with a twenty-four-year-old woman named Naomi, an Orthodox Jew. Married with a three-year-old child, Naomi rushed out as soon as class was finished to get home.

"How do you like my hair?" Naomi asked one day as they sat down at their desks.

"Looks nice," said Rebecca.

"It's a wig," said Naomi, explaining that for religious reasons she had to wear either a wig or a hat to cover her hair. "You have to go to these special places where all these old women do is make wigs.

"If you ever converted, you would have a hard time because most Jewish people don't have blond hair like you. You'd have to spend an enormous fortune on a blond wig."

She and Rebecca laughed so hard that the professor stared at them.

Rebecca's other friend was eighteen-year-old Luanna. She had four sisters and at the mid-semester break, they planned to go to Great Adventure amusement park in New Jersey.

"I've never been to Great Adventure. I'd love to go someday," Rebecca said.

"It's a nice place," Luanna answered.

Rebecca replayed the offhand conversation over and over in her head. Why didn't she ask Luanna outright if she could come along to Great Adventure? Why was she waiting for Luanna to initiate it? Rebecca was simply afraid of being direct. She felt she had no right to ask anyone to do anything with her.

And then there was the nagging fear about social situations. When people get together socially, they ask questions to get to know each other better. What if Luanna or Naomi would ask her, "What else do you do besides go to school? Do you work?"

Dr. Peters told her that no one really cares about what she does for a living. But Rebecca worried because she had no answer prepared for that question. She thought maybe it was better that she avoided any social situation where those questions might be asked; maybe it was better, after all, that she wasn't invited to Great Adventure.

During the first semester at college, she continued working in the wire room from 4:30 P.M. to 8:30 P.M. She was so busy that she managed to come into Fountain House only once every two weeks or so. When she walked into the clerical unit on a Thursday afternoon in late October, Rebecca saw at least two new members. And everyone seemed so busy. Rebecca sat down in a chair and busied herself going through the knapsack she carried everywhere.

Margie swiveled around in her desk chair. She stood and wrapped Rebecca in a bear hug.

"How have you been? It's been ages," Margie said. "I've missed you."

9

But Still, By God, They're Working

On one of those unexpectedly warm autumn days, Ralph Bilby walked eight blocks across midtown Manhattan for an appointment. He was scheduled to meet with the human resources director of an East Side law firm to discuss setting up Transitional Employment positions there. He brushed off the thought of hailing a cab, figuring it was ultimately faster to walk than to sit in gridlock traffic. And it might also impress prospective employers that Fountain House didn't fritter away its money, not even as small an amount as cab fare.

The director of employment at Fountain House, Ralph was wearing what he wore to work every day—a blue oxford shirt, a gray patterned tie, and tan slacks. He didn't have time to worry about his wardrobe. And he felt that his predictable, plain attire was an example for male members going into the workplace environment of TEs. Some women at Fountain House teased him about his lack of fashion sense, and he laughed along with them. A forty-nine-year-old bachelor, Ralph had an on-again, off-again relationship with a younger secretary who worked downtown, but he reserved his energy and deepest emotions for his work. No particular woman was picking out his clothes.

For his walk, Ralph draped his navy blazer over his arm. Once inside the air-conditioned office building, he slipped it on before he punched the elevator button for the twenty-ninth floor. The presentation he was about to make was the same as hundreds he'd given over the past fifteen years since coming to work at Fountain House. Still, each one was important.

Each presentation he made to a human resources manager was another opportunity to continue developing the TE program. So far, Fountain House had arrangements with forty-three employers who provided jobs, or placements, for 150 members. However, as corporations downsized and jobs became automated, TE placements were often casualties, so Ralph continuously worked on TE development.

The law firm's human resources manager, Bruce Rosen, a man in his mid-thirties with dark hair, came out of his office as soon as the receptionist buzzed.

"Come on in," Rosen said, extending his hand and directing Ralph into his office. Framed family photographs sat on the left corner of his desk, a stack of paper on the right. Ralph sat in a chair facing the window.

"Thanks for making time to see me," Ralph said. "Let me tell you a little about us."

He explained that Fountain House began in the late 1940s as a place for mentally ill people to get together, that John Beard structured its activities into a psychiatric rehabilitation program, and that Transitional Employment was an essential component of rehabilitation.

"In other law firms, we have indoor and outdoor messengers, or file clerks. These are the kinds of jobs that can be split into two or even three shifts a day. So we'd be able to place two or three members in that one job. You and I can talk about where would be the best place for Fountain House members to work here."

"We have a fair number of messengers, and there's some turnover in those jobs. So we could have an opening coming up," Rosen said. "What do your people generally get paid?"

"The TE placements pay whatever the prevailing wage is for that position," said Ralph. "Our average wage on TE is $6 an hour, but we have some that pay $4.50 and others in the $10- and $12-an-hour range. Whatever you pay other employees for doing the job, that's what we'd expect you to pay us."

Rosen opened a desk drawer, took out a yellow legal pad, and began making notes. He looked up and said, "Okay. That sounds good."

"You see, a member stays on a TE placement for about six months," said Ralph. "Then a new member comes on board, and we will make sure that the next member knows how to do the job."

"Tell me exactly who, that is, what kind of people come to Fountain House."

"Our members have chronic and persistent mental illness," Ralph answered slowly, clearly. He wanted to make sure that Rosen understood the nature of the members' disability. "Most of them have schizophrenia; some have manic depression. A few have other serious emotional problems.

"Most of our members are taking psychiatric medications. But medication alone can't help them get back on their feet. What they need is the experience of a job."

Ralph didn't want to lull Rosen into thinking the members weren't really sick. He never began a new TE placement by making the first worker a "ringer," someone whose mental illness was so well under control that symptoms were invisible. Instead, he wanted the employer to be aware of the disabilities—members so lacking in social experience that they can't return a greeting, the ones who worry aloud all day that they can't do the job, the ones who have to be reminded by Fountain House staff to bathe and change their clothes.

Ralph also wanted employers to be aware that some members didn't show up for work on schedule. Nevertheless, the day's work was completed by the Fountain House staffer assigned as the TE placement manager. And because of flare-ups of their mental illness or their inability to cope with the demands of holding a job, most members didn't complete the six-month TE assignment.

"Over 50 percent of our people are not going to be able to finish their TE jobs," said Ralph. "That really is the reality of the system. But we are prepared to deal with this. We provide absence coverage. We will cover the work for a couple of days, then we'll train a new member to take over."

"What we're talking about is a win-win situation for you and for us," Ralph said.

Rosen nodded in agreement. "You know, sometimes people here may be a little, well, brusque. We're good people, don't get me wrong. Fair people. But what if someone said something thoughtless, or what if we wanted to correct something that the Fountain House person was doing wrong? I mean, I wouldn't want to be responsible for our setting back someone's progress."

"A lot of our employers have that concern initially," Ralph said. "And it's a legitimate concern.

"This is a true story: I had a member come to me, all upset. He was working on a TE and I don't know what happened between him and his boss. They must've had a disagreement, or whatever. Anyway, his boss told him, 'Go jump in a lake.'"

Rosen gasped.

"The member wanted to know if the boss was telling him to commit suicide," Ralph said.

"What I usually tell employers is to balance out a problem issue by also telling the member something that he is doing well. Kind of like how we'd like our boss to treat us. It does require a more sensitive touch with most members. It takes practice. But the good employers learn."

"That makes sense," Rosen said. "Sounds like we've covered a lot of ground here. I'll have to talk to our management committee here, but I'll get back to you."

He looked down at a list of employers involved in Transitional Employment and saw the names of two major law firms. "This sounds like something we could do, especially since Baker and McKenzie, and Cleary Gottlieb are already doing it."

Rosen had one more question. "What about the chances of, well, your people being violent?"

Ralph had been expecting this question. Sometimes it was the first question he was asked. Most times, a human resources manager waited until the end of the interview before bringing up such a sensitive subject. No one wanted to stigmatize all mentally ill people as being dangerous, but it was impossible to avoid the issue. And it was documented that someone in the throes of a psychotic episode is slightly more likely to be violent than the general population.

"Employers always ask about the risk of violence," Ralph said. "We've been doing TE for thirty-five years and we've had one single incident.

"One member went back two months after his TE was finished and punched a guy in the nose whom he felt insulted him. That's it in thirty-five years. One incident. We think that our record on the risk of violence is superior to most employers' experience."

"You could be right about that," Rosen said.

He stood and shook Ralph's hand. "Thank you for coming in."

*

The Transitional Employment program that Ralph was presenting so persuasively was developed in the early 1950s by John Beard while working with mental patients in a Detroit hospital. He brought the concept of TE to Fountain House when he was named executive director in 1955.

John Beard was born and raised in Detroit, where his father was a hospital administrator. His mother was a nurse with an unsentimental, no-nonsense approach. The youngest of four children, Beard was a youngster when the family's dog grew old and died. Heartbroken, Beard sat on the grass, next to the dog's body lying in their backyard. "If you really care about the dog," his mother said, "stop sniveling and brush the flies away. Don't do nothing. Do *something.*"

After serving in the Army attached to the Corps of Engineers in Kansas during World War II, John Beard returned home and attended Wayne State University. While working on his master's degree in social work, he was assigned to work with mental patients on the back wards of Detroit's Wayne County General Hospital. In the evenings, he came home and told his wife, Marion, that he couldn't believe people could be so overwhelmed by their illness. "They have absolutely no hope," he said. To him, it was impossible to accept that their situation was utterly hopeless.

Once he received his master's degree, he was hired full-time at the hospital. At that time, Wayne County General had a permanent population of two thousand mental patients living in Eloise, its mental health complex.

At Eloise, Beard was assigned to N Building, ward 206, which was home for 150 men with chronic mental illness. Most were schizophrenic. None was on medication. (The use of Thorazine, the first antipsychotic drug, wasn't introduced until the 1950s.) Almost all patients had been through electroconvulsive treatments, commonly called electric shock therapy or ECT, but these treatment methods produced no lasting changes. The chief means of dealing with unruly, hallucinating patients was to place them in restraints to prevent them from flailing their arms or legs, hurting themselves or anyone in their way.

With the support of a young staff psychiatrist, Beard was determined to improve these patients' hopeless plight. He decided to focus on the patients' normal responses to everyday situations. After all, most patients weren't psychotic every minute of every day. They could act normal at least part of the day. For instance, a crew of patients worked as unpaid laborers, picking vegetables grown on the hospital's farm and preparing food in the hospital kitchen. They performed these tasks ably, which Beard viewed as proof that they were capable of normal behavior. Somewhere amidst the psychosis, a part of these patients was not mentally ill.

How to identify the healthy parts of patients' minds became an all-consuming challenge for Beard. He thought the best way to reveal these normal aspects was to place the patients in normal settings.

With the psychiatrist's approval, Beard took a few patients out of the hospital on day passes to do what normal people do. They took a walk in a park, looking at the trees and listening to the birds. He took some other men out to Briggs Stadium to see the Tigers play baseball. They went to dinner in a restaurant. Some of the other patrons looked at them wide-eyed when a patient plucked a dessert intended for another table off a waitress's tray, but the waitress simply returned to the kitchen for another dessert. Otherwise the patients made no disturbance.

Beard brought one or two patients at a time to his home for the afternoon. Marion was nervous about having the patients around her two babies, especially when her husband encouraged one patient to push little Margaret in her stroller around the block. But Marion swallowed her misgivings. She trusted her husband's opinion that, mental patients or not, they could act normally. And Marion soon saw that the patients' behavior was indistinguishable from that of any other visitor.

Through these outings to the ballpark, the restaurant and his home, Beard wanted to convince the patients that they had significance regardless of their pathology, that there was a place for them in normal society. For American men in the 1950s, normalcy included working at a job, and Beard wanted to see if the patients could work.

But what kind of work would be appropriate? As a teenager, Beard remembered working in a grocery store as a stock boy, a job that was demanding but not complicated. That was the kind of job Beard envisioned for the Eloise patients. He set his sights on Wrigley's, a new supermarket chain opening stores in Detroit, and made an appointment to meet with its personnel director.

Beard proposed an arrangement that was to become the essence of the TE program: a patient would come with Beard to a Wrigley's supermarket three times a week for one hour to stock shelves; the patient would be paid whatever Wrigley's other stock boys were paid; and Beard guaranteed the patient would empty as many cartons and stock as many shelves as the regular employees.

"It's terribly important to see if the patient can handle this," he told the personnel director. "I am being paid by the county and I will be there with him."

Maybe it was Beard's mention that he was a county employee that swayed the personnel manager. Maybe the manager wanted to stay on good terms with local government. Whatever the reason—and Beard never asked why, for fear that Wrigley's might reconsider its decision — the manager said yes.

As the first patient to be placed in this job, Beard selected Arthur, who'd been at Eloise for nine years. Arthur, a displaced person from Romania in World War II, came to Detroit because he had relatives there. Soon after his arrival, his mental illness became obvious. But Arthur had long periods when his hallucinations receded and he was quiet. When Beard casually mentioned he was trying to find work for a few patients, Arthur begged to be included.

On the first day of his work at Wrigley's, Arthur had to punch in his time card. But when he reached the clock, he threw up his arms and cringed. Behind the clock was the electrical equipment for the store's refrigeration. To Arthur, it looked like the apparatus for electric shock therapy and he'd been strapped up to it innumerable times. Beard had to coax Arthur to walk around the machinery and then the two of them went to work moving boxes.

Arthur liked to spend his pay immediately after work by gorging himself on food at a short-order cafe across the street from Eloise. It was Arthur's money and Beard didn't tell him how to spend it. After several months of his part-time work, however, Arthur changed his behavior. He stopped spending wildly. He wanted a new shirt and knew he had to save for it.

Arthur's decision validated for Beard the expenditure of time and effort it took to set up this three-hour-per-week job. Beard hadn't envisioned that working at Wrigley's would cure Arthur of his schizophrenia, but he had hoped the experience would help Arthur function more normally. Saving one's pay was normal behavior and Beard was thrilled.

Eventually, Arthur didn't need Beard's supervision on the job and he worked unaided. So Beard turned his attention to lining up other positions for patients. Over the next twelve months, he arranged for a few part-time jobs at the Sanders Candy Company on Oakman Boulevard in Highland Park. By the time he left for Fountain House in New York City, he'd set up seven placements for the Eloise patients.

Beard was determined to duplicate the program at Fountain House because he was convinced that offering mentally ill people the opportunity to work in the real world was an integral part of psychiatric rehabilitation. When a person with mental illness was answering the telephone, sorting mail, or delivering packages—jobs that normal people do—the person appeared less mentally ill to others and also to himself or herself.

In 1959, Beard convinced an employer in New York to try a Transitional Employment placement. That first employer, Sybert Nicholas, which published Fountain House's annual report, agreed to allow two members to make some of its local deliveries.

By the 1960s, more than fifty Fountain House members were working on TE placements at a dozen businesses. Eight positions were at a franchise luncheonette called Chock Full 'O Nuts, a place named for a brand of coffee, where members waited on counter customers. Beard and the members couldn't resist chuckling at the ironic name of the luncheonette.

In 1967, an Illinois public television station filmed a documentary about Fountain House and interviewed the co-owner of the Chock Full 'O Nuts franchise about his relationship with the clubhouse.

"In the beginning, we had some reservations about starting this project," said the co-owner. "After all, we have a successful business. The only thing that could happen was that business would go down. We couldn't see it going up because of this.

"But we had second thoughts. We decided to bring in one person at a time and it started to work out. We feel if we can help someone along the way without it causing us any trouble or costing us any money, we should help them.

"Now, about 80 percent of our help is from Fountain House. We feed three thousand people a day. During lunch hour, all the seats are taken and people are standing up. We'd like to think we turn over the seats every eight minutes.

"As far as I'm concerned, once the Fountain House people finish working in our place and prove themselves in our place with the amount of pressure they have, they can go any place to work."

By the late 1970s, the TE program had grown to include stock room positions, seasonal work in factories, janitorial jobs, and the indoor and outdoor messenger jobs at D'Arcy Masius Benton & Bowles. Not all members could complete a six-month TE placement, but that was completely acceptable. TE gave members an opportunity, including the opportunity to fail and try again, for as many times as the member wanted to try.

Rather than hire a specialist to oversee the TE program, Beard decided that Fountain House staff workers, including Esther Montanez, would serve as placement managers to teach members how to do a TE job and make sure the member's stint went smoothly. Beard maintained ultimate direction of the TE program—and all else that went on at Fountain House during his tenure.

One day in June 1979, Beard walked out of his office and was introduced to Ralph Bilby. After working for several years in industrial metal sales, Ralph was looking for a career change, possibly working with the mentally ill as he had done as a young man in Arizona. A friend of a friend had referred Ralph to Fountain House. Beard discovered that Ralph, whose master's degree was in business administration, had the personal and professional background to relate to corporate executives in their own style and language. Beard recognized that Ralph would be an ideal ambassador for Transitional Employment. Within days, he was hired.

At this point in time, Beard still tried to oversee the TE program and all other aspects of Fountain House, but his health was failing and it became too much. Eventually Fountain House slipped into a state of limbo, waiting for the inevitable. After Beard's death in 1982, his successor, Jim Schmidt, gave Ralph a free hand to run the TE program.

Ralph beefed up the list of employers with prestigious law firms and accounting firms whose TE placements were white-collar, clerical positions that paid well above the minimum wage. Often it took a year or more of gentle pressure on a firm, requiring meeting after meeting before enough key people signed off on the decision to begin a TE placement. But Ralph was seldom discouraged.

*

Ralph Bilby came out of the meeting with Eric Rosen feeling cautiously optimistic that the law firm would eventually approve at least one TE position. After nearly fifteen years' pitching TE to some of America's largest corporations, being rejected or given the runaround far more frequently than he heard "Yes, we'll try it," Ralph was still enthusiastic about his job. What kept him going were the stories of members who learned how to set their alarm clocks and get to work. Members who went on several TE placements and began to look for full-time, independent employment. Members whose triumph over an obvious disability evoked admiration in these large corporations.

"It becomes a source of pride to the employer that they are partnered up with members in their struggles to get by for their six months on TE," Ralph said. "The member binds Fountain House to the employer. The employer feels more powerful because he sees the people have special challenges, special problems, but still, by God, they're working.

"Employers become so defensive about those members. We'll go in to say, 'How's everything going?' And the employer will say, 'Jane is just fine. She is going to make it. We'll get her through the six months. She'll be a finisher.'

"I think it's there in the American character," said Ralph. "We like to be helpful, to see ourselves as generous, helpful people. I think there are hundreds of thousands of business people out there looking for ways to help. We just have to show them what's possible."

Ralph's workday extends well past 5 P.M. In addition to supervising several TEs at the *Wall Street Journal* that last until 8 P.M., he has duties within Fountain House. Every Tuesday evening, he helps organize a special dinner in the dining room for members on TE and those employed full time. Following the meal, either Ralph or another Fountain House staff worker moderates a discussion with the members on situations that they faced on the job. Frequently, an outside speaker is brought in.

On the Tuesday following Ralph's meeting with Eric Rosen, the

Fountain House dining room was decorated for the weekly TE dinner. A small white vase with pink carnations was set on every table. A large arrangement of flowers was placed in front of the podium. About eighty members and staff were waiting to hear from the invited speaker, Mike Buckley, manager of office services at the D'Arcy Masius Benton & Bowles advertising agency.

"I'd like to congratulate the dining room members and staff for making this wonderful dinner," said Esther Montanez, who was acting as the master of ceremonies. "Isn't Fountain House a wonderful place?"

Everyone clapped. Then she introduced the two placement managers at DMB&B, Arthur Burgess and Margie Staker from the clerical unit.

"We have twenty-four members working altogether over two different shifts as indoor and outdoor messengers," said Arthur. "We have people who haven't worked in their lives before. When they come to DMB&B, they find they can do a job."

"For many members, DMB&B is the best place to start on TE," Margie chimed in.

Then, Esther introduced Mike Buckley, who supervises all that happens behind the scenes at DMB&B. He stepped up to the podium. He didn't have prepared remarks, so Esther got him started talking by asking, "What do you look for in a new worker?"

"I look for someone who is willing to try, to ask questions," said Buckley. "Someone who is willing to learn. People come in new and they're nervous, but by the end of their six months, they are able to move on to another TE. I have learned not to judge someone right away. It's amazing how someone changes in just a couple of days."

The group applauded.

"It's a business environment, so it's important what you wear and how you talk to the other workers," Buckley said. "People may be abrupt when they talk to you, but that's the way it is. It's business. Most members understand that and rise to the occasion."

Someone in the back of the room raised his hand and Buckley acknowledged him. It was Larry, a middle-aged member.

"I've been on four TEs," said Larry. "One was a good experience. I was a messenger but not at DMB&B. I liked being a messenger, and I liked working in a mailroom. Then I got my own job. I had two full-time jobs. But they didn't work out. Now I am starting my own business, a house-cleaning business. I think it's a good business to be in. I think—"

"Larry," Esther said, "what is your question?"

Larry blinked. "What's it like running a business?"

"Good question," Esther said.

"What every business wants to do is move forward, to accomplish a goal," said Buckley. "Our goal is to make our customers happy."

"I have two customers at least," said Larry. "I am hoping to put an ad in the paper and—"

"Larry, give someone else a chance," Esther said.

Ralph Bilby, sitting at a table in the middle of the room, spoke up. "I'd just like to point out that DMB&B was the first employer to give a chance to deaf members on TE."

The audience applauded. Other members raised their hands to speak.

"I was a federal secretary before I got sick," said Vicki. "Then my first TE was with DMB&B. I got back on my feet."

Bill, who was currently working on a TE there, said, "When I was in the hospital, the doctors told me that I'd never go back to work. I thought, 'Never?' I went right back to work. Now the doctors ask me, how am I doing? I say, 'Fine.'"

"When I went to DMB&B," said Eddie, speaking directly to Buckley, "everyone warned me about someone in the copying room, but we got along fine. I mentioned that I liked perfume and every woman I worked with started wearing perfume. You make me feel wanted."

"Good point, Eddie," said Esther, smiling broadly, as the group again applauded. "Good point to end this evening on."

"Thank you, everyone, for sharing your experiences. Thank you, Mike Buckley."

Esther's face was glowing with pride. She put her hands around the microphone. Over the applause, she exhorted the members like an evangelist to the congregation.

"Do we walk out of here stronger because we were here together?" she asked.

"Yes!"

"We know each other. We are friends. Does Fountain House work?"

"Yes!" the members answered.

*

Through Transitional Employment, some Fountain House members gain enough self-confidence and workplace experience to move on to full-time employment. In 1994, sixty-four members were working full-time and their average annual income was $20,729.

Matthew Palmer had been on a succession of six-month TEs, working at DMB&B, in the wire room at Dow Jones, as a messenger for a law firm, and as a clerk at city hall. One day, he saw Ralph in the dining room and told him that he was ready for the next step.

"I have been patiently going along with the Fountain House program, and now I think it's time to start looking for full-time work," Matthew said.

"That sounds good," said Ralph.

"When I was at DMB&B," Matthew said, "I thought, 'Gee, I am an Ivy League graduate. Maybe I should apply for creative work.' Being a college graduate might help. It's an accomplishment. People might think I have ability. I have a hunch it'll help me get a job. But it might make me overqualified.

"But when I am working, I feel better. I've had that feeling with some of the TEs I've been on. I'd like to get that way again, and get a job and have health benefits."

"I can see that you're ready," said Ralph, tapping Matthew's sleeve for emphasis. "I'll see what I can do."

To help members look for full-time jobs, Ralph often formed an informal task force composed of staff workers and a few people from Fountain House's Employers Advisory Council. One of Matthew's first questions for the task force was whether to tell potential employers that he had mental illness. Karen Mangione, an advisory council member and an assistant manager of corporate human resources at Time Warner Inc., had experience answering this question for Fountain House members.

"My philosophy is to be up-front," she said. "A good human resources interviewer will see a gap of four years on your resume and ask you. If you hem and haw, or tell a lie, that won't work. I suggest you say, 'I had a mental illness. I am rehabilitated. I've done TEs and I feel I am ready.' It might not be a bad idea to give as your references someone whom you've worked for.

"How this is received depends on the company. Some will say, 'Oh, well, we'll let you know.' And you won't hear from them again. Others will say, 'Okay, we'll start you off at this level. We'll ease you in.' So, I recommend that you say this on a job interview. I realize it's easy for me to say, though."

Once a person discloses in a job interview that he or she has a mental illness, the employer may not discriminate against the candidate under the Americans with Disabilities Act. But Matthew felt that if there was any way he could avoid mentioning his illness, he would.

Then he worried about his skills. His professional background was in accounting, although his skills were out of date. He'd worked as a computer programmer, so the task force suggested he look into word processing. Matthew took their advice, and he took steps to prepare himself for such a job. He knew he needed to brush up on his touch typing before he would be ready to tackle a word processing program. So every afternoon, Matthew went to the education unit and practiced typing on a keyboard which, Joanna Romano, the unit leader, had found for him.

Matthew didn't want to ask his family for help. Matthew remembered how good he felt when he got his own jobs, and he wanted to feel that independent again.

Once he had prepared a resume, he had one hundred copies made.

*

Throughout the winter of 1994–1995, members and staff teased Ralph about his approaching fiftieth birthday. Margie Staker and several other female staff workers planned a party in his apartment for the Fountain House community. As was his custom, Ralph extended party invitations to both members and staff. Nearly one hundred people were expected, including Matthew Palmer.

The party was Friday, April 7 from 5:30 P.M. until whenever. The invitation said Bring Your Own Bottle, and for Matthew Palmer, BYOB meant a two-liter bottle of Diet Coke. Margie had some last-minute paperwork to do, so Matthew and a friend walked down West Forty-Seventh Street to Ralph's apartment.

Ralph lived by himself in a small one-bedroom apartment created from a converted warehouse. At the height of the real estate boom in the eighties, the neighborhood looked as if it would overcome its seedy reputation and become trendy. In the nineties, it became clear that the neighborhood would never be fashionable, but the apartment was only one block from Fountain House, so it suited Ralph's needs just fine.

When Matthew pushed Ralph's buzzer, someone immediately let him into the lobby. Inside Ralph's apartment, a CD was blasting heavy metal. Kenn Dudek was standing in the center of the living room trying to talk over the din to a member from the kitchen unit. Black balloons with white letters that said "Over the Hill" decorated the room. Matthew found a chair by the imposing brick fireplace and sat down. That's where Margie found him when she arrived.

A belly dancer had been hired to perform later in the evening and Margie couldn't wait to see Ralph's reaction. She knew he'd be mortified but enjoy the attention.

She poured white wine into a plastic cup and walked over to greet two members from the clerical unit, Martin and Craig. "I antedate this music," Martin shouted over the noise. Margie nodded and laughed.

Someone finally picked out quieter music and Craig leaned over to Margie to explain why he was happy to be attending the celebration.

"I am lucky. Because of Ralph and the brainstorming sessions he helped arrange with a task force for me, I got a permanent, part-time job," Craig said. "I work in a law firm as an outside messenger. I work 9 A.M. until 1. I am so lucky. And it's all because of Ralph."

You Don't Know Who I'm Going to Be Someday

Just after Ralph's fiftieth birthday party, executive director Kenn Dudek informed the Fountain House community that Tipper Gore, the vice president's wife, was coming to visit in early May. Mrs. Gore, who has a master's degree in psychology, made mental illness her area of interest following the 1992 election. She often visited mental health facilities, celebrating her birthday in 1993 by serving lunch to members at the Green Door clubhouse in Washington, D.C. And on a state visit to Russia, she visited a clubhouse in Moscow. Now she was coming to see where this concept of psychiatric rehabilitation originated.

Kenn Dudek's announcement of Mrs. Gore's impending visit set off a flurry of housekeeping. The unit leaders, both male and female, looked around their work areas as if for the first time and saw woodwork that needed to be touched up with paint and frayed curtains that should be replaced. Out came industrial-strength vacuum cleaners, mops, brooms, and professional floor buffers.

But the phalanx of housekeeping tools didn't prevent Secret Service agents from coming in the week before the visit to make security checks at Fountain House. Tall, very well groomed and wearing audio receivers in their ears, the agents' presence was hardly inconspicuous.

To conduct Tipper Gore's tour of Fountain House, Kenn asked Kathleen Rhoads, a staff worker in her late twenties, and a long-time member named Kay Pierson. Each year, more than a thousand people tour Fountain House, including prospective members, mental health professionals from other clubhouses and those interested in starting a clubhouse, family members, and students. These tours, which normally last ninety minutes, are led by members who explain the clubhouse operation as they visit the various units.

Kathleen Rhoads was extremely nervous about her central role. She'd only been working at Fountain House for eight months, while so many other staff workers had years of seniority. Still, she was uniquely qualified to serve with Kay as a Fountain House representative.

As coordinator of Colleague Training at Fountain House, Kathleen was in constant contact with members and staff from clubhouses around the world. To illustrate the expanding network of clubhouses, she installed in her office a world map that covered one entire wall, floor to ceiling, and placed push-pins on the cities with a clubhouse. More than two hundred pins dotted across the United States, with the remaining seventy-two in Canada, Europe, Australia, South Africa, Egypt, Japan, and Korea.

Several years before, Kathleen had been director of the first consumer-run clubhouse in the United States. And since she herself had experienced numerous psychiatric hospitalizations in her teens and early twenties, she was in the special position of having the perspective of both a consumer and a staffer.

In her job at Fountain House, Kathleen mentioned only occasionally that she had been a psychiatric patient. She didn't like to draw attention to her own experiences when members were telling her about their problems. But sometimes she referred to something that only someone who had experienced the mental health system could know.

"I don't have the need to go into it because it would take away from what I am here to do," Kathleen said. "But I'm better at my job because I have been exposed to insanity."

On the morning of Tipper Gore's arrival, Kathleen and Kay met at Kenn Dudek's office. Betsy Seidman, a Fountain House board member from Deloitte & Touche accounting firm who was instrumental in arranging Mrs. Gore's visit, was chatting with Ann Somers, the part-time public relations specialist. Several fat-free snack bars, grapes, mints, and diet sodas were arranged on a side table, as Mrs. Gore's staff had requested.

Blond, athletic, and filled with enthusiasm, Kathleen still looked like the high school cheerleader she once was. She sat down on a couch next to Kay and leaned over, "I am dying for a cigarette."

Just then, a black limousine with the presidential seal, followed by motorcycles and Secret Service chase cars pulled up to the front door of Fountain House. An agent opened the limousine door. Tipper Gore and her assistants stepped out, and the entire group moved swiftly through Fountain House's front door and up the wide, graceful staircase to Kenn Dudek's office.

"Hi, I'm Tipper Gore," she said, extending her hand.

Kay was too nervous to respond and Kathleen couldn't get past, "Hello."

"We're glad you could come," Kenn Dudek said to Tipper Gore.

After she declined Kenn's offer of refreshments, he asked her if she'd like a tour of Fountain House.

"Absolutely, I'd love to see your clubhouse," said Mrs. Gore. "You know, I've been to the Green Door. What a fabulous place!"

The Green Door clubhouse, within walking distance of the White House, is a renovated nineteenth-century mansion with antique walnut paneling in its foyer and a sleek, contemporary dining room and kitchen.

"When they remodeled, they really preserved the special features in that building," Kenn Dudek agreed. "Our building was built about thirty years ago, but we've done renovations here, too, to open up little offices into bigger spaces to get more members involved in each unit.

"Kathleen and Kay will be your tour guides."

Kay, Kathleen, and Kenn led Mrs. Gore and her aides out of Kenn's office. Several other people from Fountain House and eight husky Secret Service agents followed.

As they walked up the stairs to the clerical unit, Kathleen thought, "Should I risk it? Should I tell Tipper Gore what I was thinking when I was back in a mental hospital?"

Tipper Gore's voice interrupted the thought.

"How long have you been at Fountain House?"

"Just a short time," Kathleen said. "But I trained here to start my own clubhouse."

Then Kathleen felt she had to explain more.

"I love working in a place like this. It's just the best job. I've been in the system for years and thought there was no hope to get better. I hated the system. Now I'm working in a place where I feel comfortable. Great things happen here. We're kind of radical because members and staff really are equal here."

Tipper Gore's eyes glistened. She reached out and patted Kathleen gently on the back.

In the spacious clerical unit, some members continued to pound away on the computer keyboards while others looked up in astonishment at the entourage and said, "Oh, my God."

Mrs. Gore kept moving forward with her hand out in front of her, repeating, "Hi, I'm Tipper Gore," and shaking hands with any member or staff in her path. She looked over the shoulders of members typing articles for *Fountain House Today* and typing stencils on old-fashioned electric typewriters for use on a mimeograph machine. Inside a small room without windows, the old copying machine whirled around with its blue stencil attached to its drum.

"Running off *Fountain House Today* on a photocopy machine would cost a lot more," Kay said.

More than forty people were working in the clerical unit, some typing, some answering phones, some collating and sorting bills. Mrs. Gore stopped behind the young woman who was operating the busy Fountain House switchboard.

"Fountain House, can I help you?" the young woman asked repeatedly as she made connections and answered new calls, barely noticing the entourage behind her.

"It's amazing, how many people are working, just amazing, I've never seen anything like it," said Mrs. Gore. "And you can't really tell the members from the staff."

The group moved along, looking in other units before returning to the street. Their next destination was the HUD building, which contained the horticulture unit as well as apartments for older Fountain House members on its upper floors. Walking down the block toward the HUD building, Kathleen had something she wanted to say to Tipper Gore. She knew she might sound ridiculous, but she'd never get the chance to say it again.

"Mrs. Gore," she blurted out, "I have to tell you this. When I was in the hospital, they had me tied down one day. I remember saying to the hospital attendants, 'You don't know who I'm going to be someday. You can't judge that I'm not going to be anybody. That I'm not going to succeed. You can't judge that. You don't know that I won't be mingling someday with the president of the United States.'

"And they just kept tightening and twisting and locking and sedating."

Kathleen looked keenly at Mrs. Gore. "Then to actually meet you Mrs. Gore, this is even better."

Tipper Gore hesitated for a moment. Then she put her arms around Kathleen and gave her a big hug. Kathleen started to cry.

In the living room of the HUD building, several members, including Matthew Palmer and Linda Pierce, were seated around a table waiting for Tipper Gore to join them. Each member had undergone a background check by the Secret Service. Kathleen laughed at this. No one bothered to check her despite her extensive background as a patient because she was now a staff worker.

Matthew was nervous. He talked at length about his progress through Fountain House's housing program, moving from a supervised residence to an apartment with a lease in his own name. Linda, too, spoke longer than she intended as she tried to express her feelings about being a Fountain House member.

A White House aide whispered, "We have to leave here now." Tipper Gore, engrossed in the heartfelt story of one of the members, shook her head and murmured, "No, not yet."

When the members were finished, Mrs. Gore hugged each one. Her tour's last stop was the Transitional Employment unit, which is decorated with oversized color photographs of members and posters with statistics describing which members are on which jobs. Mrs. Gore was speaking to a member when Ralph Bilby came in from a TE placement.

"This program is just fantastic," Tipper Gore said to him.

"We'll know we really made it when our sister clubhouse, the Green Door, has a TE at the White House," he responded with a smile.

"I'll look into it," she said, smiling back.

Her tour ended back at the main building in the dining room, the single biggest space at Fountain House. Hundreds of Fountain House members and staff packed in to see the wife of the vice president.

As the entourage descended the stairs towards the dining room, Kathleen heard the members and staff cheering and clapping and hooting and hollering, just like a rock concert.

Tipper Gore entered the dining room and was surprised to see hundreds of people waiting for her to speak. She hadn't anticipated making a formal address. Everyone was standing and applauding as Kenn Dudek stepped to the microphone and introduced her.

The crowd became very quiet as Mrs. Gore hesitated a moment. She seemed moved by the intensity of the crowd.

"I am so impressed with what you are doing here with your lives and with each other."

The audience applauded.

"I feel the hope, the compassion, the love, the caring for each other." Mrs. Gore was speaking softly. Even the most restless members were still, listening carefully.

"I feel the fact that the staff is terrific and there is oneness with the staff. I think that this should be replicated. I saw the map. I visited your sister club in Russia. I will keep working hard to tell people in the United States that mental illnesses are a normal part of being human."

Mrs. Gore stepped away from the microphone to loud applause and a standing ovation from the members and staff. Kathleen and Kay helped escort Mrs. Gore to her car where she gave each of them a hug.

Ralph Bilby shook her hand and she said, "I won't forget what I said to you." Then the presidential entourage sped away.

As Kathleen walked away, she burst into tears. The combination of excitement and happiness was too much. "What a day it has been," she thought. "Not just for me, but for all these people here with their histories of abuse by the system or stigma in the community or their own internal conflicts. And here they're meeting the vice president's wife."

As soon as she got home to her apartment, Kathleen telephoned her mother in Seattle. "Mom, can you believe it? Your daughter spent two hours with the vice president's wife."

*

Kathleen, who grew up in Federal Way, a suburb of Seattle, was a high school honor student and captain of the drill team. It looked as if she had a perfect life until it all fell apart in her senior year.

Until then, no one knew that she grew up hearing voices. They weren't disturbing when she was a child. She found them comforting, like the voices of friends, and it was just nice to have the companionship. And no one knew there were lapses in her memory, that she might spend part of an afternoon giggling to herself but completely forget the episode the following day. Some of her grammar school teachers recommended that she be placed in special education classes, but her parents refused.

"Kathleen's just a very distracted child," they told her teacher.

Her voices seemed to subside in junior high and Kathleen's natural intelligence and personality emerged. But when she was seventeen, the same voices that had once been warm and friendly, turned menacing. They were screaming and yelling. Her head felt as if it was going to blow up. She wanted her head to fly off her shoulders and roll away. She couldn't stand the screaming anymore.

Then the voices changed again. *Die, die,* they said over and over. They told her to kill herself: *Drive your car off a cliff.*

One of her friends had recently committed suicide, and Kathleen thought this was the most glamorous thing she could possibly do. She planned every detail of her own funeral, down to what music would be played, but never tried to kill herself. Still, her grades in school plummeted. She dropped from an A student to a student who was just getting by.

Most disturbing was the return of her amnesia. She'd be cheering at a football game and the next thing she knew, she was coming home at three in the morning with her feet bleeding, not knowing where she'd been.

Probably she had been walking, listening to the voices. But she had no explanation for her mother, who met her at the front door of her house.

"Where have you been?" her mother asked.

"I don't know. I can't remember," Kathleen said.

"Why are your clothes dirty?"

"I can't remember."

Kathleen's condition worsened through her final year of high school. She had invited a boy to the school's Sadie Hawkins dance in the fall and he was supposed to reciprocate by inviting her to the prom in the spring. He didn't. Kathleen was devastated. Even when another boy asked her to go, it didn't lift her depression.

Her mother constantly asked Kathleen how she was feeling, if she was all right. One day, she looked at her mother blankly and said, "I have to die."

Her mother took her to her pediatrician, who referred Kathleen to a psychiatrist in Seattle. They drove to the psychiatrist's office, where Kathleen mumbled something about the little woman floating up in the corner. The psychiatrist recommended immediate hospitalization and drove behind her mother's car all the way to the hospital. Over the next week, he considered several different diagnoses: schizophrenia, manic depression, multiple personality disorder, and finally major depression. To Kathleen, none of these had any meaning. She didn't know they had repercussions and would haunt her for the next ten years.

The night of her senior prom, she was still hospitalized but stable. Her date still wanted Kathleen to come with him. So she got a pass from her psychiatrist, went home, and was picked up by her date to go to the prom at the Seattle Space Needle. The next day, she returned to the hospital.

It was far more difficult to finesse the events on graduation day. By then she'd been released from the hospital and her mother had bought her a new dress. Kathleen felt she was making a triumphant return. Her family pretended everything was back to normal, but her classmates weren't so forgiving.

"My parents said you're possessed by the devil," said the girl who'd been her best friend.

"Maybe she needs an exorcism," someone murmured as they walked by Kathleen's locker. Then a crowd of kids laughed.

"My parents said you're dangerous and I shouldn't hang around you," said another girl who was supposed to walk beside Kathleen in the graduation procession.

Kathleen was heartbroken. She knew everyone was afraid of her. In her homeroom, as everyone buzzed about the graduation parties that would follow that evening, no one spoke to Kathleen.

Over the next few years, Kathleen was hospitalized nine times. She went through a series of medications, beginning with Haldol, that left her listless and shuffling. Her pattern was to escape from the hospital and then be returned by the police. Then she'd escape again and be returned to a double-locked ward. Then she'd escape *again* and be put into a holding tank for people who were headed for the state hospital. The holding tank was the most gruesome snake pit she had ever seen.

After going through this cycle a number of times, she would eventually calm down, allow herself to become stabilized on medication, and be released.

Between bouts of illness, Kathleen attended community colleges. After each hospitalization, she explained her absences to her school friends with a new story: female troubles, back problems, migraine headaches. It was hard for her to keep all the lies straight. Then she'd transfer to another community college and begin again.

One college, which happened to be across the street from a state hospital, offered a program for students interested in mental health careers and, through it, Kathleen obtained an internship at the state hospital. She was very curious what it would be like to help patients. To her great surprise, she was assigned to an all-male ward.

Her first day, she walked up to the locked door of the ward with dread. As she was led into the noisy ward by an attendant with a huge ring of keys, Kathleen thought, "My God, will I ever get out of here alive?"

Forty men on the ward slept in large dormitory-style rooms furnished with plastic chairs and metal tables, and illuminated by harsh fluorescent lighting. There were no curtains on the windows, only bars on the outside. The patients wore gray, sleeveless pullover shirts with gray cotton pants held up by drawstrings.

A handful of patients gathered around Kathleen, all talking at the same time. "Are you a nurse or a social worker?" "A doctor?" "Are you married?" "Where do you live?"

Kathleen was overwhelmed, yet somehow amused. She responded good naturedly, although deeply moved by their look of hopelessness and enormous need for attention.

She went along when the mental health workers took the patients to a dance. She danced with the old men and the young men. The older patients sang the old songs, beginning, of course, with "I'll Take You Home Again, Kathleen." She smiled and tried to sing along. She recognized that the staff workers' behavior affected the patients' behavior. If they anticipated the patients would act crazy, they did. If they expected the men to behave sensibly, they often did.

During her internship, Kathleen tried to analyze her own experiences in mental hospitals and the treatment she received. "The more intrusive the conditions around me became, the more I rebelled," she realized. "That's what cycled it. I would behave in a very animal-like way."

She always remembered the people who were good to her. "The nice nurses and the nice doctors. Maybe they gave me a pat on the shoulder, or squeezed my hand or snuck out and got me a Diet Coke.

That's why they were my heroes, because they were nice. That should be the rule, not the exception."

In dealing with her own mental illness, Kathleen experienced many of the stages of death, but not in one orderly progression. First came shock, followed by denial. Then mourning the loss of the healthy, functioning part of herself, seemingly lost forever. Again, shock. Then bargaining with God that, "If I ever make it back, if I ever get my sanity back, I'll work in the mental health system, I'll make it better." Then mourning. Finally, acceptance.

Ultimately Kathleen got better. She found a sympathetic therapist and together, they worked hard to sort through her mental illness. Kathleen improved. Gradually, she gained more control over her own life. She transferred to a four-year college to finish her degree in psychology. She met a man, confided to him the details of her psychiatric history, and he didn't recoil in distaste. "You're one of the most mentally healthy people I've ever met in my life," he told her. Their friendship turned to romance.

In 1989, as she was completing college, she was introduced to the world of mental health advocacy. She saw a notice posted on the bulletin board outside the psych department for the monthly meeting of the Washington state chapter of the Alliance for the Mentally Ill (WAMI). Kathleen had met the executive director of WAMI through one of her psych classes. Out of curiosity, she decided to attend the meeting.

The National Alliance for the Mentally Ill (NAMI) was started in 1980 and chapters quickly sprang up throughout the country. Family members of people with severe mental illness came together with a three-pronged mission of education, support, and advocacy.

These family members saw mental illness primarily as a biological illness, advocated to change the term "mental illness" to "neurobiological illness," and urged the federal government to fund research on biological defects in the brain. Family members were often most interested in a cure, or at least more potent medications.

The patients, who called themselves "consumers," had little interest in this focus. In its earliest days, the consumer movement was composed of combative veterans of the sixties who called themselves the "patient liberation front." Consumers or "psychiatric survivors," their more radical term, had at best a grudging acceptance of psychiatric medications.

Over time, they dropped their call for the destruction of the psychiatric world—its hospitals, medications, straitjackets and electro-convulsive treatment—and demanded, often successfully, that former patients participate in the mental health world as advocates, mentors, and paraprofessionals.

Nothing characterized the differences in these movements more clearly than the annual NAMI convention and the national consumers conference. Each year, NAMI held numerous workshops dealing with the latest medications and advances in research, while the consumer conference was filled with workshops on how to start a drop-in center or how to develop housing. Medications were rarely mentioned and brain research never discussed.

When Kathleen entered the conference room for the WAMI conference, she was horrified to see signs posted around the room: Schizophrenia, Depression, Manic Depression. People were clustered under each sign.

"What's going on here?" Kathleen asked an older man standing under the Schizophrenia sign.

"These are self-help groups. We're waiting for the session to get started."

Kathleen thanked the man for his explanation but she wondered, "Does it matter what the label is? It should just be an educational seminar about mental illnesses."

Kathleen took a seat and waited for the main speaker, a woman whose son had schizophrenia. She talked about the importance of these support groups. "What was so important to me," she said, "was that you could actually meet other people with a history of mental illness in their family. That was such a killer, keeping it in such secrecy that it will eat you up. And I think the same is true for people, like my son, who have mental illness. You don't have any energy for anything else because all your energy is devoted to hiding, pretending, fantasizing that you'll get better."

Kathleen nodded in agreement. She remembered trying to keep her lies straight to explain why she took these sudden leaves of absence from college when she was hospitalized.

Then Kathleen looked around the room and recognized a few men and women whom she knew from her own hospitalizations. She cringed. Maybe she could just ignore them. No, that would be cruel, really cruel. Of course she remembered them.

After the meeting, a former patient came over to Kathleen and said, "I know you."

Kathleen said, "Hi, how are you?"

The WAMI director, who'd been standing near Kathleen, looked over.

"You know some of these people?" she asked Kathleen. "Oh, you're a consumer."

Kathleen was taken aback. She hadn't heard that term before, not unless you were talking about shopping. *Consumer,* she thought. She understood what the word meant in this setting, but she couldn't help smiling. Consumer—it sounded like you could give back your doctor and get a refund.

"Well, yes, I guess I am a consumer," Kathleen said.

"What are you doing now?"

"I'm in college and I'm about to get my bachelor's degree in psychology."

"Did you know that there's a group of people in Olympia who want to start a clubhouse program?"

Kathleen had no idea what the WAMI director was talking about. Her only thought was that a clubhouse could be a place where people might socialize. Maybe it had a Jacuzzi or a swimming pool attached to it.

"They are looking for a consumer."

"They want to hire a mentally ill person?" Kathleen asked. She couldn't imagine why being mentally ill would be a desirable trait in an employee.

"That sounds interesting," Kathleen said.

Kathleen had no idea what she was getting into. Still, she applied for the position with the Mental Health Consumers Coalition and they mailed her several articles about Fountain House so she'd understand the concept of a clubhouse.

Her first reaction after reading the articles was disbelief. "There's no way there could be any place like what's on this paper," she thought. "No way a place can run like this, that there should be this equality between the patients and staff." It seemed as if the description of Fountain House confirmed all her own thoughts about how to help people with mental illness once their symptoms were controlled by medication: Treat them like normal people and they'll act normal.

When she interviewed for the job, she discovered she was under consideration for the executive director's position. Such a job would have been unthinkable for someone like her with no work experience. But the National Institute of Mental Health grant that funded the project had specifically called for a clubhouse run exclusively by consumers. Kathleen was hired.

Immediately after her college graduation in 1989, she went to Fountain House for three weeks of Colleague Training and returned to Olympia, Washington to start Capital Clubhouse, the first consumer-run clubhouse in the country.

Kathleen and her small staff found a space for the clubhouse in a small commercial mall. She had wanted a real house, because it would be most homelike and comfortable, but this commercial space was light, bright, and, most important, affordable.

Remembering the upholstered furniture at Fountain House, Kathleen decorated Capital Clubhouse with sofas and chairs from a local furniture store. She was particularly excited about finding an old-fashioned restaurant booth for sale in a place going out of business. Then she realized the booth was welded to the floor. Her boyfriend used a crowbar to pry it loose and she proudly installed it as part of the clubhouse's dining room.

Quickly, Kathleen found out that a consumer-run clubhouse was a noble concept that, in its execution, created a community of caring peers—but one that couldn't thrive without a sense of imposed order, which contradicted the notion of a community of peers.

The greatest advantage was the almost instantaneous camaraderie among the members and staff since everyone had suffered the intense pain of mental illness. And there was a proud, giddy sense that Capital Clubhouse was a trailblazing adventure. Staff workers were hailed as consumer leaders. They spoke regularly to media and mental health agencies from around the country. Their peer advocacy was recognized as an effective way to reduce re-hospitalizations.

But after about eighteen months as executive director, Kathleen began to doubt that Capital Clubhouse could survive. The reason why people with mental illness came to the clubhouse was for help. When the people providing that help were still struggling with their own mental illness, they couldn't always provide members with the support they needed.

Another drawback was the staffers' training. Because their knowledge of mental illness was limited to their own personal experience, Kathleen felt her staff sometimes had difficulty understanding a member's illness.

As time went by, Kathleen realized she had to make accommodations for the staff. If staff workers became tired because of their medications, they were allowed to take naps at the clubhouse during the day. Occasionally, they needed to be hospitalized.

Trying to establish Transitional Employment placements was very difficult because the clubhouse's staff had very poor work histories themselves. It seemed like an insurmountable hurdle for the staff to set up an appointment with a local employer to discuss TE. After two and a half years, the clubhouse had secured only four TE placements, which were not nearly enough to create a healthy vocational experience for members.

With seven months as the average length of staff employment, it appeared to Kathleen that the staff themselves used the opportunity to work at Capital Clubhouse as their own Transitional Employment experience.

Capital Clubhouse couldn't find someone with a history of mental illness to oversee their budget and Kathleen's only financial experience was in managing her monthly SSI check. No wonder the clubhouse's financial matters were often chaotic.

When Kathleen disagreed with staff and members, those who opposed her didn't confront her objections directly. "Everything is really fine. There's nothing wrong," a staff worker told her. "You just think that something is wrong. It's your own mental illness that's kicking up."

Ultimately, she became discouraged and disgusted. After the initial National Institute of Mental Health grant expired on January 1, 1992, Kathleen resigned as executive director.

Capital Clubhouse received funding for two more years before it closed. Since then, several other consumer-run clubhouses have opened, including a growing one in Philadelphia.

The Fountain House model's approach of blending consumer and nonconsumer participants, she felt, was one of its strongest and most healing features because each person offers something valuable to the other. Once she resigned from Capital Clubhouse, Kathleen was able to assess her experience. She concluded that the consumer-run Capital Clubhouse, such a defiant gesture against the mental health system, actually created a reverse stigma by excluding nonconsumers.

Shortly after leaving Capital Clubhouse, Kathleen went to work as the coordinator of training at Genesis Club in Worcester, Massachusetts. Two years later, she was hired for the same job at Fountain House. Ralph Bilby and Margie Staker drove up to Worcester to help her move to Manhattan over Labor Day weekend, 1994.

The morning after Tipper Gore's visit, Kathleen approached Fountain House with a sense of relief. Now that the visit was over, she could focus on her work. Approximately once a month, people arrived for a three-week Colleague Training session and Kathleen had to organize their schedules and accommodations.

"Kathleen, do you have a minute?" A new member named Eric walked up to her desk. She put down her pen.

"Sure, Eric. What's up?"

Finding out what was on Eric's mind was also part of her job description, although listening to the members disrupted the work flow. Some staff workers had difficulty with this aspect of the job because it seemed to mean tolerating constant interruptions. The challenge to staff was to be accessible as a friend while engaging the member in the work of Fountain House.

Sometimes, it wasn't easy for Kathleen to remember this. She'd get so involved in her work and stressed out when the to-do pile of papers on her desk grew higher and higher. Then she'd remind herself, "Kathleen, this isn't about how well you get through your day. This is about, how well did you engage members today? You don't have a right to be so stressed out. This isn't about *you*."

Being a former mental patient made her more sensitive to the members' feelings. But in some ways, she was less tolerant than other staff workers. She could and did say to members, "My God, you have to go to the laundry room. That shirt is filthy." Other staff might tip-toe around the issue. Kathleen's style was to be blunt.

"I will just say, 'Why can't you get up to go to your job? How can I help? You need an alarm? Get an alarm.' It's a very practical approach. That's the beauty of the clubhouse, it's very practical.

"So many times we hear about the special needs of the mentally ill. But lots of what we need isn't special. Is it a special need that you want friends? That you want an intimate relationship? A social life? A job? A home? Food? A little bit of money in your pocket? Is that a special need? I don't think so.

"What we do at the clubhouse is so commonsense. It's not very fancy. People come to Fountain House for training, spend a lot of time and money, as if they're coming to Oz. And it's just commonsense."

Because Kathleen was one of the newest staff workers, Kenn

Dudek asked her to speak at Fountain House's annual theater benefit, a dinner in a midtown hotel followed by a Broadway show.

"You'll be the staff speaker and we'll also have a member speak."

"I'll be just the regular staff? Just the regular normal staff? I don't know that I have ever done that before. I don't know that I can do that," said Kathleen. She was accustomed to identifying herself as a former consumer when speaking in public.

"I would never put you in that situation or ask you to do that," he said. "You need to do what you're comfortable doing."

Kathleen didn't need to share her history of mental illness. Nor did she need to hide it. Usually it came up in conversation because of her passion about her work.

On the evening of the benefit gala, while the guests were finishing their desserts, Kathleen stepped up to the microphone.

First, she talked about the importance of work. Then she told the audience that she'd been mentally ill; that she had been told she'd never work and that if she wasn't dead by the time she was twenty-one, she'd be living off Social Security her whole life.

"When someone said these things to me, I knew it wasn't true. I wanted to work. I had ambition."

She described how she worked in the consumer-run clubhouse in Olympia before being hired at Genesis House. And she talked about what happened one day at Genesis.

It had been her responsibility to manage a TE placement. The member, Jessica, had the job of filing medical records at a local hospital. Because Jessica had been having a rough week, sounding depressed and detached, Kathleen went over to the hospital to see how she was doing.

"I am getting sick," Jessica said. "I have to go into the hospital." It was desirable and not unusual for members to recognize that their mental illness was flaring up and they needed to be hospitalized.

"Okay, I'll help you get admitted," Kathleen said.

"No, not yet. When I finish my shift," said Jessica.

Two hours later, when her shift was completed, Jessica and Kathleen walked outside the hospital building and around to the emergency department. Kathleen walked up to the reception desk and explained why they were there.

"Have a seat. Someone will be with you."

Kathleen and Jessica waited for eleven hours. They didn't go to the cafeteria for fear of missing the doctor. They took turns going to the bathroom. Whenever Kathleen asked a clerk when they'd see a doctor, she got a vague, evasive response. It became apparent to Kathleen that in this general hospital, psychiatric care was the lowest priority.

Once Jessica was admitted, Kathleen went looking for a hospital administrator whom she knew. She'd been wearing the same clothes for twenty-four hours, she was dirty and tired, but she had to tell him about the hospital staff's lack of concern for Jessica.

"We can't change that," he said. "The kind of services that you're talking about cost too much."

"You don't get it," Kathleen said. "You missed it. The kinds of things I'm talking about don't cost anything."

She went back to her apartment and before she fell asleep, she wrote down a list of the kind of services she'd been looking for.

Kathleen read the list to the audience at Fountain House's theater benefit.

"What does it cost . . .

"To smile at me. . . . To hold my hand. . . . To explain what you are doing. . . . To recognize me as a fellow human being. . . . To let me eat something. . . . To listen to me. . . . To let me call my mom. . . . To give me words of hope. . . . To touch me in a safe and gentle way. . . . To be nice.

"What does it cost?"

Membership Is Voluntary and Without Time Limits

The member waiting outside Kenn Dudek's office on a June morning was wearing a woolen overcoat and a scowl on her face. Neither was a good sign.

"Lauretha, what can I do for you?" asked Kenn, as he guided her toward a small sofa. He sat on a straight-backed chair next to her.

"I need to get this signed," she said sullenly, holding out a blue sheet of paper.

Kenn knew what she wanted. She had an account in the Fountain House "bank" where members could cash their entitlement checks and set up small savings accounts. After Lauretha paid her rent subsidy, she had only $300 remaining each month to spend on food, transportation, entertainment, and telephone bills. Her careful budgeting had been disrupted when she signed up for every premium channel offered on cable TV. Within three months, she had needed a loan from Fountain House. Now she wanted to withdraw money from her account that was earmarked to pay off the loan. According to the clubhouse rules, she needed approval from a senior staff worker and her own social worker .

"Who is your staff worker?" Kenn asked.

Lauretha kept her head down and avoided the question.

"No one is helping me here," she said.

Kenn named all the staff workers who had already tried to help her. "There's Esther and Steve Anderson and Bea—" At the mention of each name she twisted her hands tightly together.

"That's not true," she shouted. "And you're not going to help me, either."

Kenn didn't flinch.

"Just make sure you get this paper signed," he said evenly. "And you will get the money you need. But you'll have to work out another budget arrangement."

Lauretha gave Kenn a dirty look, jammed the paper in her pocket, and stalked out of the room.

Her anger didn't bother Kenn. Maybe she was entitled to it. As long as members are not harming themselves or others, Kenn believed staff should forgive many kinds of behavior. What really mattered was that this member got the help she was looking for. And that she participated in the process too.

In many ways, Kenn, who was named executive director in 1992 at age forty, is an unlikely heir to John Beard. Beard had a charismatic, domineering personality; Kenn is a soft-spoken consensus-builder. Beard was fiercely independent; Kenn wants to promote close relationships between Fountain House and public officials. Beard was wary of the mental health establishment; Kenn recognizes that the clubhouse model can flourish only by reaching out to those working and teaching in the field of psychiatric rehabilitation.

However, both John Beard and Kenn Dudek firmly believed that people with mental illness can play a meaningful role within society and that they can re-enter society through the clubhouse environment.

"I think what makes Fountain House unique is that we expect people to contribute," said Kenn. "That's significant. Any other mental health program has a service orientation. The place provides a service to the person coming in the door. They may say to the consumer, 'We want you to help us out,' but they don't necessarily expect the consumer to contribute.

"I believe your self-esteem is tied to your mastery of tasks. Simply put, if you do something well, you feel good about it. And you feel good about yourself. Unless you allow people to *do,* I don't see how they can get better."

Kenn came to know John Beard when he participated in the first Colleague Training group at Fountain House in 1977. Then he returned to Massachusetts, where he worked in several clubhouses before eventually moving on to become the community support program director of Massachusetts Department of Mental Health. With the invaluable support of family members and consumers, the program helped eighteen new clubhouses open between 1985 and 1990.

At the end of that period, Kenn was hired by Fountain House to work on clubhouse development nationwide. He assisted Rudyard Propst, an erudite man in his sixties who had a passionate belief in the Fountain House model and the political savvy to promote it worldwide.

Rudyard Propst had come to work at Fountain House in 1981 at age fifty-seven after a career in mental health administration for the states of Illinois and New York, much of which was influenced by his fifteen-year professional relationship with John Beard.

Rudyard grew up in Oak Park, a suburb of Chicago, the only child of a cardiologist. After attempting to study pre-med in college to please his father, he eventually studied at the University of Chicago to become a psychotherapist. But once in practice, he was uncomfortable with the idea that a person's problems could be solved in discrete, forty-five-minute sessions.

He gave up his practice as a therapist in 1954 and was hired by Chicago State Hospital to set up a psychiatric rehabilitation program. After four years, he became the director of rehabilitation services for the Illinois Department of Mental Health.

These were the years Thorazine and other antipsychotic drugs were introduced, when a diagnosis of severe mental illness no longer automatically meant a lifetime confined to the back ward of a state hospital. Physicians were enthusiastic about the possibility of their patients' returning to society, although there was no clear-cut vision of what form rehabilitation should take.

In 1967, the public television station in Illinois decided to film a series on psychiatric rehabilitation options and asked Rudyard to serve as a consultant. One episode was a documentary on Fountain House, and Rudyard went to New York with a film crew to interview John Beard.

The more Rudyard listened to Beard, the more he was intrigued by his concept of patients as members of a clubhouse, working side by side with staff to regain the social and vocational skills necessary for a successful transition to the real world. This theory contradicted what Rudyard had been taught to expect from forty-five-minute therapy sessions. John Beard's approach seemed practical, logical, and, as Rudyard looked around Fountain House, successful.

"Everything I didn't know how to do, he *did* know how to do," Rudyard told a friend later. "Everything I didn't know how to solve, he did. So I already knew, before we had started shooting the film, that I had walked into my world."

After completing the film, Rudyard returned to Illinois and kept in regular contact with Beard, continually exploring the ways in which a clubhouse environment could help people with mental illness. In 1970, Rudyard was hired as director of rehabilitation services for the New York State Department of Mental Health. From his office in Albany, it was only a three-hour drive to Fountain House and Rudyard made the trip several times a year. After he was appointed to an advisory committee of the Fountain House Board of Directors, his trips became more frequent.

When Rudyard retired in 1981, he joined the staff of Fountain House. John Beard, who was being treated for lung cancer at this time, was delighted to finally have Rudyard working full time in the clubhouse.

Despite his long-standing philosophical appreciation of the clubhouse model, Rudyard had no hands-on experience in this setting. So Beard suggested he spend some time as the greeter at the front door, welcoming members and staff at the beginning of the day. Quickly, Rudyard discovered what he didn't know about Fountain House.

"Where is the Transitional Employment office?"

"I don't know. I'm new here."

"Where are the keys to the closet?"

"What keys? For what closet?"

"The alarm is going off on the stairs by the dining room!"

"Oh, no, what do I do now?"

Suddenly, someone put his hand on Rudyard's shoulder. He turned, startled. It was Joe Giovanni, a member of Fountain House in his seventies.

"You look like you're new here. Can I help you?"

"You certainly can," Rudyard said, sighing in gratitude.

Afterward, Rudyard realized he'd learned an important lesson through Joe about how a clubhouse operated. He knew that the staff's job was to help members, but just as vital was members helping staff.

Nowhere was this lesson about clubhouse operation written down. While other psychiatric rehabilitation programs began as theories put into practice, the clubhouse model evolved over years of actually working with members, with John Beard adding concepts such as the work units, Transitional Employment, and a residential program as the need arose. While Beard wrote a handful of articles in the 1950s for professional journals that described his views on psychiatric rehabilitation, he never compiled a textbook describing how a clubhouse should function.

Occasionally, visiting mental health professionals asked Beard to open another Fountain House in their hometown. But in 1959, the Fountain House board of directors voted against expansion because, according to a board member, it lacked manpower and funding "to do the job properly."

Instead, Fountain House turned inward. For the next thirty years, mental health professionals and consumers interested in learning more about the clubhouse model were invited to spend time at Fountain House and learn through participation. In 1976, the National Institute of Mental Health awarded Fountain House a $160,000 grant for each of the next five years, formalizing this on-site visitation.

The participatory program, which became known as Colleague

Training, began in 1977 and continues today. The mental health professionals and consumers who come for a three-week training session are called "colleagues." They stay in the four-story, brownstone guesthouse that is part of the Fountain House complex. Colleagues spend their days working in one of the units at Fountain House for hands-on experience, visiting other New York clubhouses or touring the Transitional Employment placements. Although Manhattan-at-night beckons, most colleagues pass the evenings in the guest house kitchen, sitting around a wooden table, smoking cigarettes and drinking coffee, and analyzing the pieces that made up the Fountain House model.

In 1982, John Beard, Rudyard Propst and senior staffer Tom Malamud, who grew up on the grounds of a Massachusetts state hospital where his father was a psychiatrist, collaborated on an article for a professional journal entitled "The Fountain House Model of Psychiatric Rehabilitation." This was the first time the clubhouse concept and its program components were described in print.

Despite publication of the article, Fountain House continued to emphasize that the only way to fully understand the clubhouse model was to experience it first-hand through Colleague Training.

Generally, the colleagues were dazzled. They came away impressed with Fountain House and convinced they could duplicate its seemingly simple principles. Fountain House staff was available by telephone to advise informally on how a clubhouse runs, but there was no formal continuing training and support.

By 1988, some two hundred clubhouses had opened, almost all begun by mental health workers who'd gone through Colleague Training at Fountain House. These clubhouses formed a loose coalition with staff and members meeting at regional and international seminars. Fountain House printed a directory listing the names and addresses of clubhouses worldwide.

Throughout the 1980s, city and state officials were hard-pressed to provide services for growing numbers of homeless people, many of whom were also mentally ill. After housing was provided, the greatest need of the people with mental illness was for vocational training. Because Fountain House offered a method of integrating its members into the work world through its Transitional Employment program, mental health professionals came to Colleague Training at Fountain House. And they also looked into other programs being developed by university-based psychologists and psychiatrists.

Some community mental health centers embraced a concept called Supported Employment, which Virginia Union University had developed for the mentally retarded and which was subsequently adapted for the mentally ill. It involved a job coach accompanying the mentally ill person to the employment site for weeks or months until the person could handle the work alone.

Boston University proposed the "choose-get-keep" method to help individuals secure employment. The University of Wisconsin developed a program for Assertive Community Treatment through which case managers help mentally ill individuals get connected with services in the community. And UCLA developed training manuals, workbooks, and videocassettes for clinicians to teach social and independent living skills to people with severe mental illnesses, particularly schizophrenia.

These programs were analyzed by objective criteria in scholarly journals, which made persuasive reading for other mental health professionals and public administrators who funded these programs. Meanwhile, Fountain House was still insisting, "You have to come and experience a clubhouse to truly understand it." To Rudyard's way of thinking, it was a thick-headed, short-sighted approach.

And even more dismaying to Rudyard, word began to filter back to West 47th Street that some of the two hundred clubhouses that claimed to be based on the Fountain House model deviated in fundamental ways from John Beard's concept.

Fountain House operated on a work-ordered day. But some clubhouses had a work-ordered morning and group therapy sessions in the afternoon. Others called themselves a clubhouse without having developed a Transitional Employment program. And some clubhouses operated under a traditional staff dominance model instead of a partnership between members and staff.

In his role as director of education and training, which he began in 1982, Rudyard argued that order must be imposed among these clubhouses. "If you can't control what people are doing and they claim to be doing what you're doing, but they are not," he said, "it can generate enormous confusion and anger in families looking for a clubhouse."

To establish a formal structure in the clubhouse world, Fountain House applied to private foundations in 1987 for funding for a Clubhouse Expansion Project. It had four main objectives: (1) to develop a written set of standards that describe how a clubhouse functions; (2) to offer on-site consultations to clubhouses by a faculty of experienced members and staff; (3) to help set up additional regional training bases to complement Fountain House; and (4) to establish a center separate and distinct from Fountain House to promote clubhouse development.

The Clubhouse Expansion Project received a $600,000 grant in 1987 from the Robert Wood Johnson Foundation. With such a commitment, Fountain House was able to attract an additional $800,000 from the Pew Charitable Trust, other foundations, and federal grants.

To codify the fundamental aspects of a clubhouse, Rudyard wrote to a dozen of the strongest clubhouses, such as Gateway House in Greenville, South Carolina, and asked for their recommendations on a list of standards. Over the next year, suggestions on standards came in to Fountain House, and Rudyard was amazed at the similarity of the various proposals.

This convinced him that most clubhouses were already an unofficial federation of like-minded programs. But he urged the clubhouse community to formalize its relationship through the standards. The compelling reason was the upcoming Fifth International Seminar on the Clubhouse Model. This biennial conference of representatives from clubhouses around the world was scheduled to be held in St. Louis in August 1989.

A month before the conference, Rudyard arranged for eighteen members and staff from Fountain House and a half-dozen other clubhouses to spend a weekend at a 500-acre mountain retreat in High

Point, New Jersey. He wanted the group to thrash out the framework for the standards so that they could be brought up for consideration by the 650 conference delegates.

The retreat at High Point is a secluded, undeveloped spot where the state lines of New York, New Jersey, and Pennsylvania intersect. It was originally owned by Karl Keller, a Swiss-born manufacturer of slide rules who became a member of the Fountain House board of directors because he had a mentally ill son. This 500-acre property includes a chalet with nine bedrooms, a man-made lake, a farmhouse, and a barn, as well as a horse, cattle, pigs, and chickens. When Keller died in the late 1970s, the farm was bequeathed to Fountain House. Since then High Point has become a retreat for members and staff and for the Colleague Training program at Fountain House.

The weekend that Rudyard convened his meeting was one of those scorching hot stretches in July. Even at High Point, the heat was relentless and the meeting participants could only wonder how people back in New York City were surviving.

Rudyard, dressed casually in shorts and a sport shirt, called together the meeting on the patio overlooking the lake. Kenn Dudek took hold of a large felt-tip marker, walked over to an easel with its oversized sheets of paper, and led the process of drafting the standards.

"You can be a member forever," was the first suggestion.

"If the member wants to be," said someone else.

"That's because membership is voluntary."

"But it's important to say, 'If a member leaves, they can come back whenever they want.'"

The debate went on for hours. It was an impassioned group, members and staff shouting out suggestions and arguing. But Kenn kept taking the ideas one at a time and methodically listing them on the paper on the easel.

"It has to be active voice," insisted Rudyard. "No 'should' or 'may,' but 'is' and 'can.'"

After the weekend of brainstorming and debating, a rough draft had been created. All the essentials of a clubhouse had been written down in one form or another.

The rough draft, still on the huge sheets of easel size paper, was edited at Fountain House to thirty concise standards. These addressed membership, staff and member relationships, physical space of the clubhouse facility, the work-ordered day, transitional employment, functions of the clubhouse, and its administration.

Delegates to the Fifth International Seminar on the Clubhouse Model received a draft of the standards as they arrived in St. Louis. Divided into groups of twelve, the delegates discussed the standards and wrote a summary of their comments. At the end of the seminar, the delegates took the proposed standards back to their home clubhouses and discussed them internally. Back and forth, the draft went among clubhouses.

The standard that generated the most discussion in St. Louis and ultimately the most resistance was no. 7: All clubhouse meetings are open to both members and staff.

This cut to the heart of the clubhouse philosophy—that it is a member-driven program. It's a hard concept for mental health professionals to accept, because even if they believed in the value and vision of the clubhouse model, their training often had been in a hierarchical form of staff-patient interaction. And one of the most familiar aspects of traditional patient care is the staff-only meeting where patients' progress is assessed.

"What about member confidentiality?" an opponent of no. 7 asked during a discussion group in St. Louis. "It's one thing for the staff to be aware of someone's diagnosis or medication problems or background. Staff have been trained to maintain confidentiality and not talk about someone outside of a closed-door meeting. But why should the entire membership be privy to this intimate information about another member?"

Rudyard listened thoughtfully and said nothing.

"I don't think staff are any better than members at keeping things confidential," a member spoke up.

"Confidentiality," Rudyard said, "could be maintained simply by sharing information on a need-to-know basis, just as it would be done if the behavior of a staff person was in question."

In many discussions in St. Louis, and afterwards among clubhouse leaders, it became clear that clubhouse members and staff had to share the same agenda—there couldn't be a more important agenda for staff and a less important agenda for members.

By 1990, consensus was reached on thirty-two standards, including no. 7. (At recent seminars, four more standards have been added to bring the number to thirty-six. All are listed in the appendix.) The standards were formally adopted in 1991 at the sixth International Seminar on the Clubhouse Model in Greenville, South Carolina.

With the funding from the Clubhouse Expansion Project, a clubhouse faculty composed of staff and members from around the country, including Margie Staker, Ralph Bilby, and Rebecca Blake from Fountain House, visited various clubhouses to reinforce values and practices learned during Colleague Training.

When the clubhouse faculty went out on a consultation visit, they often found particular resistance to standard no. 7. Some clubhouse directors, once they saw in print how a clubhouse was expected to operate, either disagreed with some of the standards or found them too difficult to implement. Ultimately, 125 programs opted to be dropped from the Fountain House clubhouse directory.

Although some programs were dropping out, the demand for training in the Fountain House model remained strong. To meet the increasing need for Colleague Training, Rudyard established regional training sites at Gateway in Greenville, South Carolina; Genesis Club in Worcester, Massachusetts; Independence Center in St. Louis, Missouri; and New Frontier in Everett, Washington. As a result of increased training opportunities, new clubhouses opened throughout the country and eventually throughout the world.

To coordinate this network of clubhouses, Rudyard began in 1993 an International Center for Clubhouse Development (ICCD), financially supported in part by Fountain House and based in the Van Ameringen building which was part of the Fountain House complex. Part of ICCD's mission was to issue certification to clubhouses that operated according to the standards.

Not only did certification serve as an internal yardstick which helped clubhouses to stay focused on their mission, but it also helped preserve Fountain House's proprietary use of the term "clubhouse," a term which was increasingly being used by programs substantially different from the Fountain House model.

Around the country, state mental health officials were reevaluating the traditional day treatment programs which were funded primarily through Medicaid with a combination of diminishing federal and state dollars. Day treatment was expensive to operate on a per-patient basis and often had disappointing outcomes with patients repeatedly dropping out and then returning. A clubhouse program offered a less expensive, potentially more productive alternative.

Rudyard wanted to make sure Fountain House possessed the ability to designate which programs qualified as clubhouses and which did not. A certification process preempted a state's attempt to design its own mental health program and call it a clubhouse.

"Why are the standards a good thing?" a newspaper reporter asked Rudyard shortly after the seventh international seminar, which was held in Worcester, Massachusetts, in 1993.

"We believe we are creating the most humane, optimistic, and future-directed communities in mental health," he said. "We believe a clubhouse is most responsive to the needs and aspirations of people with severe mental illness, and more comprehensive. These standards will help members because more and more programs will be organized under these terms. The programs that exist will get better."

The reporter asked Rudyard what John Beard, who had done scant writing about the clubhouse model, would have thought of the standards.

"Probably he would have loved the idea, but he also might have thought it was dogmatic. That we should be saying, 'This is what we admire' not, 'This is the way it should be.'

"But I don't think it's dogmatic at all," Rudyard continued. "We are simply trying to ensure that what we are doing is clear to all of us."

Today a framed copy of the standards hangs inside the front door of many clubhouses. Members consider the standards to be their Bill of Rights.

The no. 1 standard, and the one over which there was unanimous agreement from the initial brainstorming session, can be traced to the Rockland State patients who called their group WANA, or We Are Not Alone: Membership is voluntary and without time limits.

There Are Many "Fire Souls" in This Room

More than eight hundred members and staff from clubhouses around the world came to Salt Lake City during the third week of October 1995 for the Eighth International Seminar on the Clubhouse Model.

People from Denmark, Sweden, Finland, Germany, Australia, Canada, Japan, Korea, England, and Russia joined with delegations from more than one hundred clubhouses in the United States.

Fountain House sent a large contingent of three dozen staff and members. Linda Pierce, Matthew Palmer, and Rebecca Blake were among the members selected to attend. Among the staffers were Margie Staker from the clerical unit, Riva K. who would talk about substance abuse, director of employment Ralph Bilby, Kathleen Rhoads, Rudyard Propst, and executive director Kenn Dudek.

Esther Montanez remained in New York at Fountain House, which was open every day as usual. Keith Hunter also stayed in New York because he'd just begun working at a new job.

During the opening session of the seminar, Lis Asklund, a frail women in her eighties from Sweden, stepped behind the podium. She had produced a film documentary about Fountain House in the late 1970s which helped popularize the clubhouse model in Scandinavia.

"I think that the best thing I've done in my life is to find Fountain House in New York and take it over to Sweden," she said in thickly accented English. "I feel like I am in a big family. That is the wonderful thing about the Fountain House movement. We are in a family."

Tears began to run down her cheeks as she spoke, recalling how she was made an honorary member of two Swedish clubhouses.

"You have many words in English that we don't have," she said. "But there is one word that you are missing . . . *eldsjäl* . . . or fire soul. A fire soul is a compassionately dedicated person who fights for the defenseless.

"There are many fire souls in this room."

✳

Linda Pierce was one of four speakers at a workshop on supported education. About thirty members and staff listened closely as she described how she enrolled in LaGuardia Community College to work toward a degree in social work.

"I hadn't been in a classroom in many, many years," Linda said. "I wasn't sure my brain would be able to learn things anymore."

She described how the clubhouse helped arrange a state education grant for her and how members advised her on which courses to take.

"Fountain House, especially the other members at Fountain House, gave me the confidence that I could do it. I am going to do it. I expect to get my associate's degree in December."

For the past fifteen months, Linda had been working on staff at Chelton Loft, a clubhouse in Manhattan that operates just as Fountain House does but on a much smaller scale. It was one of several new clubhouses that opened with funds freed up by the closing of state hospitals as mandated in the Community Mental Health Reinvestment Act. Chelton Loft occupies the fourth floor of an old office building in the garment district, where young men wheel careening racks of next year's fashions along the narrow sidewalks.

Chelton Loft is a division of a larger public mental health organization called Federation for the Handicapped, or FedCap, and its directors consulted with Fountain House to learn how a clubhouse operates. As they looked to fill staff positions, they turned again to Fountain House for advice and Linda Pierce's name was suggested repeatedly.

When Linda was approached about applying for a job at Chelton

Loft, she was frightened. She wanted to become a social worker, but she didn't know if she was ready. And she wasn't sure she was ready to leave the security of Fountain House.

"Go for it. You'll do well," said Kenn Dudek.

She had two preliminary meetings with the Chelton Loft people. Then she received a telephone call.

"We're sorry, but we already have enough people," she was told.

Secretly, she was relieved. Now she could continue being a member, going to school, and planning for the future.

Then Linda was asked back for another interview at Chelton Loft. "Maybe I *should* try to get this job," she said to Esther Montanez.

At the interview. she was asked, "What kind of salary are you looking for?"

Linda hesitated momentarily.

"$350 a week."

She thought it was a fair figure for someone who didn't have her college degree yet. And she was used to living on $5.50 a day, although she didn't tell that to the interviewer.

Ultimately, Linda agreed to accept $18,000 as her annual salary. That amount placed her above the Supplemental Security Income ceiling. The notion of losing this guaranteed financial safety net was frightening, but her new income still fell below $21,000, so she could continue receiving a monthly rent stipend from the state Office of Mental Health.

"If something happens and I fall down, I don't have to worry about losing my home," she thought.

Once Linda began working at Chelton Loft, she worried constantly about failure. When she'd been hired for other jobs, she had supplied letters of recommendation but had never felt obligated to do well for the sake of those who were recommending her. For this position, the reference letters came from people at Fountain House and she didn't want to let them down.

Taking this job was a huge leap in responsibility from working on TEs. If she fell short of expectations on a TE placement, Ralph Bilby would see that the job was covered until he could bring in someone else. Now she'd be working without that support.

During the first few weeks at Chelton Loft, Linda had a headache every day. What if she made a mistake? She was the first mental health consumer that FedCap had ever hired. Would her failure be used as a justification for not hiring another consumer? If she said she didn't understand how to fill out the mountains of paperwork, would her employers think the job was too stressful for her? Did they think she'd break under the stress? Maybe they'd say, "Get the Thorazine for her."

"Being the first is a lot of pressure," Linda acknowledged to a Fountain House friend. "I think it wouldn't be as stressful if they didn't know my background."

During her last year as a full-time Fountain House member, Linda had been annoyed by the clubhouse's reluctance to hire a staff worker directly from the member ranks. At the time she thought it was discriminatory. But after several months at Chelton Loft, she appreciated the reasoning behind this rule. She was having difficulty making the transition from consumer to mental health worker, and she was working at a place where no one had ever known her as a member. She could imagine how difficult it would be to leave Fountain House on a Friday as a member and return on Monday as a staff worker.

By the winter, Linda's headaches had subsided and her confidence had grown. Chelton Loft was much smaller than Fountain House in terms of space and membership, and she loved its intimacy. The living room was separated from the dining area by a partition. A large, blue-tinted tropical fish tank served as another divider. Within a week, she had learned the names of the twenty to thirty members who came in daily. While the other five staffers struggled to implement the clubhouse way of relating to former mental patients as members, Linda led the way by example.

She thought back to when she had first come to Fountain House, and how Clare Smith and Esther Montanez had encouraged her. Each small step she took, they applauded. And their support gave her the confidence to take the next step. Now she tried to do the same for others. Often, her bosses at FedCap told her she was an asset to their club-house and she glowed in their praise.

Eventually, Linda felt comfortable enough to tell her supervisor, Mark, that she had stopped taking all medication. Over the past year, she'd been weaned from Haldol to Prozac. Now the Prozac was gone too. Going off her meds had been her own idea, not her psychiatrist's. But the psychiatrist concurred when Linda agreed to stay in regular communication.

Mark asked Linda, "How would we know if you were, um, well—"

"Decompensating?" she filled in.

"Yeah. Decompensating."

"I would tell you. If I think I am feeling depressed or agitated, I'll talk to someone about medication. If I need it, I'll take it again without hesitation because it saved my life."

One day, a member named Art walked up to Linda as she was re-viewing a member's application to a housing program. "What would you think," he said, trying to sound off-handed, "of someone who was thinking of just ending everything?"

Linda put down her pen, took a sip of her coffee, and looked solemnly back at Art. "I would say to that person, 'Who are you to commit suicide and hurt me like that? As much as I care about you?'"

Then instantly, she recalled an experience she'd once had at Fountain House after she'd been a member for about a year. A woman who lived in her residence jumped from a sixth-floor window and died. Linda was inconsolable and blamed herself, the other residents, the residence manager, the therapist—everyone she could think of. In Esther's office, she cried bitterly. Esther waited until her tormented sobs subsided.

"Who died and made you God so that you took on this responsi-bility for someone else's life?" Esther said in her typically blunt man-ner. "If she was determined to commit suicide, you could have done nothing to prevent it."

Linda understood that Esther was telling her to care, but not to care excessively. Linda had to create a balance between listening to members and allowing members to take responsibility for their own lives.

Sometimes, Linda did feel personally responsible for making everything right for the members. Nevertheless Linda realized she had to retain a sense of objectivity, too.

One time at Chelton Loft, a member said to Linda, "You think you're so great and you know everything. I hate your ugly face."

Linda knew how to respond. When a Fountain House member spat out near-identical words to a staffer there, Linda remembered the unemotional response: "I'm sorry. It's the only face I've got."

And that's what Linda said to calm the angry Chelton Loft member.

Having watched the Fountain House staff deal with these confrontations, Linda felt confident that she could handle whatever she encountered. But there was one situation she hadn't anticipated: defining her own status within the mental health field.

Early in January 1995, mental health professionals from other agencies opening new clubhouses came to tour Chelton Loft.

"How many consumers do you have on staff?" Linda asked one of the visiting agency directors.

"Well, ah, we haven't found exactly the right person," the woman answered.

Linda said nothing, but she was unsettled. Maybe consumers weren't qualified on paper for staff positions because they didn't have college degrees. But consumers knew this illness from the inside out and they belonged on the staff. These professionals, Linda fumed, were forgetting who they're helping. These programs were supposed to be for consumers. And who better understood the effects of mental illness than a consumer? When the Chelton Loft director introduced her as a consumer working on staff, Linda was proud to be an example of successful recovery.

After working nine months at Chelton Loft, Linda received a pay raise and lost her state housing support. Now she was on her own financially. No safety net. It was scary, paying all her bills, but exhilarating. Since her paycheck came biweekly, she arranged with her land-lord to pay her monthly rent in two installments. Linda was pleased with her ingenuity.

Despite her successes, she didn't feel accepted by other mental health professionals. She believed her co-workers never forgot that she had suffered from mental illness. She felt like a staff worker with an asterisk.

One afternoon, a member named Norma got into a loud argu-ment with a staffer in the kitchen. Linda walked over to see if she could help defuse the problem. But before she could say a word, an-other staffer warned her, "Don't *you* become like Norma!"

Linda stopped. She stared at her co-worker, turned, and walked ever so slowly away from the kitchen. In the privacy of the ladies' room, she cried. Even in the heat of dealing with an angry member, Linda's co-worker hadn't forgotten that Linda, too, had been mentally ill.

The next day, Linda was still stung by the remark. A Fountain House friend happened to telephone her in the morning and they agreed to meet for lunch at a coffee shop a half block from Chelton Loft, in the shadow of Macy's department store. Over hamburgers and Diet Cokes, Linda explained how she felt.

"Because I came in to Chelton Loft as a consumer, I think there will always be a shadow there. Even though I may be an exceptional employee or whatever, it'll always be there.

"So I think someday I'd like to move on and not tell anybody at the new job that I've been mentally ill. If I move on and I disagree with another staff worker, I would be treated as an equal. Now I'm not."

When a person is addicted to drugs or alcohol, Linda told her friend, there's stigma, but it's overcome by recovery and forgiveness. But there was no forgiveness with mental illness.

"I see myself as many other things too—a good friend, a good neighbor," Linda said. "I don't want to be defined only as a mental health consumer. But that's what society does. You can't get past the stigma of mental illness.

"For instance, if something bad happened and I made the newspaper, God forbid, the media wouldn't focus on all the good things that I'm doing. They'd go right back to who I was. Someone who was in the hospital and took medication."

There was no easy way to reconcile her history as a mental patient with her present role as a mental health worker. It was something Linda Pierce was still sorting out when she was invited back to Fountain House in April 1995.

It was a rainy afternoon. As she walked down West 47th Street toward the clubhouse, she saw the large American flag hanging limply above the green door. Linda had an appointment for a job interview.

Naturally, she felt pleased that Fountain House was considering her for a position within the advocacy unit. She had no doubt that she could do the job, helping members who had problems with Social Security or other entitlement programs, and working with the public relations efforts.

Linda was treated like any other job candidate. She had formal interviews with two sets of members and staff who filled out detailed forms immediately afterward recording their impressions and recommendations. Her second interview was with Margie Staker and several members in the clerical unit.

"Linda, it's good to see you," said Margie, shaking hands and leading her over to a chair.

"Hi, Linda."

"Hi, Linda."

Maria and Lee, two members participating in the interview, remembered her from her work with Esther Montanez in the Connections program that reached out to missing members.

At the start of most job interviews, Margie and the members had to explain the clubhouse model to the applicant who might have an undergraduate degree in social work but no knowledge of this specific type of psychiatric rehabilitation. With Linda, they could skip over the explanations and delve into her own philosophy of social work within a clubhouse.

"What do you find challenging about working in a clubhouse?" Margie asked.

For the next hour, they talked about Linda's views of being a staff worker and how she could see herself fitting into Fountain House.

"I feel that my responsibility to the members," said Linda, "is to treat them as adults. With respect. They can come and talk to me about anything. Bisexual relationships, rape, hating their medication. I hear it all in a day. It's not because I am a former consumer but because I am a person who accepts them as they are. I'm available to listen. And anything they say, I never take lightly."

She had made a conscious effort each day to sharpen her listening skills. And she found that in helping members work out their problems, she was defining her own role, combining professional training and personal experience.

"We look at consumers in terms of their past history," said Linda. "But I want to know, 'What was the person going through when this incidence of violence or this depression happened?' At intake, I read the background information about new members but only so I see how I can be a facilitator and help them. The rest of it, I throw out. Their diagnosis doesn't mean anything. All I want to know is, 'Who can I be in that person's life for the brief time we will know each other?'"

By the end of the interview, Linda was drained. But talking to Margie helped clarify her thinking. "Working at Fountain House isn't the right job for me," she decided.

She thought about her decision for a week. She talked it over with Esther. Then Linda withdrew her job application.

"At first, I was going to take this job," she explained to Esther. "But I can't walk away from Chelton Loft. Whether this is self-destructive or progress, I don't know. But I have to stay there.

"Fountain House is great, don't get me wrong. I've taken everything I've learned there and brought it with me and it has been working well. But it seems like my time at Fountain House happened in a different life. It is still with me, but I have moved on.

"Fountain House is stable, established. With a new clubhouse, it's like creating something. We make mistakes. We have to go back and try it again. For me to walk away from Chelton Loft, it would be leaving before it was finished."

*

Keith Hunter was just beginning a new job, so he couldn't go to Salt Lake City. He was so excited about this new opportunity that he wasn't even disappointed about missing the conference.

Fourteen months earlier, when he completed a six-month TE assignment as an outdoor messenger in August 1994, Keith decided to work within Fountain House on an advocacy project. In the afternoons, he sat with a stack of voter registration forms at a card table on the first floor near the elevator and buttonholed each member who walked by.

"Are you registered to vote? Let me help you. I'll explain the form. It's important that we vote. That's how our leaders know what we want."

Then Kenn Dudek selected Keith as Fountain House's representative at the New York Association of Psychosocial Rehabilitation Services conference held on the Catskill Mountains. The meeting included mental health consumers and professionals from clubhouses and other psychiatric rehabilitation programs in the state.

"The fact that Fountain House thought I was capable of going by myself and they said 'Keith will be all right,' that's an honor," Keith told another member.

Over the winter of 1994–95, Keith completed a three-month course at Hunter College School of Social Work in intensive case management. The class members included students working on graduate degrees as well as mental health consumers, like himself, who hadn't finished high school but were admitted because of their life experiences. Going into psychiatric social work was his goal. It reminded him of the Alcoholics Anonymous philosophy of one alcoholic helping another.

At Linda Pierce's urging, Keith took the GED test but failed. He did well in science and reading, but needed to brush up on grammar and math. So twice a week, he took evening classes.

On the weekends, Keith often went to a nonalcoholic disco downtown with his latest girlfriend, a waitress named Olivia. "This one isn't married," Keith confided to a friend. Sometimes on Sunday mornings, he took the Number 4 train to Brooklyn and listened to Olivia sing in the choir of Bible Way church.

He applied in the summer for a part-time job as a truck loader for United Parcel Service (UPS) and was called back for a second interview. Then a staff worker at Fountain House arranged for him to be interviewed in the New York City office of AmeriCorp, the domestic Peace Corps program begun by President Clinton.

In late September 1995, Keith walked over to a nondescript building on West 60th Street. He took the elevator to the second floor and entered the Americorp office.

"We're hiring sixty-five people this year," said the interviewer. "You get $7,900 for one year that is paid monthly. You can keep your SSI and Medicaid. At the end of the year of service, you'll receive $4,800 to go to college."

Keith was excited and intrigued.

"Have you done community or volunteer work?" the interviewer asked.

He smiled and leaned back. Usually, he was nervous at job interviews, but this time he was calm. Confident, he told her about his experiences on TE and his work with the advocacy unit.

Within a week, Keith found out he'd been hired. He'd be working with Fountain House's advocacy unit which was administering a $1 million federal grant to expand outreach efforts to the homeless mentally ill. Keith would go out in a van with other Fountain House staff workers to encourage people on the streets to go into shelters for the night. The next day, Keith would follow up on their condition.

On his first day at work, Keith was out of bed and dressed before his alarm clock buzzed. He wore slacks, shirt, and a tie to look like the other male staff. Just as he was heading out the door, the telephone rang.

It was his brother, who said, "You are lucky. You have a choice between two jobs—UPS or Fountain House."

"I already made my choice," Keith said. "I am grinning from ear to ear now."

*

On the second morning of the clubhouse conference, Riva K. woke up in Salt Lake City worried she'd overslept. The clock on her nightstand said 8:15. The conference schedule was filled with meetings, seminars, and workshops, but the most important gathering to Riva was the AA Double Trouble meeting that began at 8:30 A.M. It was the thirteenth anniversary of her sobriety and she certainly didn't want to miss this meeting.

After a quick shower, Riva rubbed styling gel into her short blonde hair and combed it straight back. She looked in the mirror. Her face was slightly tanned from her summer vacation on Fire Island, augmented by a few visits to a tanning salon. "This is the best I've looked in a long time," she thought.

The AA meeting was in the hotel room of a Fountain House member named Terrell. A half-dozen people were already there waiting when Riva slipped in quietly.

Then Terrell began the meeting by reading aloud from Twelve Step materials that Double Trouble groups in New York had adapted for their meetings. "Double Trouble is a fellowship of men and women who share their experience, strength, and hope with each other that they may solve their common problems and help others to recover from their particular addictions and mental problems.

"We recognize that, for many, having addiction and mental problems represents Double Trouble. . . . Our primary purpose is to maintain freedom from our addictions and to maintain our well-being."

Another member of the group, Sam, read from a Double Trouble adaptation of the AA pamphlet *How It Works,* concluding with the familiar words, "We live one day at a time, and practice the Double Trouble Twelve Steps."

Jill, a member of a West Coast clubhouse, read the Double Trouble Twelve Steps. Only Step One and Step Twelve reflected the group's psychiatric problems.

"Number One. We admitted we were powerless over mental disorders and substance abuse. That our lives had become unmanageable."

As Jill read each step, each person in the room looked down in meditation.

"And Number Twelve. Having had a spiritual awakening as the result of these steps, we tried to carry this message to mentally disordered substance abusers and to practice these principles in all our affairs."

Then Riva spoke. "Hi, my name is Riva and I'm an alcoholic and an addict."

"Hi, Riva."

"Nine months after I stopped drinking and went through rehab, I had a relapse." She looked down at her hands. Her face reddened. But her voice didn't waver.

"I picked up a bottle of vodka and just put my head back and started drinking straight from the bottle. As the vodka poured down my throat, I felt an intense burning. I was shocked by what I had done. I was horrified. Just as quickly, I put the bottle down.

"That was thirteen years ago today. Thirteen years." She shook her head in amazement. In some ways, it seemed like yesterday. "It really scared me. It scared me so much that with the help of AA, I've been able to stay sober since then."

She smiled. "I can't believe I'm saying all these things now and I can laugh about it. When I was sneaking around and hiding in my apartment all the time, I felt so alone and ashamed. Now my life has changed so much."

After everyone had a chance to speak, Terrell stood up and read the closing. Then he reached out to Riva with one hand and to Jill with the other. In turn, everyone in the room reached out to one another.

Together, in loud voices, they said the Serenity Prayer, finishing with the refrain, "Keep coming back."

Later that day, Riva was a featured speaker at a plenary session of the seminar. The topic was substance abuse.

"About fifteen years ago I was asked to address another group of very important people as a staff member of Fountain House. That was in Madison, Wisconsin. I went there and I collapsed on stage in what I now know to be an alcoholic seizure.

"I was led off the stage by Ralph Bilby. All of this was filmed." She rolled her eyes and shook her head. The audience sighed in sympathy. "It was a very embarrassing bottom to my own alcoholism.

"Today I'm happy to say I have thirteen years in recovery from alcoholism and addiction."

The audience applauded warmly.

"Right now," Riva continued, "50 to 60 percent of people in psychiatric hospitals have a history of substance abuse, at least here in America. Many people are coming out of mental hospitals with dual diagnoses."

Riva explained how she developed education and support programs at Fountain House. "None of us has the answers at Fountain House, but we feel we're making a dent. If there is anything that I would pass on to you, it's these three things:

"Education, education, education. Learn about substances, don't be afraid of them. Learn about what's available in your community. Have people come in and talk about these things. Lift the stigma. Fountain House, and the clubhouse community, we have all been pioneers in mental health. Let's be pioneers in dual diagnosis and dual recovery.

"Start support meetings and help your members start them.

"And hire recovering staff."

Without pausing for applause, she continued, "Today on the program we have a member who is willing to talk to us. This is Matthew."

Matthew Palmer, wearing a sweater and a tie, walked to the podium. He carried notes written on index cards. He glanced up briefly at the audience, then looked down.

"Riva asked me to say a few words about a specific aspect which I feel is important. I've been going to AA meetings for fourteen years and now I have nine years of sobriety."

The audience applauded loud and hard. Margie Staker was sitting in the front row. She smiled broadly at Matthew.

"For the most part, I've been going to meetings in the community, the outside community," Matthew continued. "I was conscientious. But when I was sharing, I might discuss my hospitalizations or medication. And I just didn't feel I fit in as well as I might have.

"Since I've been going to the Fountain House meetings, I've really had a change of heart. Most of the people, except for the recovering staff, have a dual diagnosis. While I'm there, I really get the feeling I belong to something. A feeling that I didn't have when I went to the outside meetings. A more secure feeling.

"You just don't feel that you're different. You know the other people there have been through the same rough aspects of going to a hospital and those things involved in being an ex-mental patient.

"I think the new program that Riva has established at Fountain House is a really good thing and could be used at other clubhouses."

As Matthew left the podium, the audience applauded warmly. Margie wiped away tears. She was so impressed that Matthew had stood before this large audience and spoken so confidently.

She knew how far he had come from his days at Manhattan Psychiatric Center, fearful but determined to earn his release. Desperate for the chance to prove he was more than a knife-wielding assailant judged "not guilty by reason of mental disease or defect."

Now he was doing so beautifully. If only he could feel better about himself. Margie knew that Matthew, an Ivy League graduate, was still plagued by his inability to find full-time independent employment.

Matthew had spent the previous winter and spring sending out resumes, a hundred of them. He followed the advice of the task force assembled by Ralph Bilby to help him sharpen his job-hunting skills. He went on a mock interview that Margie Staker set up for him. He answered want ads in the *New York Times*. He looked up acquaintances from his youth and tried to network.

When a friend asked how his job search was going, he apologized for not having found employment yet. "I'm not pessimistic," he insisted. "I am doing the best that I can."

Margie believed ultimately he'd be successful in finding a job. Because she knew other Fountain House members who secured full-time employment despite their daunting backgrounds, she felt Matthew's search wasn't unrealistic. At the right place, he could be so good.

But he never had the chance to talk to an employer, never had to decide whether to reveal his mental illness. After answering want-ads for six straight months, Matthew had received two form letters—both rejections. Whether it was his age, his background, or his gaps in employment—or perhaps the economy—something worked against him.

"It's hard to get a job especially if you are impaired. I've got a lot of strikes against me," he once told Margie. He decided to reconsider his options. "I am not going to punish myself by looking too hard and not getting anywhere. TE is a good option. I think of TE as volunteering work."

In January 1995, Ralph Bilby found a TE spot for him, working in the mailroom of a law firm. Matthew stayed there for six months. On his last day of work, when he said, "Good-bye" to everyone in the mailroom and to the secretaries along his delivery route, they seemed sad to see him leave.

Matthew didn't begin another TE. Instead, with $4,000 in savings, he decided to take a trip with his mother to the Alpine region of northern Italy where he had lived as a boy.

Margie was hoping the trip would be everything Matthew envisioned. But there was the real possibility it would be less than satisfying, a reminder of how much of his life had been lost to his illness.

It's a shame, Margie thought, that success has to be defined by whether someone is working full-time. Each day, Matthew continued to recover from his mental illness, contributing more and more at Fountain House. Speaking before seven hundred people about his experience in AA meetings was yet another accomplishment. Even a year ago, Margie wouldn't have thought Matthew capable of making this speech. By her standards, he was truly a success.

*

After the workshop, Rebecca Blake went for a walk with her friend Kay Pierson. It was a beautiful fall day in Salt Lake City. The sun shone in a cloudless blue sky and the leaves on the trees were bright yellow. They talked about how good it was to see people from other clubhouses whom they'd met during Colleague Training.

Kay asked Rebecca about her studies. After completing a year at Queens College, Rebecca had either A's or B-plusses in all her subjects. She had decided she wanted to become a child psychologist.

Maybe she could have gotten all A's if she'd worked harder, she thought. Maybe she hadn't tried hard enough. Certainly her parents wouldn't have been pleased with anything less than an A at a public college like Queens. It wasn't exactly the Ivy League.

As they reached the corner of the hotel, Kay pushed the walk button on the traffic light. She turned to Rebecca and said, "You're doing so well, you don't have anything to worry about."

"I know I'm doing well in school," Rebecca said. "But I still can't enjoy anything."

It was the same old story. She'd been feeling depressed for so long. She'd tried ten different antidepressant medications and shock treatment and she still felt the same. It was ironic that she couldn't tolerate the only drug which ever made her feel better. When she was on Elavil, she could barely stand up without passing out.

"You should be happy," Kay said. "You're getting closer to your dream of working with kids."

"That certainly is my dream," Rebecca thought. But it was also her dream to have kids of her own. At age thirty-five, she wasn't making any progress toward that goal. Every man at Queens College seemed either too young or unavailable.

"You're right. I should be happy," Rebecca said. "So why do I go to sleep a lot of nights wishing I won't wake up the next day?"

Not giving Kay a chance to answer she quickly said, "I guess there's this life force in me that is really strong. I think it's my friends too. You and Margie and Tom Whalen and my brother Randy. That's what really keeps me going. It's my friends."

*

Kathleen Rhoads addressed all eight hundred delegates to the seminar. She was introduced as the coordinator of Colleague Training at Fountain House, but she spoke as a person who knew intimately the pain of mental illness.

Near the end of her speech, Kathleen picked up a tangle of keys and held them up at arm's length above her head.

"I want you to stop and focus on these keys for a moment," she said to the audience.

"These represent the keys which hospital staff, even as we speak, wear on their waists. These keys represented for me and many others what's locked up.

"Freedom is locked up.

"This key represents the medication room and you're not even sure you want to be on meds because you're not sure what the side effects are.

"This key represents the special little store, so you can buy some nice-smelling soap if you're a good enough patient.

"This is a key to the seclusion room.

"This is the key to the door that clangs, and you can't get that clanging of the door out of your head."

Kathleen threw the keys down on the table next to the podium. She picked up a paper and held it high.

"These are our new keys. These are our standards for clubhouse programs.

"These are our keys to a job. Keys to a life. Keys to freedom. Keys to friendships. These are our keys which open doors to life all the time. We have transformed the old ideas of people being locked up and oppressed.

"Now we are advocating for clubhouse programs, stronger than ever before."

Appendix A
Directory of Clubhouse Programs

This directory was prepared by members and staff of the Colleague Training Unit at Fountain House for the International Center for Clubhouse Development. Clubhouses in this directory are striving to comply with the Standards for Clubhouse Programs and have sent members and staff for training at one or more of seven training bases.

NOTE: Clubhouses marked ⊘ have been certified by the Faculty for Clubhouse Development of the ICCD, as of May 1996. Clubhouses marked ** are certified training bases in the clubhouse model. Clubhouses marked ++ serve persons with traumatic brain injury.

International Programs

AUSTRALIA

**BROMHAM PLACE CLUBHOUSE
10 Bromham Pl.
Richmond 3121
Victoria, Australia
Dir. Kim Kerr
61-3-9427-7377
61-3-9428-8113
FAX 61-3-9427-9308

EUREKA CLUBHOUSE
P.O. Box 711
Moonah 7009
Tasmania, Australia
Dir. Trevor James
61-2-78-9179
FAX 61-278-9901

HORSHAM CLUBHOUSE
28 Urquhart St.
P.O. Box 297
Horsham Victoria 3402
Australia
61-53-82-5430
FAX 61-53-82-5430

LORIKEET CLUBHOUSE
P.O.B 358
Wembley, 6014
Western Australia, Australia
Dir. Brian Bennett
61-9-381-9144
FAX 61-9-381-9495

PIONEER CLUBHOUSE
Quirk Rd.
Balgowlah NSW 2093
Australia
Dir. Nicola Hancock
61-2-9907-9999
FAX 61-2-9907-9999

STEPPING STONE CLUBHOUSE
9/61 Holdsworth St.
Coorparoo
Queensland 4151
Australia
Dir. Warren Sparrow
61-7-3847-1058
FAX 61-7-3847 -044

TOOWOOMBA CLUBHOUSE
P.O. Box 3108
Village Fair
Toowoomba 4350
Queensland Australia
Dir. Bryce Allcock
61-76-39-3983
FAX 61-76-39 -794

CANADA

CAMBRIDGE CLUBHOUSE
117 Main St.
Cambridge, Ontario
Canada N1R 1W1
Dir. John Jones
(519) 740-7766
FAX (519) 740-0561

CAUSEWAY
Meara St.
Ottawa, Ontario
Canada K1Y 4N6
Dir. Don Palmer
(613) 230-9557
FAX (613) 230-3436
E-mail causeway@intranet.on.ca

CLUB CENTRAL
110 Ash St.
Whitby, Ontario
Canada Lin 4A9
Dir. Andre La Flamme
(905) 430-7484
FAX (905) 430-8385
E-mail CC@mail.cyconx.com

CLUB 84
130 Queen St. E
Sault Ste Marie, Ontario
Canada P6A 1Y5
Coor. Jan Linley
(705) 759-0458
FAX (705) 945-0261

CLUB FREEDOM
358 Pinnacle St.
Belleville, Ontario
Canada K8N 3B4
Dir. Susan Scott
(613) 969-1772

CLUBHOUSE NEW HORIZONS
111 Simcoe St. N.
Oshawa, Ontario
Canada L1G 4S4
Dir. Andre La Flamme
(905) 436-8763
FAX (905) 436-1569
E-mail Horizon's@cyconx.com

CLUB NIAGARA
5841 Ferry St.
Niagara Falls, Ontario
Canada L2G 1S9
Dir. Debbie Adler
(905) 892-1991
FAX (905) 892-1993

COAST FOUNDATION CLUBHOUSE
295 East 11th Ave.
Vancouver, B.C.
Canada V5T 2C5
Dir. Tom Burnell
(604) 876-6345
FAX (604) 879-2363

CONNECTIONS CLUBHOUSE
1221 Bairington St.
Halifax, Nova Scotia
Canada B3K 4N1
Dir. Nancy Beck
(902) 496-2692
FAX (902) 496-6259

FITZROY CENTRE
170 Fitzroy St.
Charlottetown, PEI
Canada C1A 1S2
Dir. Reed Burke
(902) 566-5111

**KINGSTON CLUBHOUSE ACTIVITY
   CENTRE**
428A Barrie St.
Kingston, Ontario
Canada K7K 3T9
Prog. Dir. Ken Ohtake
(613) 542-4174
FAX (613) 542-2687

NEW FOUNDATIONS CLUBHOUSE
212 Camelot St.
Thunder Bay, Ontario
Canada P7A 4B1
Dir. Lauri Moffatt-Zawacki
(807) 345-5564
FAX (807) 345-4458

NOTRE DAME PLACE
67 Duke St.
Summerside, Prince Edward Island
Canada C1N 3R9
Dir. Pat Winchester
(902) 436-7399

OAK CENTRE
67 East Main St.
Welland, Ontario
Canada L3B 3W4
Co-Dir. Betty Farrish Ru Tauro
(905) 788-3010
FAX (905) 788-3012

OASIS
341 Kerr St.
Oakville, Ontario
Canada L6K 3B7
Act. Prog. Dir. Sandy Bray
(416) 845-5158
FAX (416) 338-9408

P.A.R. NORTH
250 Clarence St. Unit 5
Brampton, Ontario
Canada L6W 1T4
Prog Mgr. Sandra Cureton
(905) 796-9030
FAX (905) 796-9035

P.A.R. SOUTH
3181 Wolfedale Rd. Unit #3
Mississauga, Ontario
Canada L5C 1V8
Prog. Mgr. Pat Dey
(905) 270-6295
FAX (905) 270-8110

PATHWAYS CLUBHOUSE
Unit 160-5811
Cedarbridge Way
Richmond, B.C.
Canada V6X 2A8
Dir. David MacDonald
(604) 276-8834
FAX (604) 276-0342

PHOENIX CLUB
15 Wellington St.
St. Catharines, Ontario
Canada L2R 5P7
Prog. Coor. Sheila Connolly
(416) 641-5222
FAX (416) 641-8821

✪ **PROGRESS PLACE
576 Church St.
Toronto, Ontario
Canada M4Y 2E3
Dir. Brenda Singer
(416) 323-0223
FAX (416) 323-9843

S.T.E.P. CENTRE
612 Portage Ave.
Box 446
Fort Frances, Ontario
Canada P9A 3M8
Dir. Sheila Shaw
(807) 274-2347
FAX (807) 274-2473

SOURCE CLUB
6239 Walnut St.
Powell River, B.C.
Canada V8A 4K4
Coor. Justina Penner
(604) 483-3989

3-C CENTRE
111 Elm St.
Suite 202
Sudbury, Ontario
Canada P3C 1T3
Dir. Marion Quigley
(705) 675-9189
FAX (705) 675-7247

UNION PLACE CLUBHOUSE
1079 2nd Ave. E
Owen Sound, Ontario
Canada N4K 2H8
Dir. David M. Clark
(519) 376-8433
FAX (519) 371-6485

DENMARK

ENGGARDEN
Enggarden 2
7700 Hundborg
Denmark
Dir. Per Jespersen
97-937255

FONTAENE HUSET/ARHUS
Kirketoften 6
8260 Viby
Denmark
Dir. Janne Jorgensen
45-86-11-50-77
FAX 45-86-11-5470

✪ FOUNTAIN HOUSE/COPENHAGEN
Ryesgade 80/Villaen
DK-2100 Copenhagen
Denmark
Dir. Kirsten Magnild
45-31-42-8696
FAX 45-35-43-6550

✪ KILDEHUSET
  FOUNTAIN HOUSE/AALBORG
Anders Morchs VEJ 1
9400 Norresundby
Denmark
Dir. Hanne Juul
45-9819-2322
FAX 45-9819-2153

REGNBUE HUSET
Osterparken 13
Taastrup 2630
Dir. Hanne Genet
45-42-52-8036
FAX 45-42-52-8039

EGYPT

FOUNTAIN HOUSE/EGYPT
Bleeda, Aiyat, Giza
Egypt
Dir. Mohamed Gamal Abou El -
   Azayem
(202) 18 210868

FINLAND

CLUBHOUSE KARVETTI
Pl 250
Putkikatu 20
211 10 Naantali
Finland
Dir. Mika Vuorela
358-21-435781

KLUBITALO NASINKULMA
Satamakatu 7 ovi 29
33 200 Tampere
Finland
Dir. Kai Makisalo
358-31-2148239
FAX 358-31-2148239

FEDERAL REPUBLIC OF GERMANY

CLUBHAUS LICHTBLICK
Oggersheimer Str. 4
81539 Munich
Federal Republic Of Germany
Dir. Silvia Queri
49-89-680-4590
49-89-680-4595

CLUBHAUS SCHWALBENNEST
Landwehrstrasse 22
D - 80336 Munich
Federal Republic Of Germany
Dir. Vera Hahn
49-89-596728
49-89-596729
FAX 49-89-5501712

HOLLAND

STICHTING DE WATERHEUVEL
Sarphatistraat 43
1018 EW Amsterdam
Holland
Dir. Monique Geraerts
31-20-626-4642
FAX 31-20-638-85511

JAPAN

JHC SUN MARINA
4-31-12
Tokiwadai, Itabasi-ku
Tokyo, Japan
Dir. Toshiyuki Munakata
81-3-5399-4801
FAX 81-3-5399-4802

REPUBLIC OF KOREA

✪ TAIWHA FOUNTAIN HOUSE
#620-1, Ahyon-Dong, Mapo-Ku
Seoul 121-101
Republic of Korea
Dir. Jung Jim Kim
82-2-392-1155
FAX 82-2-364-5468

NEW ZEALAND

AUCKLAND CLUBHOUSE
393 Great North Rd.
Grey Lynn
New Zealand
Dir. Lyndsay Bennett
64-9 -376-6131
FAX 64-9-376-6348

NORWAY

FONTENEHUSET STAVANGER
Dronningens gt. 37
N-4008 Savanger
Norway
Dir. Vigdis Dybdahl
47-51-525393

PAKISTAN

FOUNTAIN HOUSE/LAHORE
37 Lower Mall
Lahore
Pakistan
Dir. M. R. Chaudry
7227253-352803
FAX 92-42-7572488

POLAND

KLUB GAWRA
U1 Putawska 87/89
02-595 Warsaw
Poland
Dir. Josef Sawicki
45-27-84

PORTUGAL

CENTRO COMUNITARIO
Av. Antonio Jose de Almeida, 26
1000 Lisboa
Portugal
Dir. Jose Ornealas
351-1-8409133

RUSSIA

MOSCOW CLUBHOUSE
30 Martenovskaya Str.
Moscow 111394
Dir. Igor Donenko
7-095-301-7204
7-095-301-1810
FAX 7-095-302-6353

SOUTH AFRICA

FOUNTAIN HOUSE/SOUTH AFRICA
Observatory 7425
Capetown
South Africa
Dir. Michelle De Benedictis
021-47-7409
FAX 021-470319

SWEDEN

✪ BRYGGAN
Norra Strandgatan 8
S-252 20 Helsingborg
Sweden
Dir. Swen Jeppsson
46-42-245060
FAX 46-42-143140
E-mail sj.bryggan@helsingborg.se
dm.bryggan@helsingborg.se

FONTANHUSET/LUND
Klostergatan 12
S-222 22 Lund
Sweden
Dir. Eva Husmark
46-46-18-4733
FAX 46-46-18-4003

FONTANHUSET/OREBRO
Malgatan 11-13
S - 702 16 Orebro
Sweden
Dir. Lars Pettersson
46-19-32-0520
46-19-32-2470
FAX 46-19-32-2547

FOUNTAIN HOUSE STOCKHOLM
Box 4051
S-102 61 Stockholm
Sweden
Dir. Torbjorn Althen
46-87-140160
FAX 46-87-149280

✪ **FONTANHUSET/MALMO
Engelbrektgatan 14
S-211 33 Malmo
Sweden
Dir. Bengt Jarl
46-40-120013
FAX 46-40-30-5386
E-mail fontmoe@sbbs.se

✪ GOTEBORGSFONTANEN
Andra Langgatan 25
413 28 Goteborg
Sweden
Dir. Helen Hagstrom
46-31-123001
FAX 46-31-122503

KARNHUSET
Vangavagen 36
S - 269 38 Bastad
Sweden
Dir. Carl Dandanelle
46-431-72480
FAX 46-431-72475

LAPPLANDSFONTANEN
Hamngatan 1a
S - 221 31 Lycksele
Sweden
Dir. Ulf Johansson
46-950-38960
FAX 46-950-26417

NK-VILLAN
Box 119
611 23 Nykoping
Sweden
Dir. Anette Henriksson
46-15-5268140
FAX 46-15-5268930

VANPUNKTEN
Storgatan 75
S-852 30 Sundsvall
Sweden
Dir. Gerd Isaksson
46-60-61-7531
FAX 46-60-17-1071

United Kingdom

England

○ **BRIDGE HOUSE**
15 Lower Brook St.
Ipswich, Suffolk IP4 IAO
England
Dir. Claire Smith
44-1473-230-115
FAX 44-1473-230-523

COMPASS HOUSE
84 Holland Rd.
Maidstone, Kent ME14 1UT
England
Dir. Stella Gomez
44-622-688003
44-622-677661

○ **ENDEAVOUR HOUSE**
2 Twisleton Ct.
Priory Hill
Dartford, Kent DA1 2EN
England
Dir. Julie Read
44-132-22-23335
FAX 44-132-22-289931

THE FOUNTAIN CLUB
c/o Oxton Congregational Church
Woodchurch Rd. Birkenhead
Merseyside L41 2UF
England
Coor. Lynn Webster
151-670-3042

GLOUCESTER CLUBHOUSE
The Basement
11A Spa Rd.
Gloucester
GL1 1UY
England
Dir. Jan Copcutt
44-452-381632
FAX 44-452-381632

○ **HILLSIDE HOUSE**
1 Hilldrop Rd.
London N7 0JE
England
Dir. Colin Maclean
44-171-700-6408
FAX 44-171-700-0017

HORIZON HOUSE
26 Langdon Rd.
Bromley, Kent BR2 9JS
England
Dir. Nigel Allen
44-181-466-0021
FAX 44-181-466-0028

MOSAIC CLUBHOUSE
55/57 Lewin Rd.
Streatham
London SW16 6GZ
England
Dir. Riola Crawford
44-181-677-3135
FAX 44-181-677-8242

LEATHERHEAD CLUBHOUSE
23 The Crescent
Leatherhead
Surrey KT22 8D7
England
Dir. Ben Collins
44-1372-375-400
FAX 44-1372-372349

○ **OLD FOX HOUSE**
1 Old Fox Yard
Ipswich St.
Stowmarket, Suffolk IP14 1AB
England
Dir. Margaret Stevenson
44-144-97-74966
FAX 44-144-97-75018

Scotland

S.A.M.H. CORE CLUB
92 Pittencrieff St.
Dunfermline FY12 8AN
Scotland
Dir. Cheryl Pennington
44-383-623179

United States
Alaska

QUYANA CLUBHOUSE
229 W. Fireweed La.
Anchorage, AK 99503
Dir. Maria Johnson-Klaft
(907) 265-4912

Arizona

EAST VALLEY CLUBHOUSE
1310 W. University Dr.
Mesa, AZ 85201
Dir. Stephanie Cobb Wise
(602) 835-0343

○ OUR PLACE CLUBHOUSE
39 N. 6th Ave.
Tucson, AZ 85701
Dir. Mindy Bernstein
(520) 884-5553

WEST VALLEY CLUBHOUSE
5017 N. 35th Ave.
Phoenix, AZ 85017
Act. Dir. Mary H. Jose
(602) 937-1060
FAX (602) 973-2671

Arkansas

THE N.E.W. CENTER
P.O. Box 2887
Fort Smith, AR 72913
Dir. Eleanor Clark
(501) 452-9490
FAX (501) 452-5847

REBUILDERS CLUB
1800 N. Maple St.
P.O. Box 5671
N. Little Rock, AR 72119
Dir. Ardee Eichelman
(501) 753-9583
FAX (501) 753-7428

SPRINGHOUSE
P.O. Box 1340
Springdale, AR 72765
Dir. Mick Hutchison
(501) 750-0700
FAX (501) 751-4346

California

BAYVIEW CLUBHOUSE
259 Hyde St.
San Francisco, CA 94102
Pro. Coord. Tim Mason
(415) 928-6500
FAX (415) 695-9830

++THE DAYLE MCINTOSH CENTER CLUBHOUSE
1832 N. Glassell St.
Orange, CA 92665
Dir. Cathy Demello
(714) 921-9916
FAX (714) 921-1712

HEDCO HOUSE
590 B St.
Hayward, CA 94541
Dir. Clayton Goad
(510) 247-8235

TOWNE HOUSE CREATIVE LIVING CENTER
629 Oakland Ave.
Oakland, CA 94611
Dir. Milly Alvarez
(510) 658-9480
FAX (510) 658-0811

Colorado

CHINOOK CLUBHOUSE
1441 Broadway
Boulder, CO 80302
Dir. Allan Guitar
(303) 440-4842
FAX (303) 415-0413
E-mail guitar@bcn.boulder.co.us

FRONTIER HOUSE
1103 Fifth St.
Greeley, CO 80631
Dir. Jennifer Schuster
(303) 352-1095

○ SUMMIT CENTER
10000 W. 21 Ave.
Lakewood, CO 80215
Dir. Miriam Dunnam
(303) 237-3733
FAX (303) 232-0195

WISHING WELL CLUBHOUSE
456 Bannock St.
Denver, CO 80204
Dir. Jill Lucero
(303) 733-5200
Fax (303) 733-8239

Connecticut
○ **BARRETT HOUSE**
235 White St.
Danbury, CT 06810
Dir. Sandra Harris
(203) 794-0819
FAX (203) 748-4839

○ **BRIDGE HOUSE**
880 Fairfield Ave.
Bridgeport, CT 06605
Dir. Victoria E. Furey
(203) 335-5339

LAUREL HOUSE
6 Washington Ct.
Stamford, CT 06902
Dir. Steve Dougherty
(203) 324-1816
(203) 358-0199
FAX (203) 969-7021

PRIME TIME
41 East Main St.
Torrington, CT 06790
Dir. Thomas E. Whelan
(203) 482-3636
FAX (203) 482-8816

TEAMWORKS
102 Chestnut St.
Norwich, CT 06360
Dir. Lisa Morley
(860) 885-1834
FAX (860) 885-1970

District of Columbia
○ **GREEN DOOR**
1623 16th St. NW
Washington, DC 20009
Dir. Judith Johnson
(202) 462-4092
FAX (202) 462-7562

Florida
FOCUS HOUSE
1585 NE 123rd St.
N. Miami, FL 33161
Coord. Kathy Castro
(305) 895-4800

Georgia
GENESIS
4540 Glenwood Rd.
Decatur, GA 30032
Dir. Susan Robinson
(404) 289-7701
FAX (404) 289-9188

RAINBOW HOUSE
141 W. Solomon St.
Griffin, GA 30223
Dir. Tom Abrams
(404) 229-3090

SUNRISE HOUSE
4411 Rosemont Dr.
Columbus, GA 31904
Dir. Brenda Stacey
(706) 568-0431

Hawaii
FRIENDSHIP HOUSE
P.O. Box 780
Kapaa, HI 96746
Dir. Judith A. Fields
(808) 822-3244
FAX (808) 823-0035
E-mail friends@pixi.com

Idaho
CONFLUENCE CLUBHOUSE
1002 Idaho St.
Lewiston, ID 83501
Dir. Frank Pelfry
(208) 746-1519

HARAMBEE CLUB
420 S. Main St.
Twin Falls, ID 83301
Dir. Joy Kicer
(208) 736-2114
(208) 736-2117
FAX (208) 736-2113

Illinois
○ **INDEPENDENCE CENTER**
2025 Washington St.
Waukegan, IL 60085
Dir. Michael Pierce
(708) 360-1020
FAX (708) 360-1065

Indiana

HOOSIER HOUSE
6655 E. US 36
Danville, IN 46122
Dir. Yolonda Ursery
(317) 272-3330

✪ NEW HOPE CLUB
P.O. Box 817
Kendellville, IN 46755
Dir. Rusty Shade
(219) 347-4400

Iowa

NEW HORIZONS
915 Main St.
Adel, IA 50003
Dir. Thea Applegate
(515) 993-3384

THE STATION
729 Pearl St.
Grinnell, IA 50112
Dir. Betty Murray Ludden
(515) 236-5325
FAX (515) 236-0206

✪ RAINBOW CENTER
305 15th St.
Des Moines, IA 50309
Dir. Linda Oleson-King
(515) 243-6929
FAX (515) 243-1747

Kansas

✪ BREAKTHROUGH CLUB
1005 East 2nd
Wichita, KS 67214
Dir. Barbara Andres
(316) 269-2402
FAX (316) 269-1409
E-mail break1@wichita.sn.net

GRACE HOUSE
1620 Janes Ave.
Winfield, KS 67156-2550
Dir. Mary Jarvis
(316) 221-3946
E-mail gracehouse@aol.com

Louisiana

AUDUBON FRIENDSHIP CLUB
830 Audubon St.
New Orleans, LA 70118
Dir. Wyatt Hines
(504) 865-8770
FAX (504) 865-8782

EASTBANK FRIENDSHIP CLUB
3624 Florida St.
Kenner, LA 70062
Dir. Stan Gallien
(504) 464-7948
FAX (504) 464-9753

WESTBANK FRIENDSHIP CLUB
2051 Eighth St.
Harvey, LA 70058
Dir. Gail Ritter
(504) 368-1944
FAX (504) 368-9784

Maryland

OMNI HOUSE
P.O. Box 1270
Glen Burnie, MD 21060
Dir. Lois Miller
(410) 768-6777
FAX (410) 760-6811

WAY STATION, INC.
P.O. Box 3826
Frederick, MD 21705
Pres./Ceo Grady O'Rear
(301) 694-0070
FAX (301) 694-9932

Massachusetts

✪ ATLANTIC HOUSE
338 Washington St.
Quincy, MA 02169
Dir. Linda Nardella
Regional Dir. Ellen Bruder-Moore
(617) 770-9660
FAX (617) 770-9665

✪ BAYBRIDGE
209 Main St.
Hyannis, MA 02601
Dir. Rick Eddy
(508) 778-4234
FAX (508) 778-0774
E-mail B-Bridge@capecod.net

CASA PRIMAVERA/LAH
409 Dudley St.
Roxbury, MA 02119
Dir. Maritza Berrios-Rosado
(617) 427-7175 ext. 243
FAX (617) 442-2259

✪ CENTER CLUB
31 Bowker St.
Boston, MA 02114
Dir. Mary C. Gregorio
(617) 723-6300
FAX (617) 723-1277

CORNER CLUBHOUSE
P.O. Box 2037
247 Maple St.
Attleboro, MA 02703
Dir. Calvin Seitler
(508) 226-5604
FAX (508) 226-0324

✪ CROSSROADS AT THE LARCHES
11 Williams St.
Hopedale, MA 01747
Dir. Sandy Biber
(508) 473-4715
FAX (508) 634-2602

ELLIOT HOUSE
23 Needham St.
Newton Highlands, MA 02161
Dir. Don Hughes
(617) 332-1147
FAX (617) 332-3398

✪ FAIRWINDS
510 Main St.
Falmouth, MA 02540
Dir. Mark Buchanan
(508) 540-6011
FAX (508) 457-7539
E-mail AD. .CAPE
   HOUSE@AOL.COM

FORUM HOUSE
55 Broad St.
Westfield, MA 01085
Dir. Jane Allen
(413) 562-5293
FAX (413) 562-9163

FRIENDS TOGETHER
186 Bedford St.
Lexington, MA 02173
Dir. Elaine Walker
(617)861-0205
FAX (617) 861-0899

✪ **GENESIS CLUB, INC.
274 Lincoln St.
Worcester, MA 01605
Dir. Kevin Bradley
(508) 831-0100
FAX (508) 753-1286
E-mail AD. GENCLUB
   1X.NETCOM.COM
WEB PAGE http://www.ultimate.
   org/genesis/

✪ GREEN RIVER HOUSE
37 Franklin St.
Greenfield, MA 01301
Dir. Richard Nadolski
(413) 772-2181
FAX (413) 772-2032

HAVERHILL CLUBHOUSE
44 Emerson St.
Haverhill, MA 01830
Dir. Rose Coppinger
(508) 521-6957
FAX (508) 469-9208

✪ HERITAGE HOUSE
2110 Acushnet Ave.
New Bedford, MA 02745
Dir. David Costa
(508) 995-1300
FAX (508) 998-8110

✪ HORIZON HOUSE
21 Water St.
Wakefield, MA 01880
Dir. Jay Herzog
Regional Dir. Ellen Bruder-Moore
(617) 245-7311
FAX (617) 245-1369

✪ LIGHTHOUSE
235 Chestnut St.
Springfield, MA 01103
Dir. Ruth Kaufman
(413) 736-8974
FAX (413) 785-5030

LYNN FRIENDSHIP CLUB
37 Friend St.
Lynn, MA 01902
Dir. Nancy Antonopoulos
(617) 581-2891
FAX (617) 593-5731

NEPONSET RIVER CENTER
595 Pleasant St.
Norwood, MA 02062
Dir. Catherine Taatjes
(617) 762-7075
FAX (617) 762-2409

NEXT STEP CLUB
25 Staniford St.
Boston, MA 02114
Dir. Stuart Dangler
(617) 742-6447
FAX (617) 723-3919

○ OPTIONS CLUBHOUSE
200 E. Main St.
Marlboro, MA 01752
Dir. Toni Wolf
(508) 485-5051
FAX (508) 485-8807

POINT AFTER CLUB
43 Jackson St.
Lawrence, MA 01840
Dir. Rose Coppinger
(508) 681-7753
FAX (508) 685-3891

CHARLES WEBSTER POTTER PLACE
15 Vernon St.
Waltham, MA 02154
Dir. Mark A. Crosby
(617) 894-5302
FAX (617) 891-3812
E-mail potterplace@msn.com

○ PIONEER HOUSE
34 St. Peter St.
Salem, MA 01970
Dir. Larry Marshall
(508) 741-0337
FAX (508) 745-9477
E-mail PHmembers@aol.com

PLYMOUTH BAY CLUBHOUSE
340 Court St.
Plymouth, MA 02360
Dir. Beth Wahlig
(508) 747-1115
FAX (508) 747-4199

QUABBIN HOUSE
429 School St.
Athol, MA 01331
Dir. Peter Travisano
(508) 249-2074
FAX (508) 249-0227

RENAISSANCE CLUB, INC.
21 Branch St.
Lowell, MA 01851
Dir. Larry Urban
(508) 454-7944
FAX (508) 937-7867
E-mail renclub@ultranet.com

STARPOINT
17 New South St. Ste. 7
Northampton, MA 01060
Dir. Robert Veronelli
(413) 586-5548
FAX (413) 582-9553
E-mail AD.75061.26@
  COMPUSERVE.COM

○ TOWNE HOUSE
51 Purchase St.
Fall River, MA 02720
Dir. William E. Walmsley Jr
(508) 674-5716
FAX (508) 676-5166

TRADEWINDS
102 Morris St.
Southbridge, MA 01550
Dir. Sandra K. Allen
(508) 765-9947
FAX (508) 765-9948

TRANSITIONS OF BOSTON
995 Blue Hill Ave.
Dorchester, MA 02124
Dir. Mark Moore
(617) 282-8484
FAX (617) 282-7623

WEBSTER HOUSE
20 Webster Place
Brookline, MA 02146
Dir. Veronica Besancon
(617) 739-5461
FAX (617) 739-2103

WESTWINDS
88 Boulder Dr.
Fitchburg, MA 01420
Dir. Amanda Conmy
(508) 345-1581
FAX (508) 345-3055

○ WESTWOODS
59 Hamlin St.
Pittsfield, MA 01201
Dir. Susan Doscher
(413) 443-4848
FAX (413) 448-2198

Michigan

AOI (ARENAC OPPORTUNITIES INC.)
201 Mulholland
Bay City, MI 48708
Dir. Bonnie O'Keefe
(517) 895-2300

✪ BAYSIDE LODGE
3545 Bay Rd.
Suite 7
Saginaw, MI 48603
Dir. Jere Bennett
(517) 799-1266
FAX (517) 799-1548

CENTRAL MI CMH - ISABELLA CO.
301 S. Crapo St.
Mt. Pleasant, MI 48858
Dir. Patty Ball
(517) 772-5938

CLUB CADILLAC
2105 6th Ave.
Cadillac, MI 49601
Dir. Betty Clark
(616) 775-5638

CROSS ROADS
120 Ridge
Sault St. Marie, MI 49783
Dir. Lori Pieri
(906) 632-2805

CROSSROADS CLUBHOUSE
27041 Schoenherr Rd.
Warren, MI 48093
Dir. Susan Deiter
(810) 759-9100
FAX (810) 759-9176

CRYSTAL BEACH FRIENDSHIP HOUSE
P.O. Box 276
Rapid City, MI 49676
Dir. Terri Cleis
(616) 331-4821

✪ DREAMS UNLIMITED
13200 Oak Park Blvd.
Oak Park, MI 48237
Dir. Joyce Rupp
(810) 547-7712
FAX (810) 547-0094

FISHER CENTER
2640 W. Vernor
Detroit, MI 48216
Dir. Thom Stark
(313) 961-0360
FAX (313) 961-1826

✪ FULL CIRCLE COMMUNITY CENTER
102 N. Hamilton
Ypsilanti, MI 48198
Dir. Tim Benjamin
(313) 485-2020

GENESIS HOUSE
120 Grove St.
Battle Creek, MI 49017
Dir. Vicky Lindsey
(616) 966-1885

✪ GENESIS HOUSE
209 E. Grand River
Howell, MI 48843
Dir. John Heinlein
(517) 548-3359
FAX (517) 548-0872

HEARTLAND CLUBHOUSE
611 North State St.
Station, MI 48888
Dir. Dorothy Hahnenberg
(517) 831-7521

HOPE CENTER
57418 CR 681 Suite R
Hartford, MI 49057
Dir. Ruth Campbell
(616) 621-6262

LAPEER CMH
1570 Suncrest Dr.
Lapeer, MI 48446
Dir. Alice Stoelzl-Fiebelkorn
(810) 667-0207

✪ LIGHTHOUSE
1200 N. West Ave.
Jackson, MI 49202
Prog. Mgr. Marge Rice
(517) 789-2483
FAX (517) 789-1276

NEW BEGINNINGS
131 N. University
Pontiac, MI 48342
Dir. Rodney Harper
(313) 335-8710
FAX (313) 338-3970

NEW FOCUS CLUBHOUSE
1200 North Main St.
Adrian, MI 49221
Dir. Erin McRobert
(517) 263-3577
FAX (517) 263-1683

NEW HOPE FRIENDSHIP HOUSE
17234 Robbins Rd.
Grand Haven, MI 49417
Dir. Robert Matyas
(616) 842-0076

✪ NEW VISTA CLUBHOUSE
1215 Fuller NE
Grand Rapids, MI 49505
Dir. Howard Falkinburg
(616) 451-2454
FAX (616) 242-6057

NORTHERN LITES CLUBHOUSE
1027 Ethel Ave.
Hancock, MI 49930
Coord. Bob McMullen
(906) 482-0741

✪ OPPORTUNITY CENTER
1301 N. Madison Ave.
Bay City, MI 48708
Dir. John Kinkema
(517) 895-7273
FAX (517) 895-8671

OUR HOUSE
120 S. Rochester
Clawson, MI 48017
Dir. Theresa Wick
(810) 583-9444
FAX (810) 583-9831

PATHWAYS
407 East Michigan Ave.
Kalamazoo, MI 49007
Dir. Mike Smith
(616) 342-0173

✪ PETOSKEY CLUB
555 W. Mitchell
Suite C
Petoskey, MI 49770
Dir. Kim Crane
(616) 347-1786
FAX (616) 347-1643

RIVERSIDE CLUBHOUSE
P.O. Box 429
204 S. Main St.
Three Rivers, MI 49023
Dir. Mary Herendeen
(616) 279-9407

SIGHTS UNLIMITED
1163 N. Van Dyke
Bad Axe, MI 48413
Dir. William Wells
(517) 269-2999
FAX (517) 269-7544

✪ TRAILBLAZERS
218 N. Division St.
Ann Arbor, MI 48104
Dir. Theresa Wick
(313) 665-7665
FAX (313) 665-7665

TRAVERSE HOUSE
705 W. Front St.
Traverse City, MI 49684
Dir. Marilyn Singer
(616) 922-2060

TURNING POINT CLUBHOUSE
1736 Fort St.
Lincoln Park, MI 48146
Dir. Sandra Taranto
(313) 382-7861
FAX (312) 389-7515

Minnesota
KIESLER HOUSE
220 SE 2nd Ave.
Grand Rapids, MN 55744
Dir. Connie Ross
(218) 326-5114
FAX (218) 326-8255

✪ VAIL PLACE
1412 West 36th St.
Minneapolis, MN 55444
Dir. Paul Sinclair
(612) 824-8061
FAX (612) 824-9474

✪ VAIL PLACE
15 9th Ave. South
Hopkins, MN 55343
Dir. Paul Sinclair
(612) 938-9622
FAX (612) 938-7934

Mississippi
FRIENDSHIP CLUBHOUSE
P.O. Box 1505
Greenwood, MS 38930
Dir. Lacinda Ratliff
(601) 455-3365
FAX (601) 455-5243

PINNACLE CLUBHOUSE
2214 4th St.
Meridian, MS 39301
Dir. Marshall Powe
(601) 693-5051

Missouri
○ MIDLAND HOUSE
INDEPENDENCE CENTER
9525 Midland Ave.
Overland, MO 63114
Dir. Jennifer Higgenbotham
(314) 427-5597
FAX (314) 428-6570

○ **WEST PINE HOUSE
INDEPENDENCE CENTER
4380 West Pine Blvd.
St. Louis, MO 63108
Dir. Cathy Commack
(314) 533-6511
FAX (314) 531-7372

Montana
○ MONTANA HOUSE
422 N. Last Chance Gulch
Helena, MT 59601
Dir. Gene Haire
(406) 443-0794
FAX (406) 443-7011
E-mail GeneHaire@aol.com

Nebraska
ADAMS ST. CENTER
3830 Adams St.
Lincoln, NE 68504
Dir. Marylyde Kornfeld
(402) 441-8150

CIRRUS HOUSE
1509 First Ave.
Scottsbluff, NE 69361
Dir. Doug Beezley
(308) 635-1488
FAX (308) 635-1271

FRONTIER HOUSE
P.O. Box 1209
N. Platte, NE 69103
Dir. Lori Jahnke
(308) 532-4730

IVY HOUSE
4102 South 13th St.
Omaha, NE 68107
Dir. Michelle Zuerlein
(402) 734-1614
FAX (402) 734-1749

○ LIBERTY CENTRE
112 South Birch
Norfolk, NE 68701
Dir. Mary Kay Uhing
(402) 370-3503
FAX (402) 370-3250

OPPORTUNITY HOUSE
P.O. Box 2066
Hastings, NE 68902
Dir. Bonnie Chamberlain
(402) 463-7435
FAX (402) 463-0687

Nevada
ARVILLE HOUSE
1501 S. Arville
Las Vegas, NV 89102
Dir. Bruce Adams
(702) 259-4646
FAX (702) 259-7791

New Jersey
THE CLUB
UMDNJ-CMHC
195 New St.
New Brunswick, NJ 08901
Dir. John Woods
(908) 235-6900
FAX (908) 235-6937

HARBOR HOUSE
703 Main St.
Paterson, NJ 07503
Dir. Mohammad Shafiq
(201) 754-2800
FAX (201) 345-3409

New York
ADIRONDACK HOUSE
RD 1, Box 1012
Westport, NY 12993
Dir. Robert Horne
(518) 962-8231

BOULEVARD CLUB
512 Southern Blvd.
Bronx, NY 10455
Dir. Juan Ramos
(718) 993-1078
FAX (718) 993-2016

BRIDGES
212 Williams St.
Watertown, NY 13601
Dir. Marty Smith
(315) 788-8092

THE CHELTON LOFT
212 West 35th St.
4th Fl.
New York, NY 10001
Dir. Mark Balsam
(212) 290-2300
FAX (212) 290-CLUB
E-mail Chelton@pipeline.com

CITIVIEW CONNECTIONS
42-15 Crescent St.
Suite 610
Long Island City, NY 11101
Dir. Mitch Wood
(718) 361-7030
FAX (718) 361-7031

CLUBHOUSE OF SUFFOLK
P.O. Box 373
Ronkonkoma, NY 11779
Dir. Mike Stoltz
(516) 471-7242
FAX (516) 471-5150

CLUB KWANZAA
310 Malcolm X Blvd.
Suite 306
New York, NY 10027
Dir. Gary Gibbs
(212) 831-2270
FAX (212) 316-0789

CLUBHOUSE NIAGARA
1431 Robinson Ct.
Niagara Falls, NY 14303
Dir. Evonne Clark
(716) 284-1939
FAX (716) 285-5908

EAST NEW YORK CLUBHOUSE
2697 Atlantic Ave.
Brooklyn, NY 11207
Dir. Lou Calhoun
(718) 235-5780

FEGS- BROOKLYN CLUBHOUSE
199 Jay St.
Brooklyn, NY 11201
Dir. Hyacinth Spence
(718) 488-0100 ext. 354

⊙ **FOUNTAIN HOUSE
425 West 47th St.
New York, NY 10036
Dir. Kenneth Dudek
(212) 582-0340
FAX (212) 397-1649
TTY (212) 581-2711

FOUR SEASONS CLUB
290 Front St.
Binghamton, NY 13905
Dir. Carol L. Olmstead
(607) 773-1184

FREEDOM VILLAGE
1329 Beach Channel Dr.
Far Rockaway, NY 11691
Dir. John A. Javis
(718) 337-0504
FAX (718) 868-3782

FUTURE VISIONS
344 Walnut St.
Lockport, NY 14094
Dir. Jamie Marcolini
(716) 433-1086
FAX (716) 443-6543

GEEL CLUBHOUSE
2516 Grand Ave.
Bronx, NY 10468
Dir. John Boisitz
(212) 367-1900
FAX (212) 365-0252

HARLEM BAY NETWORK
3280 Broadway
New York, NY 10027
Dir. Jackie Rivers
(212) 862-0205
FAX (212) 694-4201

HARLEM HOUSE
151 West 127th St.
New York, NY 10027
Dir. Rupert Clarke
(212) 316-1284
(212) 932-8122
(212) 932-8124

H.O.M.E.E. CLINIC CLUBHOUSE
695 East 170th St.
Bronx, NY 10456
Dir. Eleanor Clark
(718) 991-0071
FAX (718) 893-5886

HOPE HOUSE
27 North Main St.
Port Chester, NY 10573
Dir. Jim Killoran
(914) 939-2878
FAX (914) 939-3531

++HY FEINSTEIN CLUBHOUSE
65 Austin Blvd.
Commack, NY 11725
Dir. Tracy Matthews
(516) 543-2263
FAX (516) 543-2261

LIBERTY HOUSE
54 Bay St.
Glen Falls, NY 12801
Dir. Pat Geruso
(518) 798-1066
FAX (518) 798-1166

METRO CLUB
25 Chapel St.
12 Fl.
Brooklyn, NY 11201
Dir. Alan Nyysola
(718) 834-0496
FAX (718) 834-9390

OPERATION FRIENDSHIP
693 East Ave.
Rochester, NY 14607
Dir. Nancy McFarland
(716) 473-9027
FAX (716) 473-8835

RAINBOW HOUSE
514 West Dominick St.
Rome, NY 13440
Dir. Alicia Davoli
(315) 339-3870/1
FAX (315) 337-9262

SKYLIGHT CENTER
307 St. Mark's Place
Staten Island, NY 10301
Dir. Ernie Lumer
(718) 720-2585
FAX (718) 720-2601

STEPPING STONES
14 Pelton St.
Monticello, NY 12701
Dir. Judy Zigmund
(914) 794-3296
FAX (914) 791-4153

STERLING CLUB
29 Sterling Ave.
White Plains, NY 10606
Dir. Robert Litwak
(914) 949-1212 ext. 217

SUMMIT HOUSE OF BROOKLYN
1775 60th St.
Brooklyn, NY 11204
Dir. Joseph F. Donarum
(718) 256-3430
FAX (718) 256-3504

SYNERGY CENTER
210 Court St.
Riverhead, NY 11901
Prog. Dir. Wendy Fleming
(516) 369-0022
FAX (516) 369-5336

TERENCE HOUSE
218-19 98th Ave.
Queens, NY 11429
Dir. Lawrence Guice
(718) 776-9192

✪ VENTURE HOUSE
89-25 Parsons Blvd.
Jamaica, NY 11432
Dir. David Lehmann
(718) 658-7201
FAX (718) 523-0658

North Carolina
✪ ADVENTURE HOUSE
924 N. Lafayette St.
Shelby, NC 28150
Dir. Tommy Gunn
(704) 482-3370
FAX (704) 482-3383
E-mail adventureh@aol.com

ATLANTIC HOUSE
406 Arendell St.
Morehead City, NC 28557
Dir. Chris Clark
(919) 726-7983
FAX (919) 726-1055

CLUB NOVA
103D West Main St.
Carrboro, NC 27510
Dir. Karen Kincaid Dunn
(919) 968-6682
FAX (919) 968-1764
FAX (919) 918-1112

CONNECTIONS CLUBHOUSE
P.O. Box 1256
Newton, NC 28658
Dir. Beverly Bryan
(704) 466-0030

MAGNOLIA HOUSE
P.O. Box 914
Forest City, NC 28043
Temp. Dir. Sandy Padgett
(704) 248-2164

OCEAN HOUSE
317 N. 4th St.
Wilmington, NC 28401
Dir. Sheila Wood
(910) 251-6590
FAX (910) 251-6557

PIEDMONT PIONEER HOUSE
910 Roberts Dr.
Gastonia, NC 28054
Dir. Bob Davis
(704) 866-8751

RIVER CLUB
1000 Health Dr.
New Bern, NC 28560
Dir. Willie M. Franklin
(919) 633-6431

✪ SIXTH AVENUE WEST
714 6th Ave. West
Hendersonville, NC 28739
Dir. Lisa Starnes
(704) 697-1581

SMOKY MOUNTAIN HOUSE
1207 East St.
Waynesville, NC 28786
Dir. J. Meredeth Liles
(704) 452-9258

SPECTRUM HOUSE
401 East Whitaker Mill Rd.
Raleigh, NC 27608
Dir. Mike Mescall
(919) 856-6420
FAX (919) 856-5674

✪ THRESHOLD
P.O. Box 11706
Durham, NC 27703
Dir. Jonathan Beard
(919) 682-4124
FAX (919) 956-7703

UNION HOUSE
1313 E. Franklin St.
Monroe, NC 28112
Dir. Jim Shaw
(704) 289-5431

North Dakota
FRIENDSHIP PLACE
P.O. Box 13875
Grand Forks, ND 58208
Dir. Jennifer Jensen
(701) 746-4530

HARMONY CENTER
212 East Central
Minot, ND 58701
Dir. Jennifer Bartsch
(701) 852-3263
FAX (701) 838-8488

Ohio
HILL HOUSE
11101 Magnolia Dr.
Cleveland, OH 44106
Dir. Judy Peters
(216) 721-3030
FAX (216) 721-0105

PATHWAY
1203 East Broad St.
Columbus, OH 43205
Dir. Marcy Peebles-Field
(614) 251-2380
Fax (614) 251-2447

Oklahoma
ACHIEVEMENT HOUSE
4400 N. Lincoln St.
Suite 100
Oklahoma City, OK 73105
Dir. Shelly Spalding
(405) 424-7744
FAX (405) 425-0377

✪ CROSSROADS
1880 East 15th St.
Tulsa, OK 74104
Dir. Mike Furches
(918) 749-2141
FAX (918) 749-2150

Oregon
COMET CLUB
5507 N. Lombard
Portland, OR 97203
Dir. Lisa Pearlstein
(503) 283-2535

Pennsylvania
CHESTNUT PLACE CLUBHOUSE
4042 Chestnut St.
Philadelphia, PA 19104
Dir. Peggy Maccolini
(215) 596-8200
TTY (215) 382-6146
FAX (215) 596-8221
E-mail 76433,1431

LIBERTY HOUSE
1221 South 15th St.
Philadelphia, PA 19146
Dir. Christopher Bush
(215) 462-2030
FAX (215) 389-1001

++THE MOSS REHAB CLUBHOUSE
6391 Oxford Ave.
Philadelphia, PA 19111
Dir. Harvey Jacobs
(215) 533-8553
FAX (215) 533-8544

OPEN DOOR CLUBHOUSE
Collins and Cumberland St.
Philadelphia, PA 19125
Dir. Kevin Stasi
(215) 427-5763

UNITY HOUSE
2221-25 North Broad St.
Suite 500
Philadelphia, PA 19132
Dir. Troy Boyd
(215) 235-1366
FAX (215) 235-2259

WELCOME HOUSE
7700 West Chester Pike
Upper Darby, PA 19082
Dir. David Young
(610) 446-1485
FAX (610) 446-3409

WELLSPRING CLUBHOUSE
915 Lawn Ave.
Sellersville, PA 18960
Dir. Lu Mauro
(215) 257-4760
FAX (215) 257-6629

Rhode Island
○ HILLSGROVE HOUSE
70 Minnesota Ave.
Warwick, RI 02888
Dir. Jan Lorensen
(401) 732-0970
FAX (401) 732-4413

PHOENIX I
26 Spring St.
Newport, RI 02840
Dir. Mary Page
(401) 846-3135
FAX (401) 848-9151

South Carolina
○ CAROLINA CLUBHOUSE
546-N South Cherry Rd.
Rock Hill, SC 29730
Dir. Belinda Brown-McClure
(803) 327-1595

○ **GATEWAY HOUSE
P.O. Box 4241
Greenville, SC 29608
Dir. Phil Emory
(803) 242-9193
FAX (803) 242-3861
E-mail Gwhouse@aol.com
        PEmory@aol.com

○ NEW DAY CLUBHOUSE
P.O. Box 5396
189 S. Converse St.
Spartanburg, SC 29304
Dir. Bill Wilkinson
(803) 582-5431
FAX (803) 582-7111

South Dakota
5TH ST. CLUBHOUSE
100 West 5th St.
Sioux Falls, SD 57102
Dir. Jeff Hansen
(605) 335-3664
FAX (605) 336-0873

Tennessee
AIM CENTER
1903 McCallie Ave.
Chattanooga, TN 37404
Dir. Bonnie Currey
(615) 624-4800
FAX (615) 622-8102

PARK CENTER
801 12th Ave. South
Nashville, TN 37203
Dir. Jack Hollis
(615) 242-3576
FAX (615) 242-3580
E-mail parkcent@isdn.net

Texas

INDEPENDENCE HOUSE
334 Centre St.
Dallas, TX 75208
Dir. Marvin Williams
(214) 941-6054
FAX (214) 941-1753

MAGNIFICAT HOUSE
3300 Caroline
Houston, TX 77004
Dir. Russel Goodwin
(713) 520-0461

Utah

○ ALLIANCE HOUSE
1724 South Main St.
Salt Lake City, UT 84115
Dir. Margaret Currin
(801) 486-5012
FAX (801) 466-5077

BEAR RIVER CLUBHOUSE
78 West 10th North
Logan, UT 84321
Dir. Daryl Duffin
(801) 753-2080
FAX (801) 752-7433

○ THE CLUBHOUSE
P.O. Box 553
Brigham City, UT 84302
Dir. Kevin Winn
(801) 723-3176
FAX (801) 752-8102

EXCEL HOUSE
1079 East Center St.
Provo, UT 84606
Dir. Peggy Evans
(801) 375-8308
FAX (801) 344-4225

INDEPENDENCE HOUSE
960 No. Dixie Downs Rd.
St. George, UT 84770
Dir. Peggy Turnblom
(801) 628-0612

INTERACT
198 East Center
Moab, UT 84532
Dir. Sharon Relph
(801) 259-7340
FAX (801) 259-5369

NEW HEIGHTS
240 N. Cedar Hills Dr.
Price, UT 84501
Dir. Robin Potochnick
(801) 637-4246

NEW REFLECTION HOUSE
565 West 900 South
Tooele, UT 84074
Dir. Frank Reed
(801) 882-4845
FAX (801) 833-7345

OASIS HOUSE
197 West 650 South
Cedar City, UT 84720
Coord. Rosie Fletcher
(801) 586-0213

○ WASATCH HOUSE
605 East 600 South
Provo, UT 84606-5046
Dir. Ned N. Campbell
(801) 373-7440
FAX (801) 374-1064

Vermont

CARRIAGE HOUSE
135 Granger St.
Rutland, VT 05701
Dir. Michael O'Brien
(802) 775-7196

EVERGREEN HOUSE
24 Washington St.
Middlebury, VT 05753
Dir. Linda Anderson
(802) 388-3468

MOUNTAIN HOUSE
103 Burgess Rd.
Bennington, VT 05201
Dir. David Miner
(802) 447-2166

VISIONS
8 Ferns St.
St. Albans, VT 05478
Dir. Susan Wilson
(802) 527-8163

WESTVIEW HOUSE
50 South Willard St.
Burlington, VT 05401
Dir. Jacquiline Bouchard
(802) 658-3323

Virgin Islands
ST. THOMAS CLUBHOUSE
C/O CATHOLIC CHARITIES
P.O. Box 10736
#7 Kongens Gade
St. Thomas, VI 00802
Dir. Audrey Larmony
(809) 774-1733

TAMARIND TREE CLUBHOUSE
Charles Harwood Complex
　　Christiansted
St. Croix, VI 00820
(809) 773-1311
FAX (809) 773-7900

Virginia
BEACH HOUSE
3143 Magic Hollow Rd.
Virginia Beach, VA 23456
Dir. Keith Johnson
(804) 430-0368
FAX (804) 430-1950

BLUERIDGE HOUSE
Suite 10
310 Avon St.
Charlottesville, VA 22902
Dir. Evadne S. Deeds
(804) 972-1825
FAX (804) 972-1719

CHESTER HOUSE
11745 Chester Road
Chester, VA 23831
Dir. Lance Elwood
(804) 748-6787
FAX (804) 748-5490

CLARENDON HOUSE
3141 N. 10th St.
Arlington, VA 22201
Coord. Cindy Kemp
(703) 358-5236/8

COASTAL CLUBHOUSE
216 Great Bridge Blvd.
Chesapeake, VA 23320
Dir. Dwight Hendricks
(804) 547-0097
FAX (804) 547-9642

HIGHLANDS HOUSE
27018 Lee Hwy.
Abingdon, VA 24211
Dir. Carolyn Peterson
(703) 628-8513
(703) 628-9504
FAX (703) 669-9093

HOSPITALITY CENTER
5623 Tidewater Dr.
Norfolk, VA 23509
Dir. Marcellus A. Moore
(804) 441-5310
FAX (804) 441-1716

KENMORE CLUB
632 Kenmore Ave.
Fredericksburg, VA 22401
Dir. John Butler
(703) 373-7737
FAX (703) 371-3753

LAKESIDE HOUSE
5623 Lakeside Ave.
Richmond, VA 23228
Coor. Becky Blenderman
(804) 264-1007
FAX (804) 264-0984

MARSHALL CENTER
3109 W. Clay St.
Richmond, VA 23230
Dir. Gwendolyn Andrews
(804) 780-8635
FAX (804) 780-4432

PATRICK ST. CLUB
115 N. Patrick St.
Alexandria, VA 22314
Dir. John Georgopoulos
(703) 838-4706
FAX (703) 838-4953

RESTON FARADAY CLUBHOUSE
1820 Michael Faraday Dr.
Reston, VA 22090
Dir. Brenda Randall
(703) 437-1061
FAX (703) 787-0543

SUMMIT HOUSE
1888 Pear St.
Harrisonburg, VA 22801
Dir. Karla Souder
(703) 434-1816

SUNRISE HOUSE
203 South Taylor St.
Ashland, VA 23005
Exec. Dir. Frank Bognar
(804) 798-5902

TOWN HOUSE
714 East Second St.
Farmville, VA 23901
Dir. Trish Keller
(804) 392-8307
FAX (804) 392-4013

Washington
COWLITZ RIVER CLUB
537 14th Ave.
Longview, WA 98632
Dir. Dave King
(206) 423-4243

EMERALD HOUSE
1729 17th Ave.
Seattle, WA 98122
Dir. Lucille Hammond
(206) 324-9362
FAX (206) 324-9433

○ EVERGREEN CLUB
East 2102 Sprague Ave.
Spokane, WA 99202
Dir. Sue Grant
(509) 458-7454
FAX (509) 458-7449

FREEDOM HOUSE
19630 76th Ave. West
Lynnwood, WA 98026
Dir. Paula Kahn
(206) 775-8583

HARVEST HOUSE
338 N.E. Maple St.
Pullman, WA 99163
Dir. Luann Nelson
(509) 334-6873

WILSON HOUSE
224 N. 7th St.
Pasco, WA 99301
Interim Dir. Loura Waite
(509) 545-3390
FAX (509) 547-8776
E-mail wilsonhs @cbvcp.com

Wisconsin
○ GRAND AVENUE CLUB
734 N. 4th St.
Milwaukee, WI 53203
Dir. Rachel Forman
(414) 276-6474
FAX (414) 276-1606

HARBOR HOUSE
440 Main St.
P.O. Box 253
Racine, WI 53401
Act. Dir. Deborah Fritschow
(414) 636-9393

YAHARA HOUSE
802 E. Gorham St.
Madison, WI 53703
Mgr. Roger Backes
(608) 257-7757
FAX (608) 257-5214

Appendix B
Standards for Clubhouse Programs

Membership

1. Membership is voluntary and without time limits.
2. The clubhouse has control over its acceptance of new members. Membership is open to anyone with a history of mental illness, unless that person poses a significant and current threat to the general safety of the clubhouse community.
3. Members choose the way they utilize the clubhouse, and the staff with whom they work. There are no agreements, contracts, schedules, or rules intended to enforce participation of members.
4. All members have equal access to every clubhouse opportunity with no differentiation based on diagnosis or level of functioning.
5. Members, at their choice, are involved in the writing of all records reflecting their participation in the clubhouse. All such records are to be signed by both member and staff.
6. Members have a right to immediate re-entry into the clubhouse community after any length of absence, unless their return poses a threat to the community.

Relationships

7. All clubhouse meetings are open to both members and staff. There are no formal member-only meetings or formal staff-only meetings where program decisions and member issues are discussed.
8. Clubhouse staff are sufficient to engage the membership, yet small enough in number to make carrying out their responsibilities impossible without member involvement.
9. Clubhouse staff have generalist roles. All program staff share employment, housing, evening and weekend, and unit responsibilities. Clubhouse staff do not divide their time between clubhouse and other major work responsibilities.
10. Responsibility for the operation of the clubhouse lies with the members and staff and ultimately with the clubhouse director. Central to this responsibility is the engagement of members and staff in all aspects of clubhouse operation.

Space

11. The clubhouse has its own identity including its own name, mailing address, and telephone number.

12. The clubhouse is located in its own physical space. It is separate from the mental health center or institutional settings, and is impermeable to other programs. The clubhouse is designed to facilitate the work-ordered day and at the same time be attractive, adequate in size, and convey a sense of respect and dignity.

13. All clubhouse space is member and staff accessible. There are no staff only or member only spaces.

Work-Ordered Day

14. The work-ordered day engages members and staff together, side by side in the running of the clubhouse. The clubhouse focuses on strengths, talents, and abilities; therefore, the work-ordered day is inconsistent with medication clinics, day treatment, or therapy programs within the clubhouse.

15. The work done in the clubhouse is exclusively the work generated by the clubhouse in the operation and enhancement of the clubhouse community. No work for outside individuals or agencies, whether for pay or not, is acceptable work in the clubhouse. Members are not paid for any clubhouse work, nor are there any artificial reward systems.

16. The clubhouse is open at least five days a week. The work-ordered day parallels normal working hours.

17. All work in the clubhouse is designed to help members regain self-worth, purpose, and confidence; it is not intended to be job-specific training.

18. Members have the opportunity to participate in all the work of the clubhouse, including administration, research, intake and orientation, reach out, hiring, training and evaluation of staff, public relations, advocacy and evaluation of clubhouse effectiveness.

Employment

19. The clubhouse enables its members to return to paid work through Transitional Employment and Independent Employment; therefore, the clubhouse does not provide employment to members through in-house businesses, segregated clubhouse enterprises, or sheltered workshops.

Transitional Employment

20. The clubhouse offers its own transitional employment program which provides as a right of membership opportunities for members to work on job placements in business and industry. The Transitional Employment program meets the following basic criteria:

    a. The desire to work is the single most important factor determining placement opportunity.

    b. Placement opportunities will continue to be available regardless of success or failure in previous placements.

    c. Members work at the employer's place of business.

    d. Members are paid the prevailing wage rate, but at least minimum wage, directly by the employer.

    e. Transitional Employment placements are drawn from a wide variety of job opportunities.

    f. Transitional Employment placements are part-time and time-limited, generally twenty hours per week and six months in duration.

    g. Selection and training of members on Transitional Employment is the responsibility of the clubhouse, not the employer.

    h. Clubhouse members and staff prepare reports on TE employment for all appropriate agencies dealing with members' benefits.

    i. Transitional Employment placements are managed by clubhouse staff and members and not by TE specialists.

    j. There are no Transitional Employment placements within the clubhouse itself or its auspice agency.

Independent Employment

21. The clubhouse assists and supports members to secure, sustain, and upgrade independent employment.

22. Members working full-time continue to have available all clubhouse supports and opportunities including advocacy for entitlement, and assistance with housing, clinical, legal, financial, and personal issues as well as participation in the evening and weekend programs.

Functions of the House

23. The clubhouse is located in an area where access to local transportation can be assured, both in terms of getting to and from the program and accessing TE opportunities. The clubhouse provides or arranges for effective alternatives whenever access to public transportation is limited.

24. Community support services are provided by members and staff of the clubhouse. Community support activities are centered in the work unit structure of the clubhouse and include helping with entitlements, housing, and advocacy, as well as assistance in finding quality medical, psychological, pharmacological, and substance abuse services in the community.

25. The clubhouse is committed to securing a range of choices of safe, decent, and affordable housing for all members. The clubhouse has access to housing opportunities that meet these criteria, or if unavailable, the clubhouse develops its own housing program. In clubhouse housing:

    a. members and staff manage the program together;

    b. members who live there do so by choice;

    c. members choose the location of their housing and their roommates;

    d. policies and procedures are developed in a manner congruent with the rest of the clubhouse culture;

    e. the level of support increases or decreases in response to the changing needs of the member;

    f. members and staff actively reach out to help members keep their housing, especially during periods of hospitalization.

26. The clubhouse provides members education, which focuses both on basic tools such as literacy and computer skill as well as more advanced educational opportunities. As a significant dimension of the work-ordered day members serve as major resources for tutoring and teaching in the member education program.

27. The clubhouse assists members to take advantage of the adult education system in the community in support of their vocational and personal aspirations.

28. The clubhouse has a method and takes responsibility for objectively evaluating its own effectiveness.

29. The clubhouse director, staff, members, and other appropriate persons participate in a three-week training program in the clubhouse model at a certified training base. Consultations by the Faculty for Clubhouse Development are provided all programs seeking to implement the clubhouse model.

30. The clubhouse has recreational and social programs during evenings and on weekends. Holidays are celebrated on the actual day they are observed.

31. The clubhouse provides an effective reach-out system to members who are not attending, becoming isolated in the community, or re-hospitalized.

Funding, Governance, and Administration

32. The clubhouse has an independent board of directors, or if it is affiliated with a sponsoring agency, has a separate advisory board comprised of individuals uniquely positioned to provide fiscal, legal, legislative, consumer, and community support and advocacy for the clubhouse.

33. The clubhouse develops and maintains its own budget, approved by the board or advisory board prior to the beginning of the fiscal year and monitored routinely during the fiscal year.

34. Staff salaries are competitive with comparable positions in the mental health field.

35. The clubhouse has the support of appropriate mental health authorities and has required licenses and certifications. The clubhouse seeks and maintains effective relationships with family, consumer, and professional organizations.

36. The clubhouse holds open forums and has procedures which enable members and staff to actively participate in decision-making regarding governance, policy-making, and the future direction and development of the clubhouse.

About the Authors

MARY FLANNERY is an award-winning medical reporter at the *Philadelphia Daily News*. She received a 1993 Kaiser Media Fellowship from the Henry J. Kaiser Family Foundation to research Fountain House. Flannery is a former *New York Daily News* sportswriter and a graduate of the Georgetown University School of Foreign Service. She lives with her husband and their four children in suburban Philadelphia.

MARK GLICKMAN recovered from his own psychiatric illness while a member of Fountain House. He later worked on staff as the coordinator of the International Training Program. In addition, he has worked as a television reporter and has produced several documentaries about Fountain House. Glickman currently serves on the board of the International Center for Clubhouse Development. He earned his undergraduate degree from Queens College in New York City and a master's degree in broadcast journalism from Boston University. He and his wife, Cynthia, live in San Diego.